How Abstract Is It? Thinking Capital Now

Since the start of the financial crisis in 2008, the notion that capitalism has become too abstract for all but the most rarefied specialists to understand has been widely presupposed. Yet even in academic circles, the question of abstraction itself – of what exactly abstraction is, and does, under financialisation – seems to have gone largely unexplored – or has it? By putting the question of abstraction centre stage, *How Abstract Is It? Thinking Capital Now* offers an indispensable counterpoint to the 'economic turn' in the humanities, bringing together leading literary and cultural critics in order to propose that we may know far more about capital's myriad abstractions than we typically think we do. Through in-depth engagement with classic and cutting-edge theorists, agile analyses of recent Hollywood films, groundbreaking readings of David Foster Wallace's sprawling, unfinished novel, *The Pale King*, and even original poems, the contributors here suggest that the machinations and costs of finance – as well as alternatives to it – may already be hiding in plain sight.

This book was originally published as a special issue of *Textual Practice*.

Rebecca Colesworthy is a Visiting Scholar in the Department of English at New York University, New York City, USA. She has published a number of articles on literature, theory, and gender studies, and is the author of a forthcoming book on modernism and the gift.

Peter Nicholls is Henry James Professor of English and American Letters at New York University, New York City, USA. His publications include *Ezra Pound: Politics, Economics and Writing* (1984), *Modernisms: A Literary Guide* (1995, 2009), *George Oppen and the Fate of Modernism* (2007, 2013), and many articles and essays on literature and theory. He recently co-edited *On Bathos* (2010) and *Thinking Poetry* (2013).

How Abstract Is It? Thinking Capital Now

Edited by
Rebecca Colesworthy and Peter Nicholls

Routledge
Taylor & Francis Group

LONDON AND NEW YORK

First published 2016
by Routledge
2 Park Square, Milton Park, Abingdon, Oxon, OX14 4RN, UK

and by Routledge
711 Third Avenue, New York, NY 10017, USA

First issued in paperback 2017

Routledge is an imprint of the Taylor & Francis Group, an informa business

British Library Cataloguing in Publication Data
A catalogue record for this book is available from the British Library

ISBN 13: 978-1-138-29497-4 (pbk)
ISBN 13: 978-1-138-94667-5 (hbk)

Typeset in Garamond
by RefineCatch Limited, Bungay, Suffolk

Publisher's Note
The publisher accepts responsibility for any inconsistencies that may have
arisen during the conversion of this book from journal articles to book chapters,
namely the possible inclusion of journal terminology.

Disclaimer
Every effort has been made to contact copyright holders for their permission to
reprint material in this book. The publishers would be grateful to hear from any
copyright holder who is not here acknowledged and will undertake to rectify
any errors or omissions in future editions of this book.

Contents

Citation Information

The chapters in this book were originally published in *Textual Practice*, volume 28, issue 7 (December 2014). When citing this material, please use the original page numbering for each article, as follows:

Chapter 5
From capitalist to communist abstraction: The Pale King's *cultural fix*
Stephen Shapiro
Textual Practice, volume 28, issue 7 (December 2014) pp. 1249–1271

Chapter 6
The bodies in the bubble: David Foster Wallace's The Pale King
Richard Godden and Michael Szalay
Textual Practice, volume 28, issue 7 (December 2014) pp. 1273–1322

Chapter 7
Shareholder existence: on the turn to numbers in recent French theory
Emily Apter
Textual Practice, volume 28, issue 7 (December 2014) pp. 1323–1336

For any permission-related enquiries please visit:
http://www.tandfonline.com/page/help/permissions

Notes on Contributors

Emily Apter is Professor of French and Comparative Literature at New York University, NYC, USA. Her most recent publications include *Dictionary of Untranslatables: A Philosophical Lexicon* (2014), *Against World Literature. On the Politics of Untranslatability* (2013), and *The Translation Zone: A New Comparative Literature* (2006).

Timothy Bewes is Professor of English at Brown University, Providence, RI, USA. He is the author of *Cynicism and Postmodernity* (1997), *Reification, or The Anxiety of Late Capitalism* (2002), and *The Event of Postcolonial Shame* (2011). He has co-edited several collections of essays, including *Georg Lukács: The Fundamental Dissonance of Existence* (2011), and he recently edited a special issue of the journal *Novel: A Forum on Fiction* on the theme of Jacques Rancière and the Novel.

Rebecca Colesworthy is a Visiting Scholar in the Department of English at New York University, NYC, USA. She has published a number of articles on literature, theory, and gender studies, and is the author of a forthcoming book on modernism and the gift.

Richard Godden is Professor of English at the University of California, Irvine, CA, USA. His research interests lie in twentieth century and contemporary American fiction, particularly William Faulkner. His most recent book, *William Faulkner: An Economy of Complex Words* (2007), won the British Association of American Studies prize for the Best Book of 2007.

Nicky Marsh is Professor of English at the University of Southampton, UK. Recent publications include *Literature and Globalization: A Reader* (edited with Liam Connell, 2010) and *Show Me the Money: The Image of Finance, 1700 to the Present* (edited with Peter Knight and Paul Crosthwaite, 2014).

Peter Nicholls is Henry James Professor of English and American Letters at New York University, NYC, USA. His publications include *Ezra Pound: Politics, Economics and Writing* (1984), *Modernisms: A Literary Guide* (1995, 2009), *George Oppen and the Fate of Modernism* (2007, 2013), and many articles and essays on literature and theory. He recently co-edited *On Bathos* (2010) and *Thinking Poetry* (2013).

NOTES ON CONTRIBUTORS

Stephen Shapiro is Professor in the Department of English and Comparative Literary Studies at the University of Warwick, UK. His research focuses on, amongst other things, the writing and culture of the United States, particularly in the period preceding the twentieth century, cultural studies and literary theory, Marxism, and urban and spatial studies. His work includes *The Culture and Commerce of the Early American Novel: Reading the Atlantic World-System* (2008), *The Wire: Race, Class, and Genre* (with Liam Kennedy, 2008), and *Combined and Uneven Development: Towards a New Theory of World-Literature* (2015), a collaboration of the WReC (Warwick Research Collective).

Susan Stewart is the Avalon Foundation University Professor in the Humanities and Director of the Society of Fellows in the Liberal Arts at Princeton University, NJ, USA. A poet and critic, her most recent prose works are *The Poet's Freedom: A Notebook on Making* (2011), *The Open Studio: Essays on Art and Aesthetics* (2005), and *Poetry and the Fate of the Senses* (2002). Her books of poems include *The Forest* (1995), *Columbarium* (2003), which won the National Book Critics Circle Award, *Red Rover* (2008), and the forthcoming *Cinder: New and Selected Poems*. Stewart is a former MacArthur Fellow and Berlin Prize Fellow and is a member of the American Academy of Arts and Sciences.

Michael Szalay is Professor of English at the University of California, Irvine, CA, USA. His research interests include twentieth and twenty-first century literature, film and television, and the political economy of the entertainment industry. He is currently finishing a book on HBO. His first two books, *Hip Figures: A Literary History of the Democratic Party* and *New Deal Modernism: American Literature and the Invention of the Welfare State*, examine the relationship between literature, liberal governance, and economic crisis.

Alberto Toscano is Reader in Critical Theory in the Department of Sociology at Goldsmiths College, University of London, UK. He has published numerous scholarly articles, and is the author of *Cartographies of the Absolute*, co-authored with Jeff Kinkle (2015), *Fanaticism: On the Uses of an Idea* (2010), and *The Theatre of Production: Philosophy and Individuation between Kant and Deleuze* (2006).

Rebecca Colesworthy
Introduction

Capital's abstractions

> While they were looking for a smoking gun in that room, I was going to fire off a bazooka in here. (Leonardo DiCaprio as Jordan Belfort in *The Wolf of Wall Street*)

While 'they' are the Securities and Exchange Commission (SEC), Jordan's boastful confession also applies to us, the viewers of *The Wolf of Wall Street*, insofar as we, too, serve as potential victims of his misdirection. The 'bazooka' is one of the many fraudulent initial public offerings (IPOs), Belfort oversaw at Stratton Oakmont, the faux-patrician firm he created to target and fleece 'the wealthiest one percent of Americans'. Addressing the camera, Jordan begins to explain in a very clear, straightforward manner exactly what IPOs are and how he and his partners manipulated them: 'Now, as the firm taking the company public, we set the initial share price then sold those shares right back to our friends.' Suddenly, however, he cuts himself off, nominally because his explanation is already too complex for us to grasp: 'Look, I know you're not following what I'm saying anyway, right? That's OK, that doesn't matter. The real question is this, was all this legal?' Jordan's answer? 'Absolutely fucking not.' Rather than stop there, he continues, as if to excuse his transgression and, again, divert our attention: 'But we were making more money than we knew what to do with.' Is the money, then, the 'real question' or is it another smoking gun?

Directed by Martin Scorsese and released in 2013, *The Wolf of Wall Street*, like many of Scorsese's films, uses voice-over narration by its central protagonist throughout. Yet this moment is one of just two in which narration and image coincide and DiCaprio, as Jordan, breaks the fourth wall to address us directly. In the second moment, as in the first, he stops short, again while explaining a crooked IPO. This time, the

1

subject is Stratton's most profitable and notorious offering, Steve Madden Shoes: 'Of the two million shares offered for sale, a million belonged to me held in phony accounts by my rat holes. Now, once the price hit the high teens' – and here he interrupts himself – 'You know what, who gives a shit? As always the point is this.' The camera then cuts from Jordan to his partner Donnie, played by Jonah Hill, triumphantly charging into the office with champagne and two glasses as he screams, '22 million dollars in three fucking hours!' The point, the real question, on this occasion, is not legality per se, but money, albeit illegally earned money. Whether or not we could understand how they gained such near incredible profit at such near incredible speed is never broached. Instead the claim is that no one cares – the catch being that Jordan and his cronies, whom we see going to carefully contrived ends to hide their misbegotten loot, no doubt care quite a lot, which raises the question, whose interests does our supposed indifference serve? And, moreover, whose interests does the movie serve in presuming that, as the film's screenwriter, Terence Winter, has suggested, 'People don't care'[1] about the technical details? In an article in *The New York Times*, Winter recalls his conclusion while writing the script that '[t]he techno-speak goes in one ear and out the other. What they'll remember is that in the Madden deal, Mr. Belfort made $23 million in two hours.'[2] Notably, Winter's final tally is at odds with that recounted in the film, suggesting that either he or Hill's Donnie, however unintentionally, fudged the numbers. 'The point', after all, remains inscrutable. Or, more precisely, inscrutability becomes, in the context of the movie, the point.

That is not to suggest that the exact sum made in the Madden deal is, technically speaking, unknowable, but to point to the film's play with the question of what we know – of what we do know, of what we can know, of what we want to know – about the workings of finance. Indeed, Jordan's cool disregard for the details is striking, suspicious even, in the context of a film that puts so much bad behaviour on display. Of course, his disregard is also a display of sorts, part of a performance to and for the viewer of cutting to the chase, of levelling with us. In addressing the camera, in other words, he in effect makes a show of talking to us straight. That is to say, he makes a pitch, in this case, for the impossibility of understanding his misdeeds. Yet the film will not quite let us buy Jordan's pitch, for in positioning us as his clients, it reveals even as it conceals what it takes to be the secret to his success – not the stockbroking specifics that we may or may not be able to follow, but his salesmanship.

The Wolf of Wall Street never lets us forget that Jordan is, at base, a salesman: from his first high-commission sale of worthless penny stocks to his incendiary motivational speeches to his employees to his own fateful decision not to take a deal with the SEC because 'it's them selling me, not the other way around'. The film even closes with Jordan, after a luxurious stint in prison, again playing the salesman, challenging audience members at a sales training seminar to 'sell me this pen'. In implying a comparison between literary fictions and financial fictions, the pen recalls the self-penned script that Jordan uses, in an explicit homage to Melville, to 'harpoon' rich clients at Stratton, as well as the book on which the film is based, thereby suggesting the fictitiousness of that nominally true story. *The Wolf of Wall Street*, we are reminded, is not necessarily a film to be trusted. Still, in affirming that selling a stock is ultimately no different than selling a pen, both here and in an earlier moment, it takes a provocative theoretical gamble. The tools of commerce, the film suggests, have changed, the bookkeeper's pen giving way to more advanced technologies of accounting and communication, whether Stratton's boiler-room phone bank or the fibre-optic cables enabling today's high-frequency trading. Yet the process of fictionalisation – that is, the *abstraction* – underwriting capital's flows is the same.

Whether this logic holds up historically is another question. The film's account of financial capitalism is, after all, an account of (some of) its subjective effects, not its structural underpinnings. Wall Street is unknowable here apart from the addictive behaviours and Svengali-like sales skills of its presumably representative Wolf. At the same time, in returning again and again to scenes of sale, it is as if the film were returning to some primal scene of capitalism, to an originary *act* of exchange, and in this way it begins to allegorise a fundamental 'moment' of *real* abstraction. Thus, the film suggests that, while Belfort made his fortune as a 'twisted Robin Hood', he got his start as a perverse Prometheus. After his first successful sale of an improbable quantity of penny stocks, Jordan recalls, in voice-over, 'Just like that I made two grand. The other guys looked at me like I had just discovered fire.' Insofar as Jordan is 'selling garbage to garbage men', making an exorbitant profit from their loss, his primordial discovery is also a theft, not from the gods, but from a growing population of wage earners turned shareholders. This is what Randy Martin has famously called 'the financialization of daily life',[3] the generalisation of a system of abstraction perhaps 'new' in its forms of work, accumulation, and subjectivity, yet decidedly 'old' in its underlying contradictions – not as old as fire's discovery, but at least as old as its commodification and, the film further suggests, equally ripe for mythologisation. Immediately after Jordan gets off the phone, an awed co-worker asks him, 'How'd you fucking do that?' Whether rhetorical or sincere, his question suggests that what Marx called 'fictitious capital' may depend as much on our disbelief as on our belief. Jordan's co-worker, like us, has seen all there is to see, but cannot believe his eyes. So in *The Wolf of Wall Street*, the secret of finance's fictions is right in front of us, hidden in plain sight. The film's final bet is that we do not care to see it. To the question posed by this issue of *Textual Practice* – How abstract is it? – the film more or less demurs, instead preferring the question that Jordan, in his last line of narration, asks us of a world in which everything is for sale: 'Wouldn't you like to sell it?'

How Abstract Is It? Thinking Capital Now was initially conceived as a corrective to what we, the editors of this special issue, saw as a blind spot in both academic and mainstream responses to the 2008 financial crisis and ensuing global economic collapse. While the fictitiousness of finance seemed to be everywhere presupposed, the question of abstraction 'itself' – the question of just what abstraction is and does under the conditions of financial capitalism – was consistently elided. If typical of the 'economic turn' in general, this elision was especially striking in two contexts: Marxist criticism and literary studies. The first was characterised by a tension. For some critics, the crisis and related events, including social and political movements such as Occupy, marked a return of the real, an effect of the contradictions immanent to capitalism and long ago plotted by Marx, yet veiled and repressed by finance's fictions. For others, post-Fordism and its millennial afterlife constituted a 'new' economy in which 'old' oppositions – between real and fictional, concrete and abstract, material and immaterial – no longer held and which therefore called for a rethinking of earlier conceptions of labour, value, and productivity. Of course, real and fictional were never merely opposed for Marx, but converge in his work in complex ways as a result of his use of a dialectical method to represent the real of capitalism *as* a system of abstraction. Nevertheless, while critics on both sides readily echoed Marx's claim in the *Grundrisse* that 'individuals are now ruled by *abstractions*', what constitutes (an) abstraction was treated as a given.[4]

In literary studies, it was as if the pronounced fictitiousness of finance promised to renew the relevance of literary and theoretical criticism to everyday life at the very same moment that higher education was growing ever more instrumentalised and the fate of the humanities hung, as it still hangs, in the balance. If literary critics and theorists seemed especially well poised to critique finance's fictions, some critics suggested they were equally at risk of complying with them. In a special 'Theories and Methodologies' section of a 2012 *PMLA*, entitled 'Economics, Finance, Capital, and Literature', Joshua Clover identified structuralism and poststructuralism as the 'thought form' of financialisation, while Christopher Nealon cast the speculative realism of Alain Badiou and Quentin Meillassoux as the 'imagination of the conditions that would correspond to the market fantasy' of an 'equilibrium to come'.[5] Both critics, in other words, drew parallels between philosophical abstraction and financial abstraction. But something was also missing from these studies – namely, a full account of abstraction as the implicit ground of these parallels.[6]

We then set out to illuminate this ground by asking contributors how abstract 'it' is – 'it' being quite abstract in this context, even problemati-cally so, but that also being (again to cite *The Wolf of Wall Street*) the point. 'It' is, above all, abstraction 'itself', as a process and a product. Yet our question was equally how abstract are *they*, for where one finds abstraction, one assuredly finds abstract*ions*, a play of sometimes compet-ing, sometimes complementary financial, philosophical, literary, artistic, cultural, political, and still other forms. What, then, is the relationship between them and are all forms of abstraction created equal? Are they dif-ferently abstract, whether qualitatively or quantitatively, and, by the same token, how *real* are they – indeed, is 'it'? Can either abstraction or reality be calculated, measured by degrees? Whence does the real return in times of crisis and what is abstraction abstracted from? Has the real returned or has financial capitalism always already been characterised by what Alfred Sohn-Rethel referred to as the 'real abstraction' of exchange? And if abstraction is real, how can we know it when we see it?

Since posing these questions, a seemingly ceaseless string of further popular and academic takes on finance and its supposed fictitiousness has emerged – from Hollywood films such as *The Wolf of Wall Street* and other insider tales of excess to such unlikely bestsellers as the French econom-ist Thomas Piketty's *Capital in the Twenty-First Century* to a now significant body of scholarship on the history, politics, and morality of debt. (Federal take*downs* have been far less forthcoming, but that is a topic for another issue.) Across these discourses, however, the question of abstraction as such still appears to go unanswered. As Leigh Claire La Berge notes in her contri-bution to a recent special issue of *Radical History Review* addressing 'The Fic-tions of Finance', while scholars in the humanities in particular routinely 'describe finance as either abstract or as an abstraction', these terms tend to be defined differently in different contexts, if they are defined at all.[7] More often than not, 'the abstract is employed as a trope that organizes and struc-tures but that itself eludes definition and representation'.[8] The exception, in La Berge's reading, is Marxist theory, which gives us definitions ('it is there that the term has been most theorized and differentiated'), but not consensus; instead it offers 'a series of kinds or instances of abstraction that finance might be said to participate in or to reconfigure'.[9] Abstraction, then, for La Berge, may be this or it may be that, but Marxists at least work to define what it is.

The fact that so many definitions circulate within Marxist theory and so many additional usages proliferate far beyond, in other fields, begs an impor-tant question: Are we, as scholars and critics of our current historical moment, so certain that we do not already know what abstraction is? While of course rhetorical, this question is also meant to be real. With so many of finance's fictions exposed, what remains to be known? What do we still not know and, if not, why not? Does it matter? What difference does our knowing or not knowing make? Is finance too abstract – or, as popular parlance would have it, too complex[10] – for us to understand? Or is it, like Poe's purloined letter (itself a financial fiction of sorts) a little *too* self-evident? Here we might also recall another cultural response to the recent financial crisis, Woody Allen's 2013 film, *Blue Jasmine*, whose titular neurasthenic heroine would prefer not to know about her husband's Ponzi scheme, nor to remember her role in bringing it – and him – to an end. What do we, like Jasmine, know without knowing? And if we already know all we need to know, what happens to the widespread commonplace that the truth of finance's fictions must be exposed? In the introduction to the same special issue of *Radical History Review*, the editors call attention to the 'urge to demystify' driving much of the recent critical discourse on finance.[11] Is demystification the most appropriate trope for the theoretical and political work of critique today? Is it the solution or part of the problem? How are we to conceptualise the epistemological challenge before us?

The essays – and, in the case of Susan Stewart's contribution, poems – collected in this issue go a long way towards demystifying not finance per se, but the stubborn myth of its unknowability. That is not to suggest that the authors all reach the same conclusions. Rather, in approaching the question of abstraction from different angles and to different ends, they in effect enable us to get traction on a problem that remains intractable, even now – and perhaps especially now that so much information about the machinations of finance has been brought into the open. Indeed, if the essays that follow ultimately help prove one collective point, it is that the intractability of finance persists *because* of its obviousness, not in spite of it, and that we, not only as critics, but also as subjects enmeshed in financial capitalism, may already know far more about its multifarious abstractions than we think we do. Without providing a comprehensive overview of their respective arguments, it is worth briefly tracing here some of the ways the authors think beyond a familiar dynamic of concealment and revelation and reframe the question of abstraction in terms other than those of (de)mystification.

In place of a notion of abstraction as unintelligible complexity, the articles in this issue consistently set forth a notion of abstraction as intelligible, sometimes glaring fissures: the debts from which profit is drawn in a credit economy; the determinate absence of capital as an historical structure, always in flux; the missing commodity at the heart of Marx's formula for finance, $M\text{-}M^1\text{-}M^2$; and the gaps in media representations of the crisis and its aftermath. In this vein, Nicky Marsh argues in the first essay that what demands representation today 'is not the "abstract" of finance' – already 'the central task of twentieth-century aesthetic

experimentation' and a primary focus of the mainstream press in its prefer-
ence for images of forlorn bankers after the crisis – but the '"concrete" realities of labour that are now, literally, carrying their costs'. What must be
represented, in other words, is the contradictory and asymmetrical relationship between finance and production, credit and debt. To this end, Marsh
considers two films, *In Time* (dir. Andrew Nicoll, 2011) and *Looper* (dir.
Rian Johnson, 2012), that use motifs of clock time to figure and critique
'the biopolitical governance of the indebted working body'. Drawing on
recent critiques of debt, Marsh suggests that the time of this body is
twofold, corresponding to both the socially necessary labour time that
measures work and the deferral of value introduced by debt. In conjoining
these registers, both films find 'a way of recuperating the politics of work
and time in a moment that seems able to deny them'. Ultimately, for
Marsh, finance is not unknowable so much as it creates a hole in knowledge
that is filled elsewhere – a nonsynchronous, corporeal elsewhere that nevertheless insists within and resists the present order. What seems unknowable
is in fact displaced onto the indebted masses who bear the burden of the
recent crisis and who, instead of being concealed, tend not to be pictured
at all.

Timothy Bewes then illuminates the intellectual history whereby
tropes of concealment and revelation have come to dominate critiques of
capitalism, suggesting that they are symptomatic of abstraction itself. He
notes that abstraction, ever since Marx, has designated 'apparently opposing tendencies: dematerialisation and concretisation'. Abstraction, as a
concept, is reversible, 'equally applicable to our attempts to achieve intellectual understanding and our involvement in activities and practices that
prevent us from doing so'. Its reversibility derives from Marx's critique of
commodity fetishism as a form of real abstraction, located not in consciousness, but in actions, in exchanges that presuppose and reinforce
the valuation of labour for its relational properties. At the same time,
these actions extend to consciousness, for abstraction, especially in the
work of Alfred Sohn-Rethel, equally 'refers to both intellectual labour
and manual labour'. Consciousness is at once enabled and limited by
abstraction, which serves as its condition of possibility and impossibility.
The reversibility of abstraction therefore creates a potentially insuperable
problem for critical thought: 'There is nothing seeable prior to the conditions of visibility that make it so; there is no subject who "sees" and
no perception that is not, at the same time, a failure of perception.' The
question for Bewes becomes, 'What are the prospects for a thought
without abstraction?' In answer, he turns to the work of Czech-born
media philosopher, Vilém Flusser, who saw in the historical appearance
of technical images ('photographs, films, videos, television screens and
computer terminals') the promise of a form of thought that would

'dispense with abstraction altogether'. Such a thought, following Flusser, would be subject-less, without standpoint. The only standpoint would be the '*standpoint of the apparatus*: a perspective that is oblivious to any creative or political intentionality'.

Like Bewes, Alberto Toscano adopts what we might think of as a subtractive method to circumvent the supplementary logic of abstraction whereby the answer to the question of how we overcome the problem of abstraction is always, with more abstraction! While Bewes works towards a thought without abstraction, Toscano proposes a materialism without matter, or, more precisely, a materialism without an *ideal* of matter – a materialism of real abstractions, of social forms at odds with the ideologies of materiality that, in positing the primacy of matter, rest on a fundamental idealism, the presupposition of an underlying transparency or presence that must be revealed. To elaborate this materialism, also described as a materialism of absences, Toscano turns to Louis Althusser's short, yet suggestive essay on Leonardo Cremonini as a painter of real abstraction, 'straining towards a "determinate absence,"' a structural causality governing men's concrete existence. Though he praises Althusser's materialism, Toscano also puts pressure on his identification of capital as '*an* absent structure' versus a metamorphosis ('the sequence and syncopation of value *forms*'), finally asking *whom* the sought-after visibility of capital's invisible realities is supposed to be for. The answer, for Toscano following Althusser, is 'us', a projected audience that constitutes yet another absence, a gap to be assumed by 'a concreteness and collectivity to come' whose shared knowledge would consist in 'showing the gaps ... within the order of abstract domination itself'.

For her part, Stewart, in the brief exchange that serves as an introduction to her 'Abstraction set', recalls Bewes in positing two modes of abstraction. Whereas poetic abstraction concretises, economic abstraction corresponds to an ideological forgetting of knowable, specifiable particulars – the particulars of the violence of capitalist accumulation, the exploitation of workers, the sociality of exchange, and the role of human desire and volition in driving the global economy. Above all, however, what we forget is nature, which Stewart identifies as an 'infinite resource for thought', and, thus, a resource for both poetic abstraction *and* economic abstraction, which parodies poetic creativity. 'All of our metaphors', she suggests, 'come from nature'. In affirming nature as a primary cause or origin, Stewart would seem to echo the idealisation of matter at which Toscano takes aim – and yet, something curious happens when we turn to the poems. Here, it is economic abstraction that is rendered complicit with an ideal of matter. In the first poem in particular, matter figures not as a cause, but as a phantasmatic effect: 'The sailor hides a map/to hidden treasure/which leads him to believe/there will be land.' The act of concealment and the dream of revelation to which it gives rise are further figured by the two faces of the coin, bearing 'a queen's face' and 'a garland', each of which Stewart encloses in its own parentheses, as if to remind us that only one or the other is fully visible at any time. This play of concealing and revealing, which Bewes roots in real abstraction, finds a countervailing force in nature, figured by the singular face of the sea ('there is only one face to the sea'), hiding in plain sight, yet forgotten, even as the lapping of its waves in effect gives us to think the coin's liquidity.

The violence of forgetting in Stewart's critique of economic abstraction translates into the danger of distraction in Stephen Shapiro's reading of David Foster Wallace's unfinished and posthumously published 2011 novel, *The Pale King*. In part set in the Peoria, Illinois, office of the US Internal Revenue Service (IRS) in 1985, the novel casts distraction as a defence against the painful dullness of the newly 'neoliberalised IRS' and any consciousness of our fragility under corporatised governance. Such distraction, a form of abstraction most fully manifested in 'the nervous use of media', is opposed in *The Pale King* to another form of abstraction – 'the ideal of selfless dedication to unheroic, "boring" service for the collective's wellbeing'. Shapiro argues that Foster Wallace works to impart this ideal by 'train[ing] the reader to be *in* abstraction, rather than flee from it'. The ideal of being in abstraction recalls, however paradoxically, Bewes's call for a thought without abstraction, for the 'fixed, patient concentration' at which the novel aims is essentially a thought without standpoint, a thought identified with the apparatus – in this case, the apparatus of the IRS, not the new IRS, but the old IRS, 'a public service apparatus that seeks to inculcate a non-charismatic ideal of tax revenue delivery as civic responsibility'. For Shapiro, the character of DeWitt Glendenning is this ideal, a communistic 'pale king' opposed to the 'royal bourgeois subject of complex interior emotions'.

The sacrifice of the sovereign subject to abstraction assumes a less optimistic and far more ominous tenor in Richard Godden and Michael Szalay's biographically inflected analysis of the same novel. In linking Foster Wallace's suicide in September 2008 to *The Pale King*'s representation of the US nation-state's financialisation, they focus not on the old, but on the new IRS and the author's fatal immersion in it. In their reading, *The Pale King* 'embodies the state of a troubled nation' whose 'lifeblood' is derivative monies, a provocative figure suggested by Foster Wallace's text and which implies an identification of the state and, thus, the novel with the monies that flow through it. In moving through secretive financial channels, derivative flows 'obtain an opacity', yet, far from being hidden, are manifested in the bodies and bodily flows of Foster's Wallace's characters – including the character, 'David Foster Wallace'. As Godden and Szalay demonstrate through a series of fine-grained readings, these characters personify the dual nature of derivatives as both real and abstract, 'confront[ing] us with a graphic concreteness' even as 'we experience them dissolving into equivalency'. As in so many of the essays in this issue, the abstraction in question here is, at base, an absence, albeit one that is manifested in strangely excessive ways. 'Wallace's characters', they suggest, 'reference forms of value that they *can't contain*' and in this regard they at once recall the unfinished (or 'impossible to finish') form of the novel itself and prepare the way for Godden and Szalay's own detailed account of the functions and fluids running through Foster Wallace's text. For the authors, 'the deficit at the heart of finance' ultimately corresponds to a deficit at the heart of 'the contradictory structure of personhood called forth by a system of derivatives'. Like the corporeal flows that run through *The Pale King*, Foster Wallace's own sacrifice to this system leaves a residue or precipitate, both in the form of his unfinished manuscript and, more disturbingly, in the form of his own lifeless body.

If, as the third poem in Stewart's 'Abstraction set' suggests, 'numbers cannot live/in your mind', then *The Pale King* and its author's suicide cannot help but cast doubt on our ability to live in numbers, to live as the embodiment and personification of finance. And yet, Emily Apter, in the essay with which this special issue concludes, asks if there might be a number that is not destructive, but amenable to life – to a life beyond the various forms of 'shareholder existence' and 'managed life' that have concerned French theorists such as Frédéric Gros, Luc Boltanski, and Bruno Latour in their recent critiques of accountability under financial capitalism. The motifs of both sacrifice and subtraction return in Apter's essay, but are aligned here with 'pure number' and 'a subject that is unaccounted for' via a reading of Meillassoux's *The Number and the Siren: A Decipherment of Mallarmé's* Un Coup de Dés. In attempting to decode the 'enigma' of number enciphered in Mallarmé's text, Meillassoux projects a 'futural aesthetics reliant on the clairvoyance of numbers', an aesthetics of pure chance that forsakes the subject of political economy in favour of 'divine inexistence'. Meillassoux's and, by extension, Apter's return to Mallarmé's 1898 text recalls and revises the critique, voiced in different ways here, of the notion that capitalism has become *more* abstract over time. Certainly Apter, in recounting recent theoretical work by Gros, Boltanski, and Latour, is attentive to what is historically new and distinctive about today's shareholder existence. Yet in returning with Meillassoux to this earlier moment of literary production in order to gesture towards a different future, towards 'a mode of existence in which the meter is not always running', she also begins to suggest that the ontological limits of historical critique are already in view. Though the history of capital's abstractions may not yet fully be written, the thought of an alternative may already be at hand. The challenge now is to think it.

New York University

Notes

1 Quoted in Joe Nocera, 'Sex and Drugs and I.P.O.'s: Martin Scorsese's Approach in "The Wolf of Wall Street"', *New York Times*, 19 December 2013, http://www.nytimes.com/2013/12/22/movies/martin-scorseses-approach-in-the-wolf-of-wall-street.html?pagewanted=all [Date accessed: 13 April 2014].

2 Ibid.

3 Randy Martin, *The Financialization of Daily Life* (Philadelphia: Temple UP, 2002).

4 Karl Marx, *Grundrisse*, trans. Martin Nicolaus (London and New York: Penguin, 1973), p. 164.

5 Joshua Clover, '*Value* | *Theory* | Crisis', *PMLA*, 127.1 (2012), pp. 107–114, and Christopher Nealon, 'Value | *Theory* | *Crisis*', *PMLA*, 127.1 (2012), pp. 101–106.

6 Recalling the near identical titles of Clover's and Nealon's articles (see note 5 above) we might be even more precise and say that both drew parallels between 'value', 'theory', and 'crisis', while differently emphasising these three terms. But which term bears the emphasis exactly? 'Crisis' would seem to carry priority in Clover's case and 'value' in Nealon's – a point paradoxically suggested by the fact that these terms are *not* italicised in their respective titles and, arguably, borne out by their essays. What then of 'theory'? Is it equivalent to these other terms and, if so, on what ground, or, as its central placement suggests, is 'theory' in fact the middle ground, mediating between 'value' and 'crisis'? In Clover's and Nealon's essays, theories of value and crisis are taken to register the complicity of some varieties of contemporary theory with finance, but the question remains: what theory of theory, as a form of intellectual or philosophical abstraction, is operative here?

7 Leigh Claire La Berge, 'The Rules of Abstraction: Methods and Discourses of Finance', in 'The Fictions of Finance', Special Issue, *Radical History Review*, 118 (2014), p. 93–112 (96).

8 Ibid., p. 96.

9 Ibid., pp. 96–7.

10 La Berge quite cleverly suggests that '*complex* might be the vernacular equivalent of *abstract*' – 'a placeholder for a process that cannot be represented in its entirety for some unknown, and perhaps unknowable, reason'. See La Berge, 'The Rules of Abstraction', p. 105.

11 Aaron Carico and Dara Orenstein, 'Editors' Introduction: The Fictions of Finance', in 'The Fictions of Finance', Special Issue, *Radical History Review*, 118 (2014), p. 3–13 (6).

Nicky Marsh

'Paradise falls: a land lost in time': representing credit, debt
and work after the crisis

This article examines the way in which credit and debt have been explored
since the 2008 crisis: suggesting a formal analogue in which an abstracted
financial capital (credit) has been contrasted against its concrete productive
counterpart (debt). The first half of the paper traces this contrast through
the theoretical vocabularies for credit and debt that have emerged in the
wake of the crisis, in which debt has been separated from credit and the
possibility that the former can be read as resisting the latter's dependence
on financialisation has been explored. In the second half, I explore this
dyad as it is made evident in two very recent films, Andrew Niccol's
2011 *In Time* and Rian Johnson's 2012 *Looper*, which offer an alternative
model of social debt, one that uses the connection between time and work
to actively critique the movement from productive to financial capital.
These two films, I want to suggest, engage with the difficulties of representing the 'concrete' nature of productive capital by both thematically and formally foregrounding its literalism.

The memorable and lengthy opening sequence to the 2009 children's film *Up* is counter-intuitive. It not only begins with the elderly death of its most likeable youthful character but it also questions the very fabric of children's fantasy from which it is drawn, the insistence that following dreams is always heroic and will always be rewarded. The compressed narrative of Carl and Ellie's married life begins as the balloon that brought them together pops and the suggestion that real life begins only when dreams burst recurs on an ever-increasing scale until, in the film's conclusion, both their home and their fantasies have been relinquished.

It is hard not to read *Up* through the credit crisis: the film's striking visual identifier, the old man clinging fearfully to a house lifted by a gaudy cloud of balloons, suggests nothing less than the housing bubble that had burst so disastrously in the year immediately prior to its release. Bubbles and balloons have long provided credit with its most obvious metaphors, the iconography of the film is eerily similar to that of a credit card campaign, and hot air balloons, aeroplanes, rockets, mountains, waterslides and unearthly towers have long dominated the visual lexicon of the credit industry.[1] The couple dream of reaching 'Paradise Falls, a land lost in time', and the double naming both suggests and critiques the sublime of credit, its ability to free those who possess it from the constraints of space and time. Carl's eventual escape in the wake of Ellie's death is achieved not by money – the ringing coins dropped into their savings jar – but by the credit symbolised by the balloons that can safely raise their house above the ground. That the home should reach its fantasy destination by twirling intact through a storm provides an obvious allusion to *The Wizard of Oz* (whose eponymous main character was also a balloonist) and the reference is a rich one, suggesting both the allegorical critique of credit that is central to Baum's 1900 novella[2] and the doubleness of 'camp's (counter)canon' that became synonymous with Metro Goldwyn Mayer's 1939 movie adaptation of it.[3]

In the film's ending both the dream of Paradise and the house itself are abandoned as Carl becomes a father figure to the eight-year old Russell who accompanied him on his journey, and safely steered both his house and he to their end. So Carl replaces credit with debt: he is homeless but repaying Russell removes from him the very real threat of his obsolescence and gives him the future that only children, and not even his marriage, can provide. After the credit crash, the film suggests, we regain our sanity and we rebuild our lives from our debts: and the man who was created by Pixar in the shape of a 'brick, weighed down and resistant to change' is the perfect figure to do it.[4]

The commentary that the film provides on the financial crisis is ambiguous. In some ways *Up*'s apparent critique of credit accords with what Judith Halberstam dubbed the 'pixarvolt' in children's animated films. The film was directed by Peter Hans Docter, who also directed *Monsters, Inc.*, and thus was central to Halberstam's description of a computer generated imagery-led genre that makes

> subtle as well as overt connections between communitarian revolt and queer embodiment [...] the queer is not represented as a singularity but as part of an assemblage of resistant technologies that include collectivity, imagination and a kind of situationist commitment to surprise and shock.[5]

Carl's stoicism in the face of his apparent failure also fits with the broader vision that lies behind Halberstam's 'queer art of failure' that 'turns on the impossible, the improbable, the unlikely and the unremarkable. It quietly loses, and in losing it imagines other goals for life, for love, for art and for being'.[6] Yet, in other ways, the film's reliance on the father-son relationship tempers these possibilities. In identifying the future with the child it comes close to subscribing to what Lee Edelman has named the 'heterofuturity' of mainstream culture in which the reproduction of social goods depends upon the privileged innocence of the child figure.[7] The critique that the film appears to offer is immediately closed down in a move that Mark Fisher described, in relation to another Pixar film that Halberstam celebrates (*Wall-E*, 2008, dir. Andrew Stanton), as one that performs

> our anti-capitalism for us, allowing to continue to consume with impunity. The role of capitalist ideology is not to make an explicit case for something in the way that propaganda does, but to conceal the fact that the operations of capital do not depend on any sort of subjectively assumed belief.[8]

What we see at the end of *Up* is the process of accumulation, momentarily stalled by the crisis, beginning again.

The ambiguity of *Up* speaks to the difficulty of imagining a critique of contemporary finance, or at least imagining it in the vocabularies of popular culture. Most obviously it suggests the difficulty of conceptualising a future alternative to capital when the very concept of the future has been so successfully co-opted, not only by a heteronormative futurism but also by the pervasive 'pre-emption' of finance described by Randy Martin, amongst others.[9] Indeed, Joshua Clover's recent intervention in *PMLA* suggests that cultural theory might better serve the contemporary situation if it attempted to represent not the abstracting capacities of finance capital (Clover, following figures such as Michael Tratner, makes apparent the 'debt' that theory owes to it) but the 'dynamic character of the conjunction of finance and production'.[10] Grasping the 'moving contradiction of the value form, of use and exchange, production and circulation', Clover concludes, has 'proved a near-absolute limit to understanding the historical situation'.[11] We need, in other words, to acknowledge the implications of the ongoing dialectic between finance and productive (or industrial) capital, as the crisis in the former has been immediately transferred, via state intervention, to the tax-paying working classes of the latter. It is not the 'abstract' of finance that we need to find ways of representing (we might argue that this has been a recurring task of twentieth-century aesthetic experimentation) but the 'concrete' realities of labour that are now, literally, carrying their costs. Yet, as the example of Fisher's critique reminds us, this is the very thing that we find hard to do, not least because realism, its conventional historical corollary, has been so successfully emptied out.

I want to return to the cues offered by *Up* to suggest a way of representing the 'moving contradiction' that forms the relationship between finance and productive capital. The film's critique of credit and recuperation of debt can be read through a formal analogue in which an abstracted financial capital (credit) is contrasted against its concrete productive counterpart (debt). I elucidate this contention in the first half of the paper by tracing the theoretical vocabulary for the two terms that has emerged in the wake of the financial crisis, in which debt has been separated from credit and the possibility that the former can be read as resisting the latter's dependence on financialisation has been explored. In the second half, I explore these possibilities as they are made evident in two very recent films, Andrew Niccol's 2011 *In Time* and Rian Johnson's 2012 *Looper*, which offer an alternative model of social debt, one that uses the connection between time and work to actively critique the movement from productive to financial capital. These two films, I want to suggest, engage with the difficulties of representing productive capital, and the alternative future that we find so hard to imagine, by both thematically and formally foregrounding its literalism.

The counter-intuitive opening of *Up* extends to its reading of credit and debt, as it initially appears to reverse the common associations of both. If credit provides capital's spatio-temporal fix, providing it with the ability to move through time and space, then debt is associated with its opposite; it is that which it leaves behind. The languages for debt are routinely those of death or entrapment: if the images for credit speak of an abstraction, then those for debt assuredly do not. As Margaret Atwood noted in *Payback: Debt as Metaphor and the Shadow Side of Wealth*, we

> get 'into' debt, as if into a prison, swamp or well, or possibly a bed;
> we get 'out' of it, as if coming into the open air or climbing out of a

hole. If we are 'overwhelmed' by debt, the image is possibly that of a foundering ship, with the sea and the waves pouring in on top of us as we flail and choke.[12]

Debt is a death dealt to us by the banking system, John Forrester has suggested, whose symbolic presence in our lives has long since superseded the mausoleums in whose 'image they were built'.[13] Michael Rowbotham similarly begins his account of 'debt slavery' by noting that in French the word for mortgage is 'death handshake', suggesting an obligation from which one can never be freed.[14]

In *The Making of the Indebted Man* Maurizio Lazzarato theorises the relations of debt in terms of the contemporary crisis and places its eschatological register into the critique of neo-liberal governance offered by Italian autonomist Marxism. For Lazzarato debt has become the 'archetype of social relations' and the 'asymmetry of power' between creditor-debtor that it produces frames the subject, as 'debt means immediately making the economy subjective' and implies 'the moulding and control of subjectivity'.[15] Hence, for Lazzarato, indebtedness is biopolitical, requiring the indebted subject to internalise a Nietzschean language of moral edicts, of guilt, blame, duty, and conscience, and assigning to the creditor the 'power to prescribe and impose modes of future exploitation, domination and subjection'.[16] It is in this context that debt equals a kind of death: the 'principle explanation for the strange sensation of living in a society without time, without foreseeable rupture', he suggests, 'is debt'.[17]

This entrapment of debt was more wryly noted by Raymond Williams in 1983 when he observed that credit was that which we 'used to call debt' and Williams' attention to the historical slippage between the terms allows us to understand both how debt might be thought of beyond these deathly terms and the nature of its relationship to finance and productive capital.[18] For Williams the move from debt to credit signalled the identification by the indebted with finance capital, a move that the rise of home-ownership had effectively brought about. This conflation of debt with credit, and the internalisation of a shift from identifying with productive to financial capital that it involved, provides one history of the contemporary mortgage-fuelled credit-crisis. When debt is conflated with credit it is turned into an asset. Yet the virtues of this asset were, at best, ambiguous. For the actual creditor, of course, the asset was clearly quantitative: it was both interest-bearing and commodifiable and became the raw material for the derivatives which ignited the 2008 financial conflagration. This was the financialisation of debt that made risk disappear by seeding it through the entire financial sector, the subprime mortgages were the assets neatly boxed up in the derivative financial instruments which it became, literally, impossible to know or understand.[19] For the debtor who was in possession of credit the asset was more qualitative but no less ambivalent: instant loans and re-mortgages seemed to extend capital's spatial and temporal fix to all. As Williams somewhat ruefully acknowledged, credit gave 'people genuine kinds of freedom and choice and mobility which their ancestors would have given very much for'. Yet Williams is sharply explicit about the price of this freedom, noting it was reliant on the 'deterioration of the very conditions which allow it', the full employment and welfare state made possible by the postwar settlement and the restricted economies of the Bretton Woods era.[20]

Williams' remarks are suggestive not only of the unequal relations between creditor and debtor that are concealed by the conflation of the two terms under the remit of financialisation but also of the different forms that this debt has itself taken in regard to the division between public and private. He contrasts the 'mobile privatisation' of a burgeoning domestic credit against the narrowing of the State's willingness to sustain the very things – housing, education, health, employment – that this domestic credit was now required to pay for. The effect was, as Colin Crouch has argued, a privatised Keynesianism, as the 'bases of prosperity shifted from the social democratic formula of working classes supported by government intervention to the neoliberal conservative one of banks, stock exchanges and financial markets' and individuals became 'debt-holders, participants in credit markets'.[21] This interdependency of the domestic and financial economies made the bail-out of the financial sector in 2008 appear necessary and the implications of this privatisation of public credit stark indeed. In David Harvey's most succinct of terms, profits have been privatised and risks have been socialised in a process that he describes as akin to a modern enclosure.[22] The State's unwillingness to provide public credit, its reliance on the private credit of financialisation, has only been further entrenched by the austerity that has followed the financial crisis. Hence, financialisation has effectively inverted the debt trap: those in debt are still captured but they also risk being placed on the outside of the citizenship that only credit affords. These unpayable debts risk an exposure analogous to Giorgio Agamben's model of political sovereignty: finance constitutes its absolute authority by exercising a deadly ability to exclude, to condemn those without credit to the 'bare life' beyond the polity.[23]

Nowhere is this 'bare life' of indebtedness more apparent than in the two recurring images now attached to the financial crisis. The first set of images represents those who work in the financial sector, the professional creditors of the crisis. These are images of bankers who embody the crisis itself. They are routinely shown either staring in desperation at their computer monitors, clasping their heads or mouths in disbelief, or leaving their offices, clasping brown boxes of personal effects.[24] The latter image evokes the height of the first phase of the crisis, the closure of Lehman Brothers in mid-September 2008, and was seized upon accordingly in the popular press. One such figure became the 'face of the banking crisis' and a 'muse' for David Hare's play, *The Power of Yes*.[25] The second kind of image associated with the crisis, more lingering and less celebrated, is of the 'foreclosed' signs that obstruct the estate agent views of large, often American, suburban homes. These images are entirely depopulated and depict the estate agents' signs declaring the emptied ranks of newly built and abandoned homes effectively worthless.

The different registers employed by these two sets of images are telling of the ways in which the relationship between credit and debt has been imagined in the mainstream press in the wake of the crisis. The images of financial creditors suggest affect and agency, the trader's moment of dramatic recognition followed by a reckoning with individual professional precarity. They are rich with the possibility of recuperation: the stock market made an astonishingly quick and sustained revival in 2008 and when the box-carrying Lehman employee was re-employed it made national news. Yet the empty photographs of newly built homes reveal both the cost of the financial crisis and the exclusion of the indebted from its frames. In these images the subjects of this loss, a disproportionately high amount of whom were, of course, African-American and Hispanic, are removed entirely: their metonymic 'subprime' status reinforcing their dehumanising destitution. In their absence the homes of these figures not only evoke the 'prison, swamp or well' that Atwood associates with debt but they render its fluid, rushing properties, 'the sea and the waves pouring in on top of us as we flail and choke', infectiously poisonous. The untreated pools of the abandoned homes that sit behind the 'Foreclosed' signs have become a notorious host for disease-bearing mosquitoes which are now, in turn, being treated by 'foreclosure fish', described as a 'nasty invasive alien species' hungry for insect larvae but threatening to the environment.[26] The image is a clear metonym for the abjection of the indebted who, the logic suggests, have disturbed the boundaries of the community that they had no right to belong to in the first place. The absent debtor and privileged creditor apparent in the visual iconography of the crash clearly speaks to the difficulty of representing the dialectic between financial and productive capital that is at the heart of this crisis: those who work (outside of finance capital) are literally unimaginable.

In this context, *Up's* presentation of credit and debt, its critique of the flighty dangers of credit and the recuperation of debt that its inclusion of the elderly homeless man sitting on the pavement at its end implies, is worth noting. Indeed, in this sense the film chimes with the ways in which a number of theorists have begun to recast the social relations of debt by separating them from those of credit. This work has been led by the anthropologist David Graeber who represents debt as a necessary part of sociality rather than as only an articulation of an asymmetrical capital relation. Graeber argues that viewing debt solely through the language of capital involves accepting its individualism as axiomatic and rejecting that co-operation and interdependency can also function as the foundations of society. For Graeber debt is a way of organising rather than simply negating social relations: 'debt is what happens' when 'two parties cannot walk away from each other, because they are not yet equal. But it is carried out in the shadow of eventual equality'.[27] His wonderfully succinct account of the credit crisis suggests that it was produced by the financialisation of this process, the 'outcome of years of political tussles between creditors and debtors, rich and poor'.[28]

Graeber's suggestion that we can recuperate the language of debt as a social relation outside of financialisation is also evident in Atwood's *Payback* as it presents debt as a social relation that speaks to an 'innate human' propensity to evaluate 'fairness and unfairness' and that 'strives for balance: otherwise nobody would either lend or pay back'.[29] For other critics this recuperation of debt as a form of the social resides in a desire to imagine an alternative to capitalism and resist the conflation of debt and credit that financialisation successfully wrought. Credit differs from debt, Fred Moten and Stefano Harney suggested in the wake of the 2008 financial crisis, because it represents the financialisation of debt's social capacities. This was the logic apparent in their polemical manifesto 'Debt and Study' in which credit is understood as a

> means of privatization and debt a means of socialization. So long as debt and credit are paired in the monogamous violence of the home, the pension, the government, or the university, debt can only feed credit, debt can only desire credit. And credit can only expand by means of debt. But debt is social and credit is asocial. Debt is mutual. Credit runs only one way.[30]

The assumptions underpinning these claims have been elaborated in Richard Dienst's reading of Marx in *Bonds of Debt*. Dienst posits debt as a marker of social lack, as 'every socially articulable expression of the gap between what we have, what we need, and what we want' and credit as the drawing of profit from this gap, a drawing which necessarily destroys the social. Like Lazzarato, Dienst draws on Marx to suggest that debt calls forth 'concrete metaphors of the body [. . .] indebted bodies are precisely what capital takes for granted on every level' and the 'enclosure of the lived body [is] the inaugural biopolitical event'.[31] Credit, in contrast, expresses the 'abstract, even metaphysical, tendencies of capitalist accumulation and centralization', accompanying the 'generalization of exchange and property relations' and serving as the means by which 'these processes are turned into symbolic games in order to expand their domain'.[32] By separating out credit from debt in this way, Dienst is able to separate out the processes of financialisation from the experience of indebtedness. He contrasts the ways in which both imagine time, for example, suggesting that, whereas credit is 'the sweeping gesture with which capital lays claim to the present in the name of the past and the future', debt

> may be seen as a mark of the nonsynchronous, the stubborn insistence of everything resistant to economic rule. If creating credit ex nihlio is a sublime project of an economic order and system, indebtedness must be the deferral or withdrawal of value, a way to play for time in order to keep something alive.

Dienst, like Halberstam, is advocating a strategy of political resistance that calls on a counter-intuitive acceptance of failure when he asks whether indebtedness which 'seemed to be the most inescapable trap of capital, in fact offers us a lever with which to overturn it?'[33]

The time of the indebted body is, of course, also socially necessary labour time, the time of the clock. One of the reasons that playing 'for time' may act as such an effective way of keeping 'something alive' is that it presents us with a way of recuperating the politics of work and time in a moment that seems able to deny them; Dienst's rather enigmatic claim makes sense when it allows us to analyse why work itself has become a kind of failure. Noel Castree's re-reading of David Harvey outlines Marx's dual treatment of time in useful ways in this context. The first kind of time, he notes, is the 'clock time' of 'socially necessary labour time' that 'both expresses and reconfigures an ensemble of social relations' and the second is the time of 'credit and fictitious capital', the time of 'money capitalists [...] whose job it is to pool and deploy money with a view to making more of it'.[34] Castree draws on Harvey to stress the inextricability of these two forms of time: credit may allow capital to 'run ahead of itself' and be 'relatively autonomous from the primary circuit' but it is always a function of it and will contain the original 'circuit's ineluctable contradictions'.[35] Hence credit provides productive capital with a 'temporal fix', converting the 'fluidity of money into long-term' interest-bearing commitments and the contemporary crisis reveals that this 'countermand [of] the temporal contradictions of the primary circuit' is short-lived and that the 'crisis tendencies of the present stand to be amplified in years to come'.[36] As Marx had it in the third volume of *Capital*, 'credit accelerates the violent eruptions of this contradiction – crises – and hereby the disintegration of the old mode of production'.[37]

The current crisis can thus be read as the failure of credit's temporal fix: the over-accumulation that it sought to defer that has now been exponentially increased by over-leverage. The profits of the future have been realised as the losses of the present and are returned, through the bailouts of the State, to the over-indebted labouring body of productive capital, already suffering from the 'disintegration' of the 'mode of production'. It is in this sense that the present crisis can be claimed as a return to the real: the dialectical interdependencies between the 'concrete' realities of productive capital and the 'abstract' concepts of finance capital are made apparent once more. Yet this is no revolutionary moment. The politics of austerity have allowed capital to begin to financialise the remaining assets of the working class, the welfare state itself, creating a 'new field of accumulation of capital in the name of cutting public budgets to balance the books'.[38] It is no surprise that public anger is starting to focus on rapidly deteriorating and narrowing working conditions rather than on the failures of the financial class. The most telling example of the social catastrophes of the present is the sweeping phenomena of the 'zero hours' working contract, when the final commitment that made sense of the employer-employee contract, the commitment to work itself, is swept away.

I want to conclude by offering readings of two contemporary films, Andrew Niccol's *In Time* and Rian Johnson's *Looper*, that critique the relationship between clock time, debt and work as they reimagine the meaning of the biopolitical time of debt in the shadow of the crisis. The first image in both films is of the ticking clock and both immediately make sense of it by exploring how time produces and regulates the working body. In *In Time*, we see the digital clock glowing under the skin of the Justin Timberlake character, Will Salas (pronounced 'solace'), as he explains that 'time is now the currency, we earn it and spend it. The rich can live for ever. And the rest of us? I just want to wake up with more time on my hands than hours in the day'. In *Looper*, we see Joe, the character played by Joseph Gordon-Levitt, studying a silver fob watch, whilst he also waits for his working day to begin. The scales in which time and work are measured in the two films are very different. When Will clocks out of his working day in a Fordist-style factory, time is revealed to be almost impossibly tight, it is measured in minutes and social control is levered by a deflationary economy, in which productivity is required to increase as wages decrease. The scale in *Looper* is both bigger and smaller and speaks more obviously to a post-Fordist individualised regime. Joe is a contract-killer; he assassinates men delivered from the future and times his meetings with them to the very second whilst simultaneously measuring the time until he can stop working in months and years – in the film's opening he is practising the French he will need in his retired life while counting the seconds of his working life.

Yet in both films the relationship between time and work is deadly and violent. In *Looper* the assassins will only be released from their contract when they successfully kill their future selves, an act called 'closing the loop', which makes them exorbitantly rich but also ensures their certain death in exactly thirty years. In *In Time* there is simply not enough time; it has been stolen by a small elite class and the casual violence of workers being 'timed out' is demonstrated early on when Will fails by mere seconds to prevent his mother's death. The crisis in the central narrative of both films emerges as these male leads try to get more time, to resist the indebted body represented by the loop or by clocking in, in order to repay a familial debt: to save the women to whom they literally owe their lives. Hence both films use the trope of time to contrast incommensurate debts: the biopolitical debt of the labouring body against the familial debts the child owes the parent.

The dystopian settings for both films fit the description of the empty urban futuristic chaos that Mark Fisher derides in the opening to *Capitalist Realism*. Fisher is discussing *Children of Men* and the film shares with both *In Time* and *Looper* a post-apocalyptic vision of a world that both is and is not recognisably our own, a scenario that Fisher suggests denotes the collapse of a coherent response to capitalism. A world that is 'more like an extrapolation or exacerbation of ours than an alternative to it', he suggests, removes the expectations of possibility and change. It is a world in which catastrophe 'is neither waiting down the road nor has it already happened. Rather, it is being lived through'.[39] Although I want to stop short of assigning any radical significance to these two deeply generic and conventional Hollywood films I want to suggest that they exceed Fisher's 'gestural anti-capitalism' by producing a formal critique that extends the implications of their more obvious thematic critiques of work and time. The films formally enact, in other words, their self-conscious critique of the failure of the mode of production, the resistance of the indebted body, that is the invisible centre of the contemporary crisis.

For Fisher, the mimetic resources of Hollywood realism are scarce. He draws on a Lacanian vocabulary, in which the 'Real' is that which '"reality" [the symbolic] must suppress; indeed reality constitutes itself through just this repression' and hence subversion lies in 'invoking the Real(s) underlying the reality that capitalism presents to us'.[40] The symbolic order of signification is itself founded on a debt. According to John Forrester, the 'Lacanian subject becomes a subject only in incurring a symbolic debt to the father, or the element in the world which instantiates the paternal metaphor'.[41] The currency that Lacan assigns to this debt, Forrester goes on to elucidate, is measured not 'in terms of a substance, like coins or papers' but rather by 'an accounting procedure [...] a mark, by a piece of writing, like the first system of money of which we have records'.[42] Forrester describes what we already knew, the deferred nature of the sign in the symbolic, as a debt in a credit economy guaranteed by the paternal metaphor.

The critique that is offered in the near-futuristic worlds of both *In Time* and *Looper* invokes the existence of the 'Real' by evoking a literalism – a concrete debt – that disturbs both the symbolic order of signification and the familial logic of the paternal metaphor upon which it relies. *In Time* makes literalism its central conceit: it makes time money. Andrew Niccol's account of the film glosses it as 'the most sort of literal demonstration of living in the moment' and the film's clearly polemical arc echoes the '99 per cent' rhetoric of the Occupy movement and it is surprisingly blatant in its advocacy of insurrection.[43] When an interviewer suggests, for example, that the film is advocating nothing short of 'fairly radical revolution' Niccol's answer is direct: 'I wouldn't argue with that'.[44] His description of the film as 'a literal demonstration of living in the moment' could be taken to imply that its literalism is itself a kind of political demonstration. Indeed, so strangely literal are the film's effects that Niccol suggests that they provided a cover for the text's subterfuge. When explaining how the film was made by the deeply conservative Twentieth Century Fox, he suggests that 'you go in with a pitch and you say "no character's over twenty five years of age and there's a ticking clock in every scene", they just go "where do I sign?" They don't read the script'.[45]

In both films the endlessly ticking clock is a constant reminder of the indebtedness of those who work. So stark are the representations of the connection between work and time that they place both films at odds with the more obviously cinematic traditions of work and time in which they could be located. The first of these traditions, concerned with the Fordist narratives evident in *In Time*, use form to critically explore the relationship between work and time. The films that shared this interest, which range from *Metropolis* (1927, dir. Fritz Lang) to *Modern Times* (1936, dir. Charlie Chaplin) to the late-industrial angst of *The Deer Hunter* (1978, dir. Michael Cimino), experiment with cinema in order to express the alienation of Fordist work and time: Lang's claustrophobic and compressed futurism, Chaplin's physical comedy, and Cimino's ironically sublime pastoral all offer a critique of the violence of clock work. A second more recent tradition, to which *Looper* more obviously corresponds, are films that engage with the apparent plasticity and compression of time in a postmodern and post-Fordist era. These films, from *Terminator* (1984, dir. James Cameron) to *Eternal Sunshine of the Spotless Mind* (2004, dir. Michael Gondry), have been dubbed 'The Mind-Game Films' by Thomas Elsaesser, as they engender their 'own loops or Möbius strips' and their 'constant retroactive revision, new reality-checks, displacements, and reorganisation not only of temporal sequence, but of mental space, and the presumption of a possible switch in cause and effect' signify the 'effects of the new disciplinary machines of "affective labor" in a post-Fordist regime'.[46]

Yet the peculiar literalisms of both *Looper* and *In Time* keep them at a distance from these traditions. The narrative voice over in *In Time* refuses to be drawn into the machinations of its own science fiction world very early on. 'I don't have time to explain how it happened', Timberlake's voice over tells us of the genetic engineering that stopped the ageing process at 25 and required people to earn their future. *Looper* similarly denies the complexities of its form, the 'mobius strip' of time travel causality. The film's two time frames are clearly delineated and quickly brought together into a single narrative. The two versions of Joe are able to unproblematically co-exist (they can possess the same watch at the same time, for example) and the film is explicit in rejecting the philosophical questions that their face-to-face meeting involves. As the elder Joe (Bruce Willis) snaps to his younger self, 'I don't want to talk about time travel shit. Because if we start talking about it then we're going to be here all day making diagrams with straws. It doesn't matter. It doesn't matter'.

One might suggest that 'it doesn't matter' because it *is not* 'matter'. The film's thematic interest in the literal realities of work finds a correspondence in their use of language. Timberlake's opening sentence, 'I don't have time to explain how it happened', establishes the register for the film's dialogue as it both denies and underlines the significance of its own metaphors. As the phatic metaphor of time is used literally again and again it reveals how deeply rooted dialogue is in exchange as everyday interactions – 'have you got a minute?', 'I need a moment', 'don't waste my time' – become performative, and monetarised, requests. *Looper* similarly nods to the possibility that words have become things: after being threatened with a gun young Joe is confirmed in his fearlessness when the gun holder resorts to describing the weapon instead of using it, as he comments, 'it's telling. You're holding a gun and I say I'm not afraid and so you describe the gun to me. It's not the gun I'm not afraid of'.

Of course, as this example neatly acknowledges, these films do not replace figuration with the literal. This is, as Paul De Man's mocking reading of Locke's attempt to define the 'proper' use of language demonstrates, impossible. As De Man argues, 'metaphor gives itself the totality which it then claims to define, but it is in fact the tautology of its own position'.[47] Rather, both films draw attention to the literal in order to highlight the violence of a different kind of literalism, the economic literalism of the market and the violence that ensues when complex social debts are closed down by money, by the 'callous "cash payment"'

25

that drowns the possibilities of the social in the 'icy water of egotistical calculation'.[48]

In both films, paying social debts with money produces violence. Before leaving the ghetto the newly rich Will gives time-money to his heavily indebted and vulnerable friend. He gives him ten years, the length of their friendship, but by paying his debt in time-money he annuls the mutual care that their friendship otherwise involved and we later discover that his friend had drunk himself to death, with 'nine years still left on the clock'. A similar logic is at work in *Looper* where the currencies in which payment is made reveal the social exchanges that their financial worth denies. The assassins are paid in pieces of silver for a work that ends in suicide and the metal symbolises the betrayal of the self that they are complicit with. When they eventually 'close their loop' they are released from their contract, given a 'gold payday' to 'spend like crazy in the next thirty years' before they are sent back to an unwitting suicide. The annulment of self that this mocking retirement payment represents is echoed in other exchanges in the film. Joe's lover, for example, is a sex worker who is unable to keep her eyes from the clock and when they kiss she complains of being 'so tired of working everyday'. Yet when Joe offers to 'share' his silver with her so that she can stop working and care for her young son she reads this not as a release but as an offer to enter into a different kind of paid work, to becoming Joe's prostitute rather than his lover and thus losing her freedom: 'silver's got strings. I got my job and you got yours, why don't we just stick to services rendered'.

Both films resist the effects of the 'callous cash payment' whilst also complicating the nature of the familial debts that they pursue in its stead. Both men need to escape the indebtedness of their bodies to a biopolitical labour time in order to pay the familial debts that exceed this order: Will is going to 'pay back' the inhabitants of New Greenwich for the untimely death of his mother and the elder Joe is attempting to preemptively save the life of his wife who was also killed early in the narrative. Yet these family romances resist futurity and the reproduction of the symbolic order that the repayment of the paternal debt secures. Instead their psychoanalytical structures amplify the literalism of their use of language: both men are the fathers to themselves and, in the logic of the narrative, have already slept with their mothers.

In *In Time* Will and his mother appear to be the same age and their relationship is conducted through the tropes of romantic love. He gives her champagne for her birthday, meets her from work bearing flowers, and wants only to escape from the ghetto with her. The confusion of roles is made obvious in the cliché of her dying scene, in which they try, but fail, to run into one other's arms. When Sylvia (played by Amanda Seyfried) becomes Will's actual lover later in the film she does so wearing his mother's clothes and, indeed, sleeping with Sylvia is Will's most effective form of vengeance for his mother's death: he steals the daughter of the man who stole his mother in a world in which the difference between mothers and daughters and fathers and sons is impossible to determine. As Sylvia's father (played by Vincent Kartheiser) notes of precisely this difficulty, these are 'confusing times'.

A parallel set of complexities exists in *Looper*. The relationship between the elder and younger Joe is complicated not by the machinations of time travel but by the oedipal drama that is being played out between them. Their meeting is framed as a tense conversation between a son and father rather than between two versions of the same self, with the younger Joe initially ruefully accepting of advice but sarcastically hostile about enquiries about his schooling, 'are you going to tell me that I ought to be learning Mandarin?' Hence saving the elder Joe's wife is equivalent to saving the younger Joe's mother (who is thus also his lover) and the language with which the elder Joe attempts to persuade the younger Joe to fall in with his plan suggests this. Like Carl and Ellie, Joe and his wife were unable to have a child (the single instance in which the film does play with the possibility of false memory is in the scene in which the elder Joe appears to joyfully remember a baby's cry) and as he describes his wife he recalls that 'for a long time she thought we were going to have a baby. She would have been a great mother. She wanted it so much'. The jarring use of the future perfect tense in the first sentence leaves open the possibility that they *did* actually have a baby and when he loses his temper with younger Joe it implies that, indeed, they now have, albeit a profoundly ungrateful one: 'Shut your fucking child mouth. [...] she's going to clean you up. You're going to take her love like a sponge'.

In Time and *Looper* use clock time to critique the biopolitical governance of the indebted working body. They overcome the difficulties contemporary culture has in presenting the indebted worker by literalising its 'concrete metaphors', drawing attention to the very contradictions of such representations. They also seek to illustrate the violence of these debts by contrasting them against other kinds of debt, specifically social and familial debts, which exceed the logic of the 'callous cash payment' and offer the possibility for recuperating debt in the face of its economic violence. The films' literalism extends to its psychoanalytical structures and thus the repayment of these familial debts disturbs the heteronormative centrality of the child or the futurity of the paternal metaphor. In both cases the films' pervert the family romance; they remove its debts from the economic sphere whilst also making the ideal of familial reproduction an impossibility.

The contemporary crisis has made apparent the profound limitations of considering economics only through the self-referential abstractions of finance capital. Credit's apparent ascendancy over the productive world of work has been revealed as a dangerous fantasy: its temporal-fix has failed and its over-leveraged costs are being paid for by the already over-indebted body of the worker. Yet this worker remains persistently absent in the iconography of this crisis, where they are represented by their absence, by the effects of their failure to pay their debts upon finance capital. Cultural theory's intervention in these debates, its reflection on the meanings of credit and debt and its attempt to recuperate the latter in order to resist the financialisation of the former, has offered one fruitful response to this absence. The attempt to find ways of representing not simply workers but their dialectical relationship to credit that this response implies has also been taken up in popular culture. It is in the near-worlds of contemporary science fiction, in films such as *Looper* and *In Time*, I have argued, that we see the contradictions between credit and debt, and the desire to offer an alternative to them, being put into play through a literalisation of the 'concrete metaphors' of the indebted worker.

University of Southampton

Notes

1 The Lloyds' campaign, 'For the Journey', which began in 2007 shares both an uncanny visual similarity and a set of tropes with the iconography of *Up*. An analysis of financial adverts written during the crash noted that in their self-representations financial institutions are 'shown to exist above, outside, or across and beyond the cityscape' and their employees are subject to an '"architectural inflation" where the consulting partners are shown walking and talking casually on a platform or floor that towers above the towers'. Christian De Cock, James Fitchett, and Christina Volkmann, '"Myths of a near Past": Envisioning Finance Capitalism Anno 2007', *Ephemera: Theory & Politics in Organization*, 9.1 (2009), pp. 8–25.

2 Hugh Rockoff, 'The "Wizard of Oz" as a Monetary Allegory', *Journal of Political Economy*, 98.4 (1990), pp. 739–60.

3 Corey K. Creekmur and Alexander Doty, 'Introduction', in Alexander Doty and Corey K. Creekmur (eds), *Out in Culture: Gay, Lesbian, and Queer Essays on Popular Culture* (Durham, NC: Duke University Press, 1995), p. 3.

4 http://www.pixar.com/features_films/UP [Date accessed: August 2014].

5 Judith Halberstam, *The Queer Art of Failure* (Durham, NC: Duke University Press, 2011), p. 29.

6 Ibid., p. 88.

7 Lee Edelman, *No Future: Queer Theory and the Death Drive* (Durham, NC: Duke University Press, 2004).

8 Mark Fisher, *Capitalist Realism: Is There No Alternative* (London: Zero Books, 2009), pp. 12–13.

9 Randy Martin, *American War and the Financial Logic of Risk Management* (New York: Duke University Press, 2007).

10 Joshua Clover, 'Value/Theory/Crisis', *PMLA*, 127.1 (2012), p. 112. See also Michael Tratner, 'Derrida's Debt to Milton Friedman', *New Literary History*, 34 (2004), pp. 791–806.

11 Clover, 'Value/Theory/Crisis', p. 113

12 Margaret Atwood, *Payback: Debt as Metaphor and the Shadow Side of Wealth* (Toronto, Anansi, 2009), p. 81.

13 John Forrester, *Truth Games: Lies, Money and Psychoanalysis* (Cambridge: Harvard University Press, 1997), p. 161.

14 Michael Rowbotham, *The Grip of Death: A Study of Modern Money, Debt Slavery and Destructive Economics* (London: Jon Carpenter, 1998).

15 Maurizio Lazzarato, *The Making of Indebted Man* (London: Semiotexte, 2011), p. 33.

16 Ibid., p. 34.

17 Ibid., p. 34.

18 Raymond Williams, 'Problems of the Coming Period', *New Left Review* (July/August 1983), p. 16.

19 John Lanchester, *Whoops! Why Everyone Owes Everyone and No One Can Pay* (London: Allen Lane, 2010).

20 Williams, 'Problems of the Coming Period', p. 16.

21 Colin Crouch, *The Strange Non-death of Neoliberalism* (London: Polity Press, 2011).

22 David Harvey, *The Enigma of Capital: And the Crises of Capital* (London: Profile Books, 2010).

23 Giorgio Agamben, *Homo Sacer: Sovereign Power and Bare Life*, trans. Daniel Heller-Roazen (Stanford, CA: Stanford University Press, 1998).

24 The image of the stricken trader has become infamous, partly due to the wittily blank tumblr 'Brokers-with-their-hands-on-their-faces', http://newsfeed.time.com/2011/08/09/tumblr-of-the-week-brokers-with-their-hands-on-their-faces/ [Date accessed: August 2014].

25 http://www.telegraph.co.uk/culture/theatre/theatre-news/6262486/Sir-David-Hare-manages-to-find-beauty-in-the-financial-crisis.html [Date accessed: August 2014].

26 http://www.newscientist.com/blog/environment/2008/06/foreclosure-fish.html [Date accessed: August 2014].

27 David Graeber, *Debt: The First 5,000 Years* (London: Melville House Publishing, 2011), p. 122.

28 Ibid., p. 373.

29 Atwood, *Payback*, p. 17.

30 Fred Harney and Stefano Moten, 'Debt and Study', *e-flux*, 14.3 (2010).

31 Richard Dienst, *The Bonds of Debt* (London: Verso, 2011), pp. 149–50.

32 Ibid., p. 150.

33 Ibid., p. 152.

34 Noel Castree, 'The Spatio-Temporality of Capitalism', *Time and Society*, 18.27–62 (2009), p. 41.

35 Ibid., p. 46.

36 Ibid., p. 48.

37 Karl Marx, *Capital: A Critique of Political Economy*. Vol. III (London: Lawrence and Wishart, 1962), p. 432.

38 Ursula Huws, 'Crisis as Capitalist Opportunity: New Accumulation through Public Service Commodification', *Socialist Register 2012: The Crisis and the Left*, 48 (2012), p. 65.

39 Fisher, *Capitalist Realism*, p. 2.

40 Ibid., p. 18.

41 Forrester, *Truth Games*, p. 143.

42 Ibid., p. 163.

43 http://collider.com/andrew-niccol-eric-newman-in-time-interview/ [Date accessed: August 2014].

44 http://collider.com/andrew-niccol-in-time-the-host-interview/ [Date accessed: August 2014].

45 http://collider.com/andrew-niccol-in-time-the-host-interview/ [Date accessed: August 2014].

46 Thomas Elsaesser, 'The Mind-Game Film', in Warren Buckland (ed.) *Puzzle Films: Complex Storytelling in Contemporary Cinema* (London: Wiley, 2009).

47 Paul De Man, 'The Epistemology of Metaphor', *Critical Inquiry*, 5.1, (1978), pp. 13–30.

48 Karl Marx and Friedrich Engles, *The Communist Manifesto* (Chicago: Charles H. Kerr and Company, 1910), p. 15.

Timothy Bewes

To think without abstraction: on the problem of standpoint
in cultural criticism

Within the Marxist critical tradition, abstraction has figured as a reversible
concept, designating two apparently contrary tendencies: dematerialisation
and concretisation. Thus, for Adorno, 'the extreme abstraction' represented by Hegel's thought consists in 'its ideal of presentation, the negation of presentation', while for Lukács abstraction is a principle of
reification, meaning concretisation. This essay begins by outlining the
implications of this reversibility of abstraction, using Marx, Adorno, and
Lukács, as well as the recent work of Vivek Chibber, whose *Postcolonial
Theory and the Specter of Capital* helps clarify some of the contemporary
misuses of the term 'abstraction'. The second half of the article turns to
the question of the possibility of a thought without abstraction. The key
figure for this discussion is the theoretician of new media Vilém Flusser,
whose book *Into the Universe of Technical Images* outlines an account of
technical images that, I argue, enables us to think both the reversibility
of abstraction and the possibility of a thought that is not subject to
abstraction.

'Are you the undergraduate of today?'

'I wish I were. I should love to be quite abstract'. (Elizabeth Bowen, *The Last September*)

1. Abstraction and reversibility

Abstraction designates the representation of a process as a noun, the presentation of a relation between entities as an entity in itself. As such, 'abstraction' is itself one of the great abstractions of modern critical thought, a term whose endlessly recursive quality is liable to induce a sense of vertigo. For who or what is the agent, the *subject* of abstraction – considered as such, in the abstract? History? Capitalism? Human consciousness, in forms such as the tendency to conceptualisation? And who or what is its *object*; that is to say, how may we best conceptualise the domain that is subjected to abstraction, transformed by it? As the 'real'? The 'concrete'? It is difficult to think of notions more abstract than these.

Within the Marxist critical tradition, the word 'abstraction' designates two apparently opposing tendencies: dematerialisation and concretisation. Thus Theodor Adorno, in the context of a positive assessment of Hegel, writes that the 'extreme abstraction' represented by Hegel's thought consists in 'its ideal of presentation, the negation of presentation'.[1] Hegel's texts are 'antitexts'; both the abstraction and the substance of his thought are found not in their content but in their quality as 'reverberations'. In Hegel, says Adorno, 'process ... wants to express itself as process' (p. 121). Hegel's philosophy expresses the moment at which thought arrives at a positive state of abstraction *as such* – the moment when thought is released from its imprisonment in form. In this usage, abstraction signifies dematerialisation, the positive liberation of thought from (as Hegel puts it in his *Aesthetics*) 'its entanglement in matter'.[2]

For Georg Lukács, on the other hand, abstraction is the principle of 'reification', Lukács's term for the fetishistic logic (derived from Marx's analysis of the commodity in the first chapter of *Capital*) that explains the fate of all social relations under capitalism. The 'phantom objectivity' that appears as a negation of process and relation is the crystallisation of an abstraction, 'an autonomy that seems so strictly rational and all-embracing as to conceal every trace of its fundamental nature: the relation between people'.[3] In the usage that establishes abstraction as an element in the logic of reification, then, abstraction is a mode of concretisation. As Marx himself was aware, when individuals seem independent, they appear so 'only for someone who abstracts from the *conditions*, the *conditions of existence* within which these individuals enter into contact'.[4] The crystallisation, the very stepping forth of individuality is a process of abstraction. What is produced in that moment of *abstraction from* is an entity in all its self-evident, reified, concrete reality.

The fact is that abstraction is a reversible concept. As a one-way process, considered to have a subject (an agent), an object, a historicity and thus to be embedded in a spatial relationality, abstraction has already succumbed to the greatest abstraction. The enigmatic or vertiginous quality of abstraction persists as long as we think of it as an event or an 'effect' of capitalism – for example, as a condition that *increasingly* defines labour in a capitalist economy. Adorno, by contrast, is especially aware of the implications of the reversibility of abstraction; the entire text of his *Minima Moralia* is organised around the observation that the very 'streak of independence' that we need in order to resist is extended to us only according to the logic of the order we are resisting: political economy itself.[5] Abstraction signifies both the 'power of images over man' (abstraction from the conditions of relationality) and the 'freedom from images' (the historical possibility of a thought capable of transcending images) (p. 140). 'Late capitalism' is a condition in which the latter is subject to ever more pressure by the former. Thus, 'amid the network of now wholly abstract relations of people to each other and to things, the power of abstraction is vanishing' (p. 140).

It is in this context that the proposition of 'real abstraction' exerts a strong contemporary appeal as an expression of the logic of commodity fetishism and of its extension to every facet of human existence – including that which enables us to resist it.[6] For both Alfred Sohn-Rethel, the figure responsible for the formulation of the concept, and Vivek Chibber, a figure writing more recently, 'real abstraction' is not a contemporary development, particular to the world of late capitalism; it is a central element in the theory of labour developed by Marx, not only in the *Grundrisse* but in the 'official' text of *Capital*. Commenting on Marx, Chibber observes that 'it is impossible to separate concrete labor from abstract labor, except as an abstraction'.[7] In his recent work *Postcolonial Theory and the Specter of Capital*, a critique of the field of postcolonial theory, Chibber clarifies the role of abstraction in Marx's account of capitalism. For Marx, abstract labour and concrete labour are in every case the same labour. Abstraction is not, then, a descriptive term for the transformation of labour under capitalism, in forms such as the progressive 'homogenization' of the labour force, or the 'de-skilling' associated with 'Taylorist' production processes. Abstract labour, writes Chibber, 'comprises a dimension of all actual, concrete labors that go into the production of commodities' (p. 135). The 'tectonic shift' of the abstraction of labour is a shift not in how labour is utilised, or in how labourers are treated by employers, but rather in 'how labor is viewed'; and the explanation for that transformation is profit ('surplus value'). It is on the basis of how labour is recompensed, for example, that labour becomes 'abstract':

> The market does not reward the labor on the basis of particular characteristics. It is rewarded on its *relational* properties – how well it performs *relative* to those of its competitors, and in particular, how productive it is compared to other labors. ... Labor, in other words, is rewarded in the market on its *general* features, not its particular ones. It is rewarded as *abstract* labor – labor as such, general labor, average labor, even though it must be mobilized in its concrete forms.

> Hence, abstract labor is not a distinct kind of labor. It is not another species of labor called 'homogeneous labor', as postcolonial theorists imply ... Marx's argument is that the emergence of abstract labor is specific to capitalism because capitalism creates a social mechanism that takes the dispersed, disparate laboring activities of producers, and forces them onto a common metric. (pp. 139–40)

Chibber is writing in opposition to commentators such as Lisa Lowe and Harry Braverman who conceive of abstraction as a term that applies to labour *descriptively* rather than definitionally or logically. As Marx has it, 'the abstraction, or idea, is nothing more than the theoretical expression of those material relations which are their lord and master' (*Grundrisse*, p. 164). Abstraction is not a quality of labour as such; it would be truer to say that abstraction is nothing other than the coming into appearance of labour as a distinct epistemological category, an appearance that we owe to the emergence of political economy as a discipline. Abstraction is the mode that attaches to labour when it is no longer conceived in relation to its particular properties, but is considered, instead, as an element within that larger abstraction of the modern world, the economy.[8]

2. The problem of standpoint

Abstraction, then, is a reversible concept. But that reversibility testifies not to the incoherence of the concept, but to its historicity; that is to say, its existence as a historical, and therefore concrete, formation. The reversibility of abstraction is an effect, to be precise, of Marx's critique of commodity fetishism, for it is with Marx's critique that abstraction becomes 'real', located in the actions of people, rather than in consciousness.[9]

However, this reversibility of abstraction, a discovery of Marx, signifies far more than simply the 'metaphysical subtleties and theological niceties' of commodity value. As with all social and conceptual forms, something fundamental is expressed by the reversibility of abstraction. Ever since Marx, abstraction has been equally applicable to our attempts to achieve intellectual understanding and our involvement in activities and practices that prevent us from doing so. That is to say, abstraction, in Sohn-Rethel's terms, refers to both intellectual labour and manual labour. The relationship thereby established between two movements of abstraction, which is also the moment of Marx's 'inversion' of Hegel's dialectic,[10] has further implications, for at that point it is no longer possible to name a sphere of activity or consciousness that is assuredly free of abstraction. The reversibility of abstraction, then, amounts to the universalisation of the terrain, both physical and conceptual, that is susceptible to abstraction. Abstraction becomes a condition of possibility of intellectual work, for example. Even naming is established as a form of abstraction. Sohn-Rethel's coinage 'necessary false consciousness' implies the inevitability of abstraction. Necessary false consciousness, he writes, 'is not faulty consciousness'; it is a consciousness that 'is called false, not against its own standards of truth, but as against social existence' (p. 197). The false consciousness of abstraction is an 'unavoidable illusion' grounded in the 'spatio-temporal reality of social being' (p. 203), one which even Marx saw as necessary for the analysis of economic forms.[11]

The predicament that this situation creates for critical thought, however, seems all but insuperable. In its starkest articulation, the predicament takes the form of a dilemma: Is abstraction located on the side of comprehension or the failure of comprehension? In other words, does abstraction, in advanced capitalist societies, characterise the aspiration to totality, or the refusal of it in the face of an increasingly atomised reality? Many of the key debates in twentieth-century critical thought may be explained by reference to this dilemma. Take, for example, the debates of Western Marxists in the 1930s and 1940s on aesthetics and politics. There, Lukács rejects modernism on the basis of its celebration of a fragmented perception, the very basis of which – monadological consciousness – is for Lukács an abstraction. The realism of Thomas Mann, for Lukács, is founded on the awareness that 'thoughts and feelings grow out of the life of society and [that] experience and emotions are parts of the total complex of reality'.[12] Following on from Lukács's earlier work on reification, abstraction here implicates all categories of experience that reaffirm or consolidate the boundaries of the subject. When Bertolt Brecht objects to Lukács's commitment to realism with an insistence on historicity – 'Even the realistic mode of writing ... bears the stamp of the way it was employed ... ' – the abstraction, by contrast, is situated with Lukács's conception of objective 'reality'.[13]

To take another example, how should we understand the supposed 'meaninglessness' in Samuel Beckett's works: as a flight into abstraction, the *ne plus ultra* of the renunciation of objectivity (as Lukács has it);[14] or, with Adorno, as a 'historical' development that we resist only by an abstract attachment to categories (such as character, narrative, plot and significance) that have lost their historical legitimacy?[15] Similarly, how should we approach the theory of 'polyphony' put forward by Mikhail Bakhtin to explain the power and originality of Dostoevsky's works: as an event that speaks to Dostoevsky's prophetic anticipation of the historical collapse of the 'monologically perceived and understood world',[16] or a symptom of the writer's merely subjective flight from the obligation of historical understanding? Again, the difference dramatises the distinction between associating abstraction with the construction of meaning or with its absence; and that distinction depends on whether ethical or political commitments are connected to a belief in human agency or predicated upon a vacation, or critique – however paradoxical – of that category.

This situation affects the discipline of literary criticism most decisively when the insuperability of these alternatives is accepted as the condition and limit of critical thinking. When contemporary critics of the novel express their resignation to the abstraction or poverty of concepts and, consequently, to the 'loss' involved in any 'theoretical' understanding; when they extrapolate approaches to reading predicated upon the inevitability of that loss – for example, expanding the 'scale' of literary analysis, treating the text not as the primary object of study but as a term within a larger conceptual field (say, nineteenth-century British detective novels, epistolary novels, the *Bildungsroman*, or the 'core' or 'periphery' of the literary world system); when they thereby renounce any concern with the expressive quality of the work, declaring such qualities to be beyond the competence of the critic – they too confirm their alliance with one side of the division: with human agency as against the capacity for thought *of the work*; with the vocation of the critic and his or her separation from the critical object; with the fundamental illegibility of the text.[17]

Everything depends on standpoint. From a 'philosophical' standpoint, these dilemmas appear undecidable; but, as such, they too attain an abstract reality (as, for example, a 'faultline' running through twentieth-century critical thinking) once we reconcile ourselves to occupying the position of critical diagnostician.

3. A historical thesis

Everything depends on standpoint. The problem of abstraction is the problem of standpoint; as such, it is not a problem to be solved but a situation to come to terms with. Abstraction is a predicate of our existence as perceiving, contemplating, calculating beings. As a merely chronological narrative, 'abstraction' would tell the story of a progressive isolation of the subject from the 'life world'.[18] But that kind of transcultural, transhistorical explanation is in tension with Marx's use of 'abstract' to denote the consequences of regarding labour as a term in the field of political economy, the point at which labour is valued not for its productive capacity but for its 'relational' properties: its capacity to generate profit.

The first task in the project of disturbing the 'insuperability' of the relation between abstraction and thought is to disarticulate these two uses of abstraction, or rather, to rearticulate their relation. Only the non-chronological use, denoting the methodological abstraction of taking something or someone as an object – an abstraction that describes both the approach of political economy to labour and that of capital itself – is properly Marxist. Abstraction, as we have already observed, is not a quality that *increasingly* applies to labour in Marx's analysis; it applies to labour *immediately* as a consequence of the capitalist mode of production, which is to say, the mode (which is not a 'tendency', or a 'predisposition', but an inevitable consequence) of viewing labour, or indeed capital, in its economic rather than its productive significance. The term 'abstract', for Marx, does not describe, it merely designates. Abstraction is a condition of knowledge, but it is also a practice, a corollary of Marx's ideal of a 'scientific' approach to the analysis of capital. The categories of Marxian knowledge – 'total social capital', 'total surplus value' – are abstract, but not in the sense in which Lukács later uses the term in connection with the theory of reification.[19] Every such abstract concept, notes Louis Althusser,

> provides knowledge of a reality whose existence it reveals: an 'abstract concept' then means a formula which is apparently abstract but really terribly concrete, because of the object it designates. This object is terribly concrete in that it is infinitely more concrete, more effective than the objects one can 'touch with one's hands' or 'see with one's eyes' – and yet one cannot touch it with one's hands or see it with one's eyes.[20]

The object of Marx's analysis, clarifies Althusser further,

> is an abstract one: which means that it is terribly real and that it never *exists* in the pure state, since it only exists in capitalist societies. Simply speaking: in order to be able to analyse ... concrete capitalist societies ... it is essential to know that they are dominated by that terribly concrete reality, the capitalist mode of production, which is 'invisible' (to the naked eye). 'Invisible', i.e. abstract. (p. 49)

Althusser's observation helps us distinguish the use of abstraction as a purely designative term – a use that, in Althusser, is also a 'practice' – from another that is weighed down with pejorative suggestion, i.e. that condemns particular intellectual operations (although, logically, all intellectual operations are thereby condemned – we will return to this theme) for transforming relations into objects, or for presenting a particular perspective as a universal one. Both uses are found in Marx, although the latter is more common in Marx's early writings, such as the unpublished 1844 *Manuscripts.*[21]

For Althusser, the 'practice' of abstraction, which can be theoretical as well as artistic (as in the work of the painter Leonardo Cremonini), facilitates the grasping of relations, 'real relations', in all their invisibility.[22] The second, generalizing and pejorative use is not tolerated by Althusser (nor, for different reasons, by Chibber), on the grounds that it elaborates thinghood itself as the very problem of capitalism, a situation in which it is impossible for any intellectual activity whatsoever not to be tainted by the charge of abstraction.[23] With the generalisation of abstraction, the logic of capital is extended to the organisation of perception, to the distinction between subject and object, to the expression or perception of an anchored subject.

In a fascinating passage in *The Theory of the Novel*, written before his own turn to Bolshevism and the famous essay on reification, Lukács talks about the abstraction – 'in a Hegelian sense' – of every element of the novel:

> Abstract, the nostalgia of the characters for utopian perfection, a nostalgia that feels itself and its desires to be the only true reality; abstract, the existence of social structures based only upon their factual presence and their sheer ability to continue; abstract, finally, the form-giving intention which, instead of surmounting the distance between these two abstract groups of elements, allows it to subsist, which does not even attempt to surmount it, but renders it sensuous as the lived experience of the novel's characters, uses it as a means of connecting the two groups and so turns it into an instrument of composition.[24]

The significance of abstraction in this passage is not necessarily pejorative, in the sense intended above. What Lukács is analysing are the conditions in which the novel is able to make an ideational presentation; those conditions register a limitation to the form; and they involve 'dangers', which are most acute when the 'formal' qualities of the novel are confused with 'content' (p. 71). However, the limitations of the novel are understood by Lukács to be productive, inasmuch as the novel is 'a true-born form in the historico-philosophical sense' (p. 73). For Lukács, the novel is defined by the paradox that the 'intelligibility' of experience that is its very premise is not fulfilled or delivered in the form itself; intelligibility is only a presupposition, not a consequence of the novel. J. M. Bernstein explains this proposition as follows:

> The principle of totality governs the novel's aesthetic ambitions on the formal level. What, however, legitimates the operation of this principle? It is ... the idea that we *presuppose* the *in principle* intelligibility of experience; that is, if not in fact then at least in principle life should be intelligible. In life, *counterfactually but in principle life is intelligible.* This is the principle behind aesthetic form-giving which gives it its weight; it is the principle that makes the aesthetic ethical, but the aesthetic can be ethical only because the ethical itself has already been rendered aesthetic (fictional).[25]

With this development – which is a historical development, according to Lukács, not simply an aesthetic one – abstraction becomes reversible, applicable equally to intelligibility and unintelligibility. The novel has no hope of attaining 'adequacy'. That is to say, the novel is the form that gives form to the historical situation in which form has no hope of attaining adequacy. The world of the novel is the world, as Lukács defines it, of 'absolute sinfulness' (p. 152). This is what Lukács means by abstraction in the novel; it is clear that he is using the term to mean not reification, but dematerialisation (the 'Hegelian sense'). For, in its essence, the novel, in Lukács's reading, is a form that is inimical to reification. The novel enables a presentation to take place in the interval between intelligibility and unintelligibility – and it is the 'abstraction' of its elements that makes this possible. What Althusser says of the human faces in Cremonini's paintings might equally be said of the utterances of characters in Lukács's novel: 'not the expression of their "souls", but the expression ... of an absence, visible in them, the absence of the structural relations which govern their world, their gestures, and even their experience of freedom' (p. 164). Lukács's theory of the novel has nothing to say about the decisions made by certain writers, or the sentiments uttered by certain characters; it is the theory of an objective, 'historical' loss of faith in the capacity of writing to speak, a loss that the novel itself emerges historically in order to embody, to make concrete.

Althusser objects to the reversible notion of abstraction in the name of a 'rigour' that insists upon giving concepts a 'strict' meaning. In so doing, Althusser appears to retain the critical prerogative of the intellectual: 'Without the rigour demanded by its object there can be no question of *theory*, that is, of theoretical practice in the strict sense of the term' (*For*

Marx, p. 164). What if, however, the reversibility of abstraction were to violate the pronouncements of the theoretician and take on 'historico-philosophical' reality in itself, not only within the form of the novel, but as a backdrop against which all intellectual and conceptual work had to take place? What if it were no longer possible to insulate our own inclination towards commentary and meaning-making from what Lukács calls the 'incomplete nature of the world as ultimate reality' (p. 71)? 'True-born' forms, after all, cannot be policed against. And who is to say that my dissatisfaction with the poverty of concepts is any less a true-born form 'in the historico-philosophical sense' than the resignation to their inevitability?

It is against such a backdrop, the potential universalisation of the field of abstraction, that Michel Foucault, in his introduction to *The Birth of the Clinic* in 1963, announces his departure from the mode of 'commentary'. For commentary assumes that the textual object has a 'deeper' meaning which, if it were to be produced, would enable the text 'to achieve an identity with itself, supposedly nearer to its essential truth'.[26] Foucault imagines instead 'a structural analysis of discourses that would evade the fate of commentary by supposing no remainder, nothing in excess of what has been said, but only the fact of its historical appearance' (p. xix). This mode would avoid, therefore, all abstraction, including the premise of 'an unformulated remainder of thought' slumbering within every discursive object (to use Foucault's colourful phraseology) (p. xviii). In such a mode, which Foucault will later systematise as the 'archaeological' method, the very presumption of critical subjectivity is abdicated.

Foucault's intervention is emblematic of a generation of thought that was formed by the reversibility of abstraction – by its application to intelligibility as well as to the failure of intelligibility. Moreover, it is apparent that Althusser's disciplined insistence on the first, methodological or 'scientific' use of abstraction maintains its discipline only by adherence to the second, pejorative sense; for abstraction (in the first sense) is thereby defended against its own abstraction (in the second). That is to say, Althusser's adherence to the *second* use of the term *is maintained precisely by his rigorous refusal of it.*

In a sense, the shift in the meaning of abstraction from dematerialisation to reification, from a one-way process to one that potentially implicates everything, all action and all thought, parallels another shift that we can follow, then, in the work of the thinkers of Foucault's generation, from the phenomenological world to the post-phenomenological one, from 'anchored' consciousness to decentred consciousness, from the world in which the philosopher 'thinks' and the artist 'sees' to one in which thinking, seeing, are dependent on a non-thinking, a non-seeing, that are immanent to them. In this 'incomplete' world there is no longer any object of knowledge; all such knowledge, extracting itself from the conditions that allow it to be constructed as such, is an abstraction. There is nothing seeable prior to the conditions of visibility that make it so; there is no subject who 'sees' and no perception that is not, at the same time, a failure of perception.

If there is a 'chronological' component to abstraction, therefore, it consists not in the narrative of a progressive abstraction attaching to labour under capitalism, but in a momentous reversibility, a point at which abstraction comes to apply not only to unintelligibility but to intelligibility also. This reversibility is anticipated in Hegel's philosophy – for example, in Hegel's appraisal of the power of Christian painting not for its capacity to depict the absolute, but for conceiving the absolute in the limited form of 'visibility as such' (p. 87). It is registered in Marx's analysis of the commodity, when for the first time alienation is conceived not in relation to human consciousness but to human activity; and it is present in Lukács's theory of the novel, in which the intelligibility of the world ('the extensive totality of life')[27] is established as a premise only alongside its categorical removal from the work and from consciousness. Each of these practices announces the arrival of a thought that is coextensive with the forms in which it takes place. In each case, a work or a practice (Christian painting for Hegel, the materialist dialectic for Marx and Sohn-Rethel, the 'abstraction' of the novel for Lukács) offers a mode of grasping conceptually, and thereby dissolving, an abstraction that looms over it. The reversibility of abstraction is registered, finally, even in Althusser's refusal of it, a refusal in which the spirit of reversibility is so deeply embedded that it has no need of being either named or acknowledged.

4. Thought without abstraction? Vilém Flusser

What are the prospects for a thought without abstraction? The very proposition seems to depart from historical materialist principles, as well as from the post-Saussurean tradition of twentieth-century thinking around language. For, presumably, an abstractionless thought would be radically autonomous: singular and hence incommunicable. In order for communication to take place, some abstraction – some loss of singularity, with a corresponding gain in transmissibility – is inevitable. Any post-Saussurean (for example, Derridean) account begins, still more radically, from the principle that abstraction is a condition of possibility for the event of thought; that writing (that is to say, abstraction) precedes thought, just as it precedes speech.

In *Intellectual and Manual Labour*, his great Marxist study of epistemology, Sohn-Rethel addresses the question of whether there can be abstraction 'other than by thought' (p. 17), but he does not mention the inverse

proposition, a thought without abstraction. As long as our model of thinking remains discursive, that is to say dialectical, it seems that we are caught
in a paradoxical relation to abstraction: regretting its falsity but resigned to
its necessity. Similarly, as long as we accept the inevitability of standpoint,
we remain condemned to, at best, a compensatory relation to the positionality of the 'other' and to its ultimate inaccessibility.

The proposition of abstraction's 'reversibility', therefore, like any
number of recent theoretical-linguistic innovations, is a form in which
the very imperfection of language, its violence, is forced into a necessary
relation with its utility. To dispense with abstraction *tout court* one
would have to dispense with agency, with the spatial differentiation of
subject and object, with time and space as categories for the organisation
of knowledge, with instrumental rationality itself. Verbal linguistic forms
would have to be transformed, conjugated only in the infinitive. A
language (or use of language) without abstraction is inconceivable; the
most that can be achieved are the kinds of elaborate, incessantly reflective
and strategic usages that have been a hallmark of twentieth-century theoretical writing, especially in the post-Marxist and poststructuralist traditions. To recover or maintain the sense of abstraction as a deleterious
entity, and as a linear, one-way process, it would be necessary to give up
the attachment to discourse as the model for thought.

Such, in fact, is the project of the Czech-born philosopher of media
Vilém Flusser, whose writings have begun posthumously to appear in
English translation, in which form they are being marketed as a prophetic
commentary on the implications and promise of the 'new' – especially
digital – media. Flusser himself does not especially celebrate the arrival
of the digital. *Into the Universe of Technical Images* was published in
1985, before the likely reverberations of the new image technologies had
become apparent. Flusser rests no part of his argument on an epistemic distinction between analogue and digital media. For Flusser, the important
shift happened earlier, with the appearance of 'technical' images, a category
that includes images in 'photographs, films, videos, television screens and
computer terminals' (p. 5). It is computers that have enabled Flusser to
conceptualise the 'essence' and potentiality of technical media; yet, even
today, the implications of the shift are, in Flusser's terms, far from
having been realised.

In the face of its 'reversibility', Flusser restores to abstraction its linear
quality by correlating abstraction with history itself. Abstraction, for
Flusser, means, very simply, 'the alienation of human beings from the concrete' (p. 6). Cultural history, from animistic and 'primitive' societies to the
contemporary world of technical images, has been a story of continual
ascent 'from the concrete towards higher and higher levels of abstraction'.
Flusser describes five stages in this trajectory, each of which is characterised

by a dominant type of activity. The first is a 'pre-historical' stage in which animals and 'primitive peoples' exist in a 'four-dimensional' world of 'concrete experience', a world unstratified by levels of meaning or variations in significance. (In this stage, implicitly, there is no abstraction at all.) The second stage, beginning around two million years ago, 'somewhere in East Africa' (p. 11), inaugurates the long story of 'civilisation', as the possibility of determined action 'abstracts' the subject from the 'life world'. A three-dimensional world of 'graspable objects' and 'problem[s] to be solved' comes into being, dividing the world into subject and object (p. 8). The third stage is the world of 'appearances', a two-dimensional world of 'observing and imagining', when the subject 'further withdraws into its subjectivity' and images take on all the significance of 'magical action' (pp. 8–9). Flusser locates this moment (somewhat facetiously) 'in a cave in southwestern Europe', 40,000 years ago (p. 11). With the development of Platonic individuality, the subject 'is once again in doubt about the objectivity of its circumstances'. Out of this doubt, Flusser continues, 'come observations and images' (p. 11). The cave paintings at Lascaux, or those in Mesopotamia or Egypt, exemplify the still 'pre-historical' consciousness in which 'everything carries meaning [and] everything must be appeased' (p. 13).

The fourth stage, the world of linear texts, dates from 4000 years ago, and is responsible for creating the world as we know it. As the stage of 'understanding and explanation', it is the one 'to which human beings . . . owe most of their insights' (p. 7). With linear textuality comes 'conceptual, historical consciousness'; this is yet another moment in the trajectory of progressive abstraction, and the point at which 'imagination' enters into a relation with conceptual thinking, whether in servitude or opposition (p. 13). That is to say, 'images of our time are infected with texts; they visualize texts' – which, again, implies a further alienation from the concrete. Finally we have the 'dimensionless', imagined, still emerging universe of *technical images*, which comes into existence with the realisation that texts 'have shown themselves to be inaccessible'; that the rules they obey (rules of orthography, logic and mathematics, for example) lack any referential authority; that they emanate, rather, 'from our own scientific texts' (p. 9). What ushers in the universe of technical images is a broad recognition of the arbitrariness of the rules of discourse:

> In this way, we lose faith in the laws of syntax. We recognize in them rules of play that could also be other than they are, and with this recognition, the orderly threads finally fall apart and the concepts lose coherence. In fact, the situation disintegrates into a swarm of particles and quanta, and the writing subject into a swarm of bits and bytes, moments of decision, and molecules of action. What

remains are particles without dimension that can be neither grasped nor represented nor understood. (pp. 9–10)

With this development, history itself becomes 'posthistorical' (p. 6). Flusser's hypothesis is dependent upon standard, scientistic accounts of the origins of human civilisation, which it makes no attempt to complicate or critique. Flusser appends to those accounts a version of the Cartesian theory of subjective development that is reminiscent of the one so effectively mocked by Samuel Beckett towards the end of *The Unnamable*.[28] For Flusser, however, there is little at stake in these historical narratives, for the simple reason that the trajectory they describe is at an end. The more important and contentious shift that concerns Flusser is the final one: from the world of texts to that of technical images, the stage whose very substance is hypothetical rather than historical. We are not there yet, maintains Flusser at various points in his essay;[29] yet our not being there yet turns out to be a substantial quality of this moment, its secret essence. In order for us to leave history it is necessary, perhaps, for the departure itself to be perpetually under way. 'Posthistory' would be a state that, from this point on, is always emerging.

In this light, it is worth noting that this last stage in Flusser's version of things bears crucial similarities with the moment, described earlier in this essay, when abstraction becomes 'reversible' – applicable to both comprehension and the failure of comprehension, to both intelligibility and unintelligibility. The universe of technical images, indeed, comes into existence in the same period in which Lukács's analysis of reification (a theory based on the extension of abstraction from the ideational realm to the realm of activity as such, to labour) becomes a compelling hypothesis. The reversibility of abstraction, a historical thesis, is simultaneous with the 'cultural revolution' during which, according to Flusser, the entire regime of linear textuality and its 'laws', meaning our faith in the connections between representations and concepts – connections that facilitate and make possible our 'understanding and explanation' – collapse, to be superseded by a new awareness of the particulate and aleatory quality of the world we live in.

There is nothing tragic about this supersession, for Flusser, nor does it imply a relation to meaning condemned to paradox. On the contrary, it is a 'fabulous new way of life' that is 'emerging around technical images' (p. 7). The condition of its emergence seems to be that we give up our attachment to writing as a basis of thought: the form that supports and gives expression to 'linear, directional thinking'.[30] The universe of technical images is a moment – an extreme one – in the progressive history of abstraction. It is formed by that history, but it is also a mode in which the collapse of the rule-bound universe, when 'all recognizable orientation points hav[e] become abstract', finds a material form that is adequate to it, and in which 'we may again experience it, recognize it, act in it' (p. 23).

> One cannot live in such an empty and abstract universe, with such a dissociated and abstract consciousness. To live, one must try to make the universe and consciousness concrete. One must try to consolidate the particles to make them substantial (graspable, conceivable, tangible). Those who invented calculus in the seventeenth century already solved this problem of filling in the intervals, integrating the infinitesimal, resolving differentials. But at the time, the problem was methodological, and today, it has become existential, a question of life and death. I suggest that we regard technical images as an answer to this problem. (pp. 15–16)

Space constraints prevent a full discussion of Flusser's ideas here. What especially demands consideration is the suggestion that the forms of information processing that are possible in the world of technical images, although currently imperfect, have the potential to dispense with abstraction altogether. The mode of rationality peculiar to the universe of technical images, where all abstract concepts have dissolved into particles that are neither 'visible, graspable nor comprehensible' (p. 23), is 'calculation and computation'. In the mode of calculation, thought without abstraction is for the first time a possibility; and the means of such thought is the apparatus. For the apparatus has no *interest* in grasping, representing, or understanding particles; indeed, from *its* standpoint, Flusser writes, a technical visualisation is 'just another possible function' (p. 16), of no superior (or inferior) value in itself. A technical image – for example a photograph, made by manipulating 'the effects of photons on molecules of silver nitrate' – is 'a blindly realized possibility, something invisible that has blindly become visible' (p. 16). Thus, Flusser dispenses with the problem of standpoint, the problem of the subject, by adopting, as a methodological and historical principle, *the standpoint of the apparatus*: a perspective that is oblivious to any creative or political intentionality.

The principle of agency in the world of technical images is the 'key', an instrument for manipulating an apparatus but one that, in essence, operates 'in a time unrelated to everyday human time' – 'in the infinitesimal universe of particles, in the realm of the infinitely small' (p. 23). To talk about the 'infinitely small' is to talk about something that has no mathematical existence, whose very substance is negative.[31] Existing keys are 'relatively primitive', says Flusser; their 'actual character' has not been understood, and, insofar as they retain a positive function within themselves, they have not been 'properly installed' (p. 29). Thus, there are still two types of keys: those that send messages (the transmission apparatus of a television station) and those that receive (the keys on a television). One symptom of the imperfection of keys is that their operation continues to be beset by a 'double ambience': on one hand, a kind of subjective 'rapture' characterizing the feeling of artistic creation; on the other, a subjective sense of being manipulated (p. 29). Both the intoxication of artistic expression and the sense of outrage or resistance that accompanies and fuels ideology-critique are hence obsolete affects, reminiscent of an older form of cultural criticism modelled on discourse.

> The difference between sending and receiving, between productive and reproductive keys, is therefore to be viewed as provisional. The typewriter is only a forerunner of the telewriter, the control panel of the washing machine only a forerunner of a feedback loop linking manufacturers and the users of washing machines. And the current state of keys in general is only a forerunner of a telematic society. (p. 30)

What role remains for the human actor in Flusser's vision of telematic society? Flusser distinguishes between two modern types of image-maker, which correspond to the distinction between 'depiction' and 'visu-alisation'. On one hand are the producers of traditional images, which includes writers, who work with the premise that the apparatus is merely a neutral tool of artistic expression. This is the conception of image production that is formed by the world of linear textuality, by 'dis-course'; a conception according to which texts (that is to say, concepts) saturate images, 'infect' them (p. 13). On the other hand we find the work of 'envisioners', which takes place entirely within the materiality of the apparatus, and with no agenda that preexists it or that arises in a situation that is alien to it. 'When I write, I write past the machine toward the text; when I envision technical images, I build from the inside of the apparatus' (p. 36).

Are envisioners identifiable by name? Is it possible to invoke contem-porary envisioners, or figures who, in an artistic mode, anticipate the arrival of the envisioner as a general principle of cultural production? And to what extent can Flusser's notion of envisioning operate as a model for criticism? 'Envisioners press buttons that set events into motion that they cannot grasp, understand, or conceive', writes Flusser.

> The images they visualize are produced not by them but by the apparatus, and, in fact, automatically. In contrast to writers, envi-sioners have no need for deep insight into what they are doing. By means of the apparatus, they are freed from the pressure for depth and may devote their full attention to constructing images. (p. 36)

Envisioners, he continues, 'stand at the most extreme edge of abstraction ever reached in a dimensionless universe' – the point at which the abstractions themselves collapse – 'and they offer us the possibility of again experiencing the world and our lives in it as concrete' (pp. 37–8). The 'revolutionary new attitude toward the world' that emerges is one in which we no longer 'bend over the world as over a text' in an attempt to understand it (p. 46); instead, we 'project meaning on the world. And technical images are such projections. Whether they're photographs, films, videos, or computer images, all have the same meaning: to give absurdity a meaning' (pp. 46–7).

By this point in the discussion it should be clear that Flusser's theory of keys is best understood as a theory not, primarily, of new media, but of reversibility as a solution to the problem of standpoint. This theory priorities neither artistic production nor criticism, for in Flusser's theory of keys, meaning is transmitted only at the instant in which it is produced. So far as Flusser himself is concerned, reversibility becomes *thinkable* with the invention of digital media; however, its implications extend to the art and the thought of historical periods that long precede it. Insofar as we are able to think the principle of reversibility, we are always thinking from the point of view of the interval. The reversibility of abstraction, for example, is thinkable when we denominate two ideas (themselves abstract) of abstraction: one that limits abstraction to the sense of *dematerialisation*, and another, only apparently opposed to it, that limits the term to the sense of *concretisation*. The standpoint of reversibility is not that of the critic, but an abstract point of infinite smallness that is located between two positivities. Flusser thinks this abstract point through the speculative proposition of an immaterial entity, inaccessible to human consciousness, that achieves its earliest realisation with the digitally produced image. However, older thinkers have thought the same principle by reference to different media. For example, Henri Bergson thinks the possibility of a substanceless, purely hypothetical standpoint through the existence of photography ('Is it not obvious that the photograph, if photograph there be, is already taken, already developed in the very heart of things and at all the points of space?') (p. 31); Deleuze does the same thing with cinema ('The brain is nothing but ... an interval, a gap between an action and a reaction').[32] Lukács uses the novel ('In the created reality of the novel all that becomes visible is the distance separating the systematisation from concrete life') (*Theory*, p. 70); and even Hegel, writing on the cusp of the invention of photography, thinks the same possibility through Christian painting ('The visibility and the making visible which belong to painting ... free art from the complete sensuous spatiality of material things by being restricted to the dimensions of a plane surface') (p. 87).

One of the implications of Flusser's own work, indeed, must be that different media do not need to be limited by qualities that are historically specific to them;[33] even writing does not have the necessary relation to abstraction that Flusser, writing in the discursive mode, has no choice but to attribute to it. The same possibilities for 'envisioning' apply to writing as to any other media technology. When Flusser talks about the 'future', on one hand, and the 'obsolescence' of writing, on the other, he is himself, perhaps, aspiring to the status of 'envisioner', renouncing 'deep insight' and inhabiting a form, discourse, 'from the inside'. Writing is thereby treated as a technical apparatus, a form in which all expression takes on a provisional quality. As Flusser says in the final chapter of the book, any attempt (such as the one he himself has under-taken) to predict telematic society – prediction being a mode of writing that is formed by and limited to the discursive mode – is 'contradictory and self-referential' (p. 160).

For the time being, says Flusser near the beginning of *Into the Universe of Technical Images*, 'I cannot become enraptured about the keys on the television or the washing machine. ... But we can expect to be enraptured by all keys at a later stage of automation because they will all be instruments that permit us to join with all others, giving meaning to the whirring chaos of the particulate universe' (p. 31). The proposition of a 'time being' and 'a later stage of automation', however, does not survive Flusser's reflections on his own practice at the end of the book; nor is it consistent with the contex-tualised reading of Flusser that I have tried to put forward in this essay.

Flusser's work on technical images impacts less directly, then, upon our understanding of digital media than on certain historical transform-ations in the conditions of meaning itself, transformations that I have been exploring here through the notion of abstraction. Flusser's writing stages the quandaries inherent in any argument predicated on the notion of abstraction *as such* – or, to put this slightly differently, he demonstrates and enacts the conditions under which a usable (non-reversible) concept of abstraction may be retained. Flusser retrieves a stable notion of abstraction from the momentous reversibility that assails all terms and concepts as the epoch of linear textuality comes to an end; and he does so by recasting the reversibility of abstraction in linear terms: as the (potential) universalisa-tion of abstraction, its completion, which is also the point of its 'collapse'. Against that eventuality, Flusser posits the reversibility of keys. The lesson of Flusser's work is that we do not need to become resigned to the 'paradox' of abstraction, or the historical motif of its 'inevitability', for that history is over. In order for criticism to escape implication in abstraction, criticism itself must be renounced, along with its correlates: the expression of the artist, the positionality of the critic, the spatial, unbridgeable gap between the two, and the hierarchy of artist, critic and reader. Every such presupposition can be understood as an abstraction from the reality of the technical images that now 'lie at the center', having pressed into private space, blocking off all public spaces completely (p. 52). The issue, for Flusser, is not one of political necessity but of empirical actuality. 'Not only are authors no longer necessary', he writes, 'they are not even possible' (p. 99).

Flusser helps us imagine the form that 'the coming cultural criticism' (p. 52) might take. Many questions remain: Do the intoxicating, aesthetic qualities of Flusser's own writing indicate the distance still to be travelled if criticism is fully to inhabit the world of technical images that, at present, it can only imagine – or are those aesthetic qualities a sign of how near we are to arriving? And what of causality? Is the world of technical images *responsible for* the dissolution of the older social and cultural forms, 'of lines into particles, of processes into quanta' (p. 135), or a *response to* it? Are the developments narrated by Flusser evidence of supreme attentiveness to history or of a headlong flight from it?

Such questions are versions of the theoretical dilemmas mentioned near the beginning of this essay. Like them, they depend on 'standpoint', the category from which Flusser – intoxicatingly – announces our liberation; in other words, they are products of abstraction. When it comes to answering questions posed from an abstract standpoint, no one is more bracing or challenging than the young Karl Marx. Addressing those who would refute the thesis of man's 'self-mediated being with recursive questions about the origins of man, he writes: 'If you ask about the creation of nature and of man, then you are abstracting from nature and from man. You assume them as non-existent and want me to prove to you that they exist. My answer is: Give up your abstraction and you will then give up your question' ('Economic and Philosophical Manuscripts' 357). Flusser's work suggests that the moment has arrived in which giving up abstraction may involve giving up standpoint altogether.

Brown University

Notes

1 Theodor W. Adorno, 'Skoteinos, or How to Read Hegel', in *Hegel: Three Studies*, trans. Shierry Weber Nicholsen (Cambridge, MA: MIT Press, 1993), p. 119. Publication details of all references will be provided in a footnote on first appearance in the essay; thereafter page numbers will appear in parentheses in the text.

2 G. W. F. Hegel, *Aesthetics: Lectures on Fine Art*, trans. T. M. Knox (Oxford: Clarendon, 1975), Vol. I, p. 88.

3 Georg Lukács, *History and Class Consciousness: Studies in Marxist Dialectics*, trans. Rodney Livingston (London: Merlin, 1971), p. 83.

4 Karl Marx, *Grundrisse: Foundations of the Critique of Political Economy*, trans. Martin Nicolaus (Harmondsworth: Penguin, 1973), pp. 163–4.

5 Theodor W. Adorno, *Minima Moralia: Reflections from Damaged Life*, trans. E. F. N. Jephcott (London: Verso, 1978), p. 148.

6 See Slavoj Žižek, *The Fragile Absolute* (London: Verso, 2000), pp. 15–16; Alfred Sohn-Rethel, *Intellectual and Manual Labour: A Critique of Epistemology* (Atlantic Highlands, NJ: Humanities Press, 1977), pp. 19–22.

7 Vivek Chibber, *Postcolonial Theory and the Specter of Capital* (London: Verso, 2013), p. 135.

8 See Susan Buck-Morss, 'Envisioning Capital: Political Economy on Display', *Critical Inquiry*, 21.2 (Winter 1995), pp. 434–67.

9 Alfred Sohn-Rethel is the clearest exponent of this narrative:

> The essence of commodity abstraction is that it is not thought-induced; it does not originate in men's minds but in their actions. And yet this does not give 'abstraction' a merely metaphorical meaning. It is abstraction in its precise, literal sense. ... While the concepts of natural science are thought abstractions, the economic concept of value is a real one. It exists nowhere other than in the human mind but it does not spring from it. Rather it is purely social in character, arising in the spatio-temporal sphere of human interrelations. It is not people who originate these abstractions but their actions. (p. 20)

10 Karl Marx, 'Postface to the Second Edition', in *Capital*, trans. Ben Fowkes (Harmondsworth: Penguin, 1990), p. 103.

11 Karl Marx, 'Preface to the First Edition', *Capital* (Harmondsworth: Penguin, 1990), p. 90.

12 Georg Lukács, 'Realism in the Balance', in Ernst Bloch, Georg Lukács, Bertolt Brecht, Walter Benjamin, and Theodor Adorno, *Aesthetics and Politics*, trans. Rodney Livingstone (London: NLB, 1977), p. 36.

13 Bertolt Brecht, 'Against Georg Lukács', in Ernst Bloch, Georg Lukács, Bertolt Brecht, Walter Benjamin, and Theodor Adorno, *Aesthetics and Politics* (London: NLB, 1977), p. 81. For Brecht, as for Marx, abstraction is not only an objective event, it is also a critical practice. Far from being irreconcilable with the concrete, abstraction is closely interconnected with it, an indispensable tool for 'discovering the causal complexes of society'. Brechtian realist art, therefore, involves 'making possible the concrete and making possible abstraction from it' (p. 82).

14 Georg Lukács, *The Meaning of Contemporary Realism*, trans. John Mander and Necke Mander (London: Merlin, 1963), p. 31. David Cunningham has noted a fundamental shift in Lukács's conceptualisation of the relation between abstract and concrete which amounts to 'a far more straightforward opposition of abstraction to the concrete' in later works such as *The Meaning of Contemporary Realism*. Thus, abstraction for Lukács 'comes to mean little more ... than a straightforward "negation of outward reality"' itself'. See David

Cunningham, "'Very Abstract and Terribly Concrete": Capitalism and *The Theory of the Novel*, *Novel: A Forum on Fiction*, 42.2 (Summer 2009), p. 313.

15 Theodor W. Adorno, *Aesthetic Theory*, trans. Robert Hullot-Kentor (Minneapolis: University of Minnesota Press, 1997), p. 153.

16 Mikhail Bakhtin, *Problems of Dostoevsky's Poetics*, trans. Caryl Emerson (Minneapolis: University of Minnesota Press, 1984), p. 285.

17 Thus critics such as Franco Moretti or Mark McGurl, invoking the inevitability of abstraction, circumscribe their commentary on literary works within abstract categories of knowledge (genres, literary forms, disciplines, institutions) to which, by implication, the significance of their work is limited. What is ruled out of consideration is any access to the 'illegibility' of the work as, say, an indication of the existence of forms of (non-abstract, non-situated) thought that would be incommmensurable with those categories. For Moretti, the price paid for theoretical knowledge is 'the text itself', which consequently 'disappears' as a proper concern of the critic (*Distant Reading* [London: Verso, 2013], pp. 48–9). For McGurl, 'thinking can only really begin with a reduction of complexity, and with the imposition of a certain frame of analysis'. Thus, 'for all its variety, postwar American literature can profitably be described as the product of a system, though one ... ingeniously geared to the production of variety' (*The Program Era: Postwar Fiction and the Rise of Creative Writing* [Cambridge, MA: Harvard University Press, 2009], p. x). These critics, this is to say, see no way, rhetorically, out of the regime that equates knowledge with the abstraction of forms, and criticism with the limitations of perspective. Of his own categories of analysis ('technomodernism', 'high cultural pluralism', 'lower-middle-class modernism') McGurl writes:

> They are ... the self-consciously 'reductive' instruments of a scholar reviewing the situation from a point of critical remove and trying to organize it afresh, and would ideally be thought of not as separate baskets into which individual works can be placed but as principles around which they gravitate at a greater or lesser distance. (p. 32)

Incidentally, McGurl's critical writing is notable for its many 'loopholes' – to use Bakhtin's term for the ways in which Dostoevsky's heroes retain 'the possibility for altering the ultimate, final meaning of [their] own words' in the words themselves (*Problems*, pp. 232–3). The phrase 'self-consciously "reductive"' in the sentence above, or the words 'the flagrant abstraction of the diagram' (p. 31) and 'barbarous neologisms' (p. 32) to characterise his own critical procedures, indicate that the dialogism of Dostoevsky's Underground Man has crept into McGurl's own discourse in such as way as to undermine the *cordon sanitaire* that his work appears to sustain between the critical and the novelistic registers. McGurl, I would go further, is aware of the novelistic quality of his critical persona even as he ignores it. This internal conflict is especially apparent in the moments when, almost Kinbote-like, he contravenes the conventions of formal academic discourse (for example, by issuing casual aesthetic judgements such as 'awesome' and 'excellent' – even while acknowledging the rhetoric of 'excellence' prevalent in the neoliberal university) (pp. 406–7). As Bakhtin says of the language of Dostoevsky's Underground Man, such 'accents of the most profound conviction ... are actually one side of an internal dialogue and meant to convince the speaker himself' (*Problems*, p. 261).

18 The term 'life world' comes from Vilém Flusser, *Into the Universe of Technical Images*, trans. Nancy Ann Roth (Minneapolis: University of Minnesota Press, 2011), p. 11 and *passim*. I will return to this text in the final section of this essay.

19 See, for example, *History and Class Consciousness*, p. 105.

20 Louis Althusser, 'Preface to *Capital* Volume One', in *Lenin and Philosophy and Other Essays*, trans. Ben Brewster (New York: Monthly Review Press, 2001), pp. 48–9.

21 Karl Marx, 'Economical and Philosophical Manuscripts', trans. Gregor Benton, *Early Writings* (Harmondsworth: Penguin, 1992), pp. 356–7.

22 Louis Althusser, 'Cremonini, Painter of the Abstract', *Lenin and Philosophy and Other Essays*, trans. Ben Brewster (New York: Monthly Review Press, 2001), p. 158.

23 No category, says Althusser, is more foreign to Marx than 'thing'. *For Marx*, trans. Ben Brewster (London: Verso, 2005), p. 230n.

24 Georg Lukács, *The Theory of the Novel: A Historico-Philosophical Essay on the Forms of Great Epic Literature*, trans. Anna Bostock (Cambridge, MA: MIT Press, 1971), p. 70.

25 J. M. Bernstein, *The Philosophy of the Novel: Lukács, Marxism and the Dialectics of Form* (Brighton: Harvester Press, 1984), p. 100.

26 Michel Foucault, *The Birth of the Clinic: An Archaeology of Medical Perception*, trans. A. M. Sheridan (London: Routledge, 2003), p. xviii.

27 Lukács, *The Theory of the Novel*, p. 56.

28 Samuel Beckett, *Molloy, Malone Dies, The Unnamable* (New York: Alfred A. Knopf, 1997), especially pp. 399 ff.

29 See, for example, p. 29: 'Of course, th[e] condition ... in which keys will free human beings to make meaning ... has so far not been reached'; p. 31: 'for the time being, the freedom to choose therefore contradicts existential freedom'.

30 Vilém Flusser, *Does Writing Have a Future?* trans. Nancy Ann Roth (Minneapolis: University of Minnesota Press, 2011), p. 6.

31 I am using 'mathematical' in the same sense as Henri Bergson when he defines what he means (and does not mean) by the present: 'There can be no question of a mathematical instant ... ' Henri Bergson, *Matter and Memory*, trans. Nancy Margaret Paul and W. Scott Palmer (London: George Allen and Unwin, 1911), p. 176.

32 Gilles Deleuze, *Cinema 1: The Movement-Image*, trans. Hugh Tomlinson and Barbara Habberjam (London: Athlone, 1986), p. 62.

33 This becomes especially clear in the final chapter of *Into the Universe of Technical Images*, where chamber music and jazz turn out to serve as models of a telematic social structure (p. 163). Why not, in that case, cinema and literature too? The question arises of the extent to which Flusser's philosophy of new media is really, or also, a general philosophy of aesthetics. Lending credence to this reading, Flusser writes: 'The universe of technical images can be seen as a universe of musical vision. This essay is an argument in support of this proposition' (p. 165).

Alberto Toscano

Materialism without matter: abstraction, absence and social
form

In light of the contemporary theoretical infatuation with 'new' materialisms, matter and materiality, this essay revisits the heterodox Marxian
thesis according to which materialism may, in Étienne Balibar's formulation, have 'nothing to do with a reference to matter'. The article explores
variants of this materialism without matter: Antonio Gramsci's objections
to Bukharin's 'Marxist sociology', Theodor W. Adorno and Alfred Sohn-
Rethel's critiques of epistemology, and Isaak Illich Rubin's elucidation of
the categories of Marx's value-analysis. It foregrounds a shift in this
counter-intuitive materialism from subjective praxis to the categories of
capital, in which 'not one atom of matter enters' (Marx). This recovery
of an understanding of materialism as the critical analysis of real, social
abstractions concludes with a reconsideration of Louis Althusser's 'aesthetic' reflections on the materialism of absence, as featured in his philosophical appreciation of the paintings of Leonardo Cremonini.

1. The uses of ideology

The terms 'materialism' and 'materiality' are subject to a bewildering variety of uses in contemporary theory. Many of these uses serve not to define a particular field of research, or a specific method, but to orient and demarcate; they often repeat, in attenuated guise, that polemical impetus (against religion, idealism, spirit, transcendence and abstraction or even nobility and good taste) which has led many an anti-systemic thinker to emblazon 'materialism' on their banner.[1] Yet even as the explicit echoes of philosophical combats – trespassing into cultural and political ones – fade, there is still a certain aura, in the field of theory, which attaches to the declaration, be it in thought or discourse, of the primacy of matter.

In what follows, I wish to consider some of the ways in which this polemical affirmation of matter's anteriority to thought has been unsettled by theorists grappling with the stakes of the intellectual tradition that for many became, across the late nineteenth century and throughout the twentieth century, the only truly contemporary materialism: Marxism. My title is borrowed in part from an illuminating provocation in Balibar's *The Philosophy of Marx*, which tells us that 'Marx's materialism has nothing to do with a reference to *matter*'.[2] The notion of a 'materialism without matter' is silently borrowed by Balibar from a famous letter of Jacobi to Fichte, whose philosophy of the act and subjectivity Balibar does identify as a crucial precursor for the primacy of praxis. In order to shore up his own anti-dialectical and non-philosophical defence of faith against the claims of an omnivorous reason, Jacobi interestingly rehearsed a theme that many a critic of materialism as a philosophy (or an ontology) has since advanced, namely that it is but a specular inversion of idealism.[3]

In Balibar's own estimation, Marx's displacement of the materialism/idealism distinction, which involved mining the resources of idealist philosophy to structure a materialist critique and catalyse a materialist politics, itself rested on a related inversion, or dialectical chiasmus: while traditional materialism, in its contemplation and representation of matter, showed itself to be haunted by an idealist foundation, modern idealism, with its stress on the activity of the subject, could be transmuted into a truly contemporary materialism. What Marx proposed then 'is quite simply to explode the contradiction, to dissociate representation and subjectivity and allow the category of practical activity to emerge in its own right'.[4] A fixed image of a system of material causality, impervious to human action – which would stand revealed as a mere illusion or epiphenomenon – can thus be regarded as idealist, to the very extent that it purports to offer an exhaustive and incontrovertible representation of the world. Contrariwise, the primacy of action – a thesis drawn from German Idealism at its most Promethean, even hubristic – could be the starting point for a materialism that grounds our representations, including those of matter itself, in collective life, social relations and human practices. But what happens to a materialism without matter when social practice appears in all its antagonism, opacity and unconsciousness, as determined by forms and forces that are not transparent or even available to the activity of individuals or collectives? What happens when materialism turns out not to reduce ideal fantasies to bodies and objects, but to demonstrate the specific ways in which the latter are dominated by abstractions – abstractions through which capitalism conjures up, in Chris Arthur's formulation, 'a world of pure form' in which 'value emerges from the void as a spectre that *haunts* the "real world" of capitalist commodity production'?[5] I want to suggest that the materialism of practice of the early Marx, as captured in Balibar's *détournement* of Jacobi's formulation, must be pulled away from the humanist myth of a transparency of praxis, in the direction of a materialism attentive to the potent *immateriality* of capital's social forms, in other words, a *materialism of real abstractions.*[6]

It is not so difficult to see how 'matter', 'materiality' and 'materialism', in their claim to immediacy, firstness and incontrovertible facticity could be deeply ideological nouns. The literary theorist Marc Shell begins his erudite exploration of *The Economy of Literature* with this astute observation:

> Those discourses are ideological that argue or assume that matter is ontologically prior to thought. Astrology, for example, looks to the stars, phrenology to the skull, physiognomy to the face, and palmistry to the hand. In the modern world, ideological discourses look to the biochemistry of the brain, sexual need, genes, and social class; they seek to express how matter 'gives rise to' thought by employing metaphors such as 'influence', 'structure', 'imitation', 'sublimation', 'expression', and 'symptom'. Every ideology would demonstrate that all other ideologies are idealist expressions of the basic matter to which it alone has real access.[7]

The critique of materialism as an ideology is at the core of Gramsci's lengthy critical annotations in the *Prison Notebooks* on Bukharin's attempt to popularise historical materialism. For Gramsci, the grafting of a Marxist 'sociology' onto a materialism of matter, deriving as it does from an uncritical picture of the natural sciences, misses the core Marxian teaching, to wit that for a critique of political economy matter is always, as Gramsci writes, 'historically and socially organised for production'.[8] Where for Marx natural forces are to be thought of as social, not abstractly ahistorical, Bukharin distorts the 'philosophy of praxis', turning it into the '"sociology" of metaphysical materialism', a political and social-scientific supplement of sorts to a naturalist materialism.[9] In Bukharin, we can observe how a supposedly desecrating ultra-materialism flips over into an abstract idealism when it tries directly to apply concepts extracted from the scientific domain, for instance atomic physics, to refute the claims of bourgeois ideology, say the robinsonnades of individualism.

It was around the same time that Karl Korsch, whose *Karl Marx* is quoted in manuscript form by Benjamin in *The Arcades Project*, was recalling Marx's disparaging comments about 'the philosophical phrases of the Materialists about matter'.[10] For Korsch too, it was the passage from the determinate abstractions of historical materialism as a theory of capitalism to a 'universal sociological theory' which posed the problem. A materialism that is not reflexive about its political, polemical and pedagogical function, as well as about its social rather than metaphysical character, can only repeat the idealist gesture that hypostasises, divinises and abstracts an unmediated ground. Here matter, there Spirit – which has the obvious advantage for Gramsci as for Marx of at least foregrounding practice and relationality. Aside from hammering home the danger for historical materialism of ignoring its crucial difference from metaphysical materialism, and thereby turning into an inverted idealism, an ahistorical ontology that overlooks or underplays historical process, Gramsci also incorporates into his critique of Bukharin a number of interesting historical notations about the manner in which the primacy of matter can take different political complexions, progressive in one conjuncture, regressive in another. Thus, a materialist realism, advocating the rights of the empirical world against the fancies of the subject, is a feature of reactionary strains of Catholic philosophy, just as it can also make up the conservative common sense of certain popular classes.

A not entirely dissimilar intuition, roughly contemporary with Gramsci, lies behind the programmatic pronouncement by Adorno, in his study of Husserl, that the target of relentless dialectical critique should be the very idea of a *first philosophy*, a *prima philosophia*, whose 'original sin' is to eliminate everything which exceeds its judgement 'in order to enforce continuity and completeness' – where 'firstness' is also understood to define the idea of philosophy as closed system.[11] The elementary Hegelian lesson, according to which every first is an abstraction, a simulacrum of immediacy that can only appear as such through the dissimulation of the complex mediations which make its appearance possible, is one that for critical theory should apply with equal rigour to the claim of materialism; the problem, as Adorno notes about phenomenology, is not to replace the foundation with a firmer one, but to question the 'philosophical compulsion' to seek final grounds.[12] But what is a dialectical materialism or 'last philosophy' if, as Adorno writes: 'Nothing immediate or factical, in which the philosophical thought seeks to escape mediation through itself, is allotted to thinking reflection in any other way than through thoughts'?[13] Can the polemical gesture of demarcation, which in the case of material- ism, is crucially linked to some form of 'reduction', survive the passage from first to last philosophy, the abandonment of the basic structure of metaphysics?

I want to propose that if we follow the thread of a materialism without matter, from the initial position of the problem in terms of sub- jective practice to the understanding of social forms and relations in terms of the power of 'real abstractions' – that is, to the critique of pol- itical economy understood as a *critique of the ideologies of materiality* – it is possible to maintain the imperative of reduction (or perhaps more pre- cisely of correlation and displacement); yet this reduction will turn out to be *a reduction of form to form*, of cognitive or ideal abstractions to real or practical ones. I will turn to the works of Isaak Illich Rubin (1886– 1937) and Alfred Sohn-Rethel (1899–1990) to sketch out what it might mean to extract from Marx's critique of political economy such a materialism of social forms. In a second moment, I will consider the way in which such a materialism throws up an 'aesthetic' question: how is one to represent, or indicate, the social powers of intangible forms, of real abstractions? I will home in on one of Louis Althusser's most singular and scintillating essays, 'Cremonini, Painter of the Abstract' – following Warren Montag's powerful if unorthodox sugges- tion that the encounter with Cremonini is crucial to Althusser's articula- tion of materialist theory.[14]

2. Social forms and the critique of philosophy

In the *Grundrisse*, Marx defines capitalism as a social system in which human beings are ruled by abstractions, first and foremost.[15] The overcom- ing of a merely philosophical – which is also to say ethical, moral and ideal – criticism of contemporary capitalist society requires refitting or refunc- tioning many of the conceptual and methodological tools of philosophy, in order to delineate and undermine the domination of social life by abstractions, and above all by the form of value. Without entertaining the melancholy conviction, voiced by Theodor Adorno, that philosophy perseveres in a guilty form because the hour of its realisation was forever missed, we can perhaps ask how things stand today for a discipline con- cerned above all with abstractions at various degrees of purity with regard to Marx's challenge. As socio-economic demystifications of philoso- phical practice fall out of favour, we can identify three broad tendencies in the current articulation of philosophy, capitalism and abstraction.

The first, of a militant type, enlists the resources of ontological and metaphysical abstraction to erect a rational infrastructure for a broadly voluntarist anti-capitalist politics (the eminent example would here be Alain Badiou). The second, rife in social theory, incorporates the legacies of post-modernism and post-structuralism in seeking to replace cold, Cartesian abstractions, with 'warm' abstractions. Materiality, bodies, diagrams, scapes, networks and assemblages are its catchwords.[16] Generally, its invocations of materialism betray a remarkably dematerialised thinking, while its abstractions seem parasitic on a palette of experiences easily referred to the contemporary predicaments of intellectual labour. A third approach, which some have dubbed speculative realism or materialism, and is associated with a disparate host of philosophers – among them Graham Harman and Quentin Meillassoux[17] – seeking to move away from 'Continental' phenomenology and hermeneutics, has tried to combine polemics against idealism and critical philosophy with a call for an unabashed return to the speculative or the absolute after the hesitations of deconstruction and the interdisciplinary hybrids spawned by much post-68 thought. About this recent tendency, we could perhaps unkindly repeat the quip by Alfred Sohn-Rethel, at the end of his *Intellectual and Manual Labour*, according to which the materialist who embarks on speculative philosophy is a bit like the man who throws himself into a fire in order to put it out.

In all three cases – in this admittedly *ad hoc* taxonomy – the question of the relationship between social being and forms of thought, or between capitalism and cognition, remains obscure. Either it is ignored, for the sake of a robust renewal of philosophy or a purely political use of abstractions, or it is sublimated, as social theory is transformed into the cheerfully acritical description of a network of relations seemingly awash in myriad forms of abstraction, ones ultimately indistinguishable from concreteness – a trend that could be termed, harkening back to the post-Kantian philosopher Friedrich Albert Lange, a 'materio-idealism'.[18]

I want to argue that in this intellectual context returning to the Marxian discussion of 'real abstraction', and in particular to the writings of Alfred Sohn-Rethel – *in primis* his *Intellectual and Manual Labour* – can allow us to renew the neglected question of philosophy's place in the understanding and critique of capitalism as a system of abstract domination.[19] In Sohn-Rethel's critique of epistemology – which posits the origin of philosophical thought and modern subjectivity in the non-mental practice of commodity exchange and the mediations of the money form – it is the extra-mental logic of commodity exchange which underlies 'Western thought', and, to put it in hyperbolic, but I think pertinent terms, while the essence of capitalism is not metaphysical, the essence of metaphysics is capitalist. Whereas earlier iterations of materialism countered metaphysics, and its attendant ideologies, by revealing it to be a spectre of matter, or of practice, a materialism of social forms that takes its cue from this notion of real abstraction tries to take seriously the thesis that our social life does not merely appear to be but *actually is* 'metaphysical'.

Against any Eurocentric pieties about the singularity of philosophy's Greek origin, this requires that we begin with a radically profane expatriation: it is the contingent emergence of entirely mundane forms of social abstraction, pivoting around monetary exchange, which permitted the kind of idealities characteristic of ancient Greek philosophy to emerge, not any mysterious spiritual features of that civilisation. Money is abstraction made tangible and visible, the representative, equivalent and medium of a fundamentally impersonal exchange, a relationship without qualities. Ideal abstraction (philosophy) is derivative, but also in a way identical to, the real abstraction of exchange.

According to Sohn-Rethel, the

> act of exchange has to be described as abstract movement through abstract (homogeneous, continuous and empty) space and time of abstract substances (materially real but bare of sense-qualities) which thereby suffer no material change and which allow for none but quantitative differentiation (differentiation in abstract, non-dimensional quantity).[20]

The same underlying schema accounts for the fecund heuristic fiction of homogeneous spatio-temporal individuation, and for the fact that 'in the market-place and in shop windows, things stand still', immersed as they are in the separation between the practices of use and the acts of exchange in time and space.[21]

It is this spatio-temporal distinction between use and exchange that makes it possible to locate a 'material' and historical basis for formal and ahistorical modes of thinking and practice. In a classical meaning of the verb 'to abstract', the exchange abstraction subtracts from, is indifferent to, or suspends, the 'materiality' of the commodity – and it does so not through a cognitive act but through unconscious social practice. In Sohn-Rethel's elucidation:

> The form of exchangeability applies to commodities regardless of their material description. The abstraction comes about by force of the action of exchange or, in other words, out of the exchanging agents *practicising their solipsism against each other*. The abstraction belongs to the interrelationship of the exchanging agents and not to the agents themselves. For it is not individuals who cause the social synthesis but their actions. And their actions do it in

such a way that, at the moment it happens, the actors know nothing of it.[22]

The 'moment' of exchange is a most unusual moment. 'The exchange-abstraction', Sohn-Rethel notes, 'is the historical, spatio-temporal origin of atemporal, ahistorical thought'.[23] The nature of exchange is such that the 'abstract' activity of equivalence and commensuration is concrete, while use-value becomes a matter of ideal representation, and thus turns out to be abstract. This separation has to do with the purely social postulate that things can indeed be instantaneously frozen, a logical requirement for the exchange of commodities which is 'then' projected onto the natural world. The 'mental' reflection of commodity exchange takes place through money as an abstract thing. Coined money is the value-form made visible, and the token of a socially unconscious practice:

> Abstraction is therefore the effect of the action of men, and not of their thought. In reality, it takes place 'behind their backs', at the blind spot, so to speak, of human consciousness, that is there where the thinking and efforts of men are absorbed by their acts of exchange.[24]

Unlike binding and embedded forms of pre-capitalist sociality, money as a social nexus is 'formally unlimited'.[25] This is a formal and logical echo of Marx's reflections about how money poses itself as the antithesis of any community, other than itself. Money is not just formally unlimited but tendentially exclusive of other standards of commensuration or mediums of intercourse.

In the second notebook of the *Grundrisse*, from November 1857, Marx noted the way in which money

> directly and simultaneously becomes the *real community* [*Gemeinwesen*], since it is the general substance of survival for all, and at the same time the social product of all. But as we have seen, in money the community [*Gemeinwesen*] is at the same time a mere abstraction, a mere external, accidental thing for the individual, and at the same time merely a means for his satisfaction as an isolated individual. The community of antiquity presupposes a quite different relation to, and on the part of, the individual. The development of money ... therefore smashes this community.[26]

Or, as the mention of 'mere' abstraction suggests (which we could juxtapose to the *real* abstraction of money), it recodes the pre-monetised community as an auxiliary resource for the real community of money, deployed or curtailed in keeping with the shifting imperatives of accumulation.

But money is not just real community, it is also a *sensus communis*.[27] Monetised exchange structures a socially transcendental aesthetic, which is not solely a matter of commensurability (and of its dialectical reliance on singularity, or the appearance of uniqueness[28]), but also that of a practical arrest of time and evacuation of space, which the customary tools of psychology, or indeed of philosophy itself, are ill-prepared to analyse. This monetised abstraction is an activity that is simultaneously relational and impersonal, rather than in any sense primarily mental. It also for Sohn-Rethel differentiates between socialised men and animals. In a vignette from *Intellectual and Manual Labour*, he writes:

> Money is an abstract thing, a paradox in itself – a thing that performs its socially synthetic function without any human understanding. And yet no animal can ever grasp the meaning of money; it is accessible only to man. Take your dog with you to the butcher and watch how much he understands of the goings on when you purchase your meal. It is a great deal and even includes a keen sense of property which will make him snap at a stranger's hand daring to come near the meat his master has obtained and which he will be allowed to carry home in his mouth. But when you have to tell him 'Wait, doggy, I haven't paid yet!' his understanding is at an end. The pieces of metal or paper which he watches you hand over, and which carry your scent, he knows, of course; he has seen them before. But their function as money lies outside the animal range.[29]

The crucial thing to grasp is that Sohn-Rethel's derivation does not move from the density of empirically observable and palpably material social relations to the supposedly distorting and transcendent illusions of philosophy; rather, it takes its cue from Marx's conception of value as a social form to ground ideal abstractions in real abstraction. Philosophy can thus be seen to develop from the 'socialised mind of man'. As Sohn-Rethel declares, in one of the most peremptory and provocative of his formulations, philosophy 'is money without its material attachments, immaterial and no longer recognisable as money and, indeed, no longer being money but the "pure intellect"'.[30]

The aim here is that of 'putting Kant back on his feet', by analogy with Marx's notorious statement on Hegel, to show how the synthetic powers of the transcendental subject are really social powers. Or, as Adorno argued in *Negative Dialectics* – partially acknowledging the considerable impact of Sohn-Rethel's thesis on the development of his own thought ever since their first contact in the late 1920s – the transcendental subject is society unconscious of itself.[31] The elimination of society from abstract philosophical thought is a product of society itself; it is an abstraction that society makes from itself, in the exercise of intellectual labour and in the primacy of exchange as form of mediation. Capitalism is an abstract society, where the social nexus is not generated primarily by custom, reciprocity or tradition – though these remain the material and forms of appearance of capitalist society – but in the indifference of exchange. The profound theoretical originality of Marx is thus to be sought in the fact that he provides 'the first explanation of the historical origin of a pure phenomenon of form'.[32]

Around the time of Sohn-Rethel's first theoretical epiphany, this was also an important dimension of Isaak Illich Rubin's pioneering discussion of 'social form' in his *Essays on Marx's Theory of Value* (1928). From this last flowering of critical Marxism in the USSR, I only want to retain, for the purposes of this discussion, Rubin's stress on the fact that Marx's critique of classical political economy hinges on distinguishing between 'material categories' concerned with 'technical methods and instruments of labour', on the one hand, and 'social forms' concerned with specifically capitalist relations, on the other. The blind spot of political economy is precisely its inability, evidenced by the theory of commodity fetishism, to think why *these particular value-forms* are generated in bourgeois society, and wrongly supposing that it is in transhistorical 'material categories' – labour in general rather than labour-power, exchange separate from capital, and so on – that one can look for the clues to the structure and development of the mode of production. Contrariwise, it is 'the social *function* which is realized through a thing [that] gives this thing a particular social character, a determined social *form*, a "determination of form" (*Formbestimmtheit*), as Marx frequently wrote'.[33]

Marx's remonstrations against those political economists who, in Rubin's terms, cannot see the 'social forms' lying 'beneath' the 'technical functions in the process of material production' are legion. *Historical materialism is predicated on the rejection of the spontaneous materialism of the political economists.* This is the impetus behind such seemingly 'idealist' declarations as this famous passage from the first volume of *Capital*:

> The value of commodities is the very opposite of the coarse materiality of their substance, not an atom of matter enters into its composition. Turn and examine a single commodity, by itself, as we will, yet in so far as it remains an object of value, it seems impossible to grasp it. If, however, we bear in mind that the value of commodities has a purely social reality, and that they acquire this reality only in so far as they are expressions or embodiments of one identical social

substance, viz., human labour, it follows as a matter of course, that value can only manifest itself in the social relation of commodity to commodity.[34]

Earlier in the *Grundrisse*, Marx had criticised political economists for simply beginning with labour and seeking to build the forms of value out of it in a linear manner. His argument there was unimpeachably Hegelian, suggesting that the positing of the labour process as a point of departure was marred by its 'abstractness, its pure materiality'.[35] This is an abstractness and materiality that of course becomes 'concrete' with the apotheosis of abstract labour, when, to quote again from the *Grundrisse*,

> particular skill becomes something more and more abstract and irrelevant, and as it becomes more and more a purely abstract activity, a purely mechanical activity, hence indifferent to its particular form; a merely formal activity, or, what is the same, a merely material [*stofflich*] activity, activity pure and simple, regardless of its form.[36]

The critique of 'materialism' is also a key methodological postulate in the second volume of *Capital*, for instance, in Marx's sardonic attack on those who think that fixed capital should be understood as 'fixed' in a commonsensically material sense of the term. This is how political economists go astray:

> Firstly, certain properties that characterize the means of labour materially are made into direct properties of fixed capital, e.g. physical immobility, such as that of a house. But it is always easy to show that other means of labour, which are also as such fixed capital, ships for example, have the opposite property, i.e. physical mobility. Alternatively, the formal economic characteristic that arises from the circulation of value is confused with a concrete [*dinglich*] property; as if things, which are never capital at all in themselves, could already in themselves and by nature be capital in a definite form, fixed or circulating.[37]

3. A materialism of absences

Discussions of the correlation or homonymy between the social forms of capital and the aesthetic forms of art are rife with fallacies, above all the one between the progressive abstraction of art and the increasing abstraction of capital. It is all the more interesting that one of Althusser's most fertile inquiries into the problem of representing capital emerges from his attempt to articulate and defend the figurative practice of the Italian painter Leonardo Cremonini, against both the primacy of 'abstract painting' and social-realist denunciations of Cremonini's putative expressionist or existentialist orientation. It is in the displacements of the aesthetic and methodological vocabularies of form, visibility and abstraction that the originality of Althusser's intervention is to be located. In an earlier text, Althusser had signalled the specificity of art as that of making visible, through a process of allusion, *retreat* and *internal distantiation*, the ideology in which these works bathe.[38] Making visible, but not making known.

The stakes of the Cremonini are considerably higher, as the Italian artist's work comes to represent not just a sectoral materialism but a kind of allegory for the materialist method as such. For Cremonini's painting tackles, in the artistic register, *the* problem of a materialism without matter; in Althusser's evocative words:

> Cremonini 'paints' the *relations* which bind the objects, places and times. Cremonini is a *painter of abstraction*. Not an abstract painter, 'painting' an absent, pure possibility, but a painter of the real *abstract*, 'painting' in a sense we have to define, real relations (as relations they are necessarily *abstract*) between 'men' and their 'things', or rather, to give the term its stronger sense, between 'things' and *their* 'men'.[39]

This painting of relations is further entangled in a kind of non-specular reflection, once we consider that the painting is also the painting of the relations between the painter and 'his' work.

A number of observations are in order. To begin with, figuration, as a modality of representation, is here a *conditio sine qua non*, for 'alluding' to or 'indicating', relations which are intangible. One will encounter a curiously contiguous iteration of this argument in Deleuze's book on Francis Bacon, where instead of the structures of capital and ideology, it will be vital forces and intensities which figuration allows one to crystallise. For Deleuze:

> The task of painting is defined as the attempt to render visible forces that are not themselves visible. Likewise, music attempts to render sonorous forces that are not themselves sonorous. That much is clear. Force is closely related to sensation: for a sensation to exist, a force must be exerted on a body, on a point of the wave. But if force is the condition of sensation, it is nonetheless not the force that is sensed, since the sensation 'gives' something completely different from the forces that condition it. How will sensation be able to sufficiently turn in on itself, relax or contract itself, so as to capture

these nongiven forces in what it gives us, to make us sense these insensible forces, and raise itself to its own conditions?[40]

Cremonini's problem is, in its own register (but this register is not easily cordoned off from that of science, contrary to what Althusser's earlier letter on art seemed to suggest), analogous to the problem of a Marxist theory of capital as a theory of real abstractions – including in terms of the question of how one is to confront the anti-humanist reversal which takes place in the 'inter-objectivity' of fetishism, once things not only appear to but *really determine* 'their men'. Yet far from arranging this aesthetic of abstraction in terms of a dialectic of the abstract and the concrete, Cremonini *appears* to unfold his plastic project in terms of an ascension, a chain of being, moving from the mineral, to the vegetable, to the animal (and the human).

What Althusser identifies in this 'progression' is something like a disjunctive synthesis of materialisms: a materialism of matter that begins in the inorganic is limned or shadowed by a materialism of the immaterial, of the invisible. This duality is tangible in Althusser's own prose, which here draws on delectable poetic resources to describe materiality only in order to reduce it to an effect through which we can read the traces of an absent presence. From the geological to the vegetal to the animal we move, at the figural level, across 'the armatures and articulations, consolidated by weight and by history, of the passive body of an island, dormant in the heavy oblivion of the rocks, at the edge of an empty sea, a matter-less horizon' to 'the sharp growth of a bulb, the long shriek of the dumb stems' and at last, as dehumanised men commingle with dissected beasts to 'dismembered animals scattered among men collecting bony carcases, men like the carcases they bear on their emaciated shoulders'.[41] Yet the focus is elsewhere, off-screen, off-canvas – the rocks' 'difference', which makes them the 'ground' of men; the absences in the presences of the flowers, the invisible 'time of their growth'. And throughout the ponderous materiality – rocks like stems like bones like people – is really the site for a kind of 'materialist' similarity whose urge is rather 'abstract': to distance men from our ideology of men, and to do this by distancing us, in the arrangement of this 'natural' ascension and progression, from our very idea of progress; to paint *difference from this ideological project of the descent of forms.*[42]

In order to move us towards a showing of real abstraction, through a displacement of our ideological vision, Cremonini also needs to transit through a kind of extreme materialism, the anti-humanist *identification* of men with their things: men

fashioned from the material of their objects, circumscribed by it, caught and defined once and for all: faces corroded by the air, gnawed and seemingly amputated (almost *too much* faces), gestures and cries congealed into immutable weight, a parody of human time reduced to eternity, the eternity of matter.[43]

This phase, crushing the humanism of natural progress under the impress of matter, is followed for Althusser – reviewing Cremonini's exhibition at the Venice Biennale – by the introduction of a painting of the relations among men, relations that appear in the metaphor of displacement, deformation or that favourite Althusserian term, *décalage*.

Althusser excels here in an exploration of the role of the mirror in Cremonini's work, which far from any 'reflection theory' is caught up in a complex play of delays, misrecognitions, over-identifications, a play shaped by a definite space: the interiors in which Cremonini arranges the gravity of lives through tall vertical lines and makes visible the laws of their relation in the arrangement of circles.[44] These spaces of displaced reflection – in which individuals are fixed to objects that mirror them and the sites that they inhabit – have left behind the line of descent of the antecedent series. But for Althusser Cremonini is getting at something more, and something other, than the bad, infinite relay between men and their things; he is straining towards a 'determinate absence'. And it is here, in an act not of reflection but perhaps of forced projection, that the Italian painter's aesthetic problem becomes nigh-on indistinguishable from the aesthetic problem of a Marxist theoretical practice that moves from a materialism of matter to a materialism without matter. In Althusser's words:

> In their 'finite' world which dominates them, Cremonini thus 'paints' (i.e. 'depicts' by the play of the similarities inscribed in the differences) the history of men as a history *marked*, as early as the first childhood games, and even in the anonymity of faces (of children, women and men), by the *abstraction* of their sites, spaces, objects, i.e. *in the last instance* by the *real abstraction* which determines and sums up these first abstractions: the relations which constitute their *living conditions*. I do not mean – it would be *meaningless* – that it is possible to 'paint' 'living conditions', to paint social relations or the forms of the class struggle in a given society. But it is possible, through their objects, to 'paint' visible connexions that depict by their disposition, the *determinate absence* which governs them. The structure which controls the *concrete* existence of men, i.e. which *informs the lived ideology* of the relations between men and objects and between objects and men, this structure, *as a structure*, can never be depicted by its presence, *in person*, but only by traces and effects, negatively, by indices of absence, *in intaglio (en creux)*.[45]

Among such effects are the deformations (and not the deformity) of the faces in Cremonini's paintings, which is a *determinate absence of form* for Althusser, as well as an erasure of the features of humanist ideology. But curiously, the absence which at one level appears as the determinate absence of structural causality, the 'positive, determinate absence which determines' these 'men', 'which makes them the anonymous beings that they are, the structural effects of the real relations which govern them' is at another, in a strange aesthetic reversal, the absence of ideology itself, what Althusser calls 'a purely negative absence, that of the humanist which is refused'[46] these faces which cannot be seen, which do not take the *form* of individuality or subjectivity – whence Althusser's provocative remark that all of 'man' is present in Cremonini in the guise of a double absence, the positive absence of capital and the negative absence of the human.

As far as the positive absence of capital is concerned, it is striking how Cremonini's problem both foreshadows and displaces – in the complexity and specificity of his dispositions of matter, forms and figures – Althusser's formulation, itself anticipated by the play of the visible and the invisible in *Reading Capital*, of the visibility of capital as a real abstraction. In his preface to the first volume of *Capital*, notorious for its suggestion that the reader bypass the value-form core of Marx's theory of abstraction, Althusser writes of how the 'apprenticeship' to thinking with abstractions is rendered particularly daunting by the fact that none of its grounding concepts – total social capital, surplus-value and so on – are ones that one can 'touch with one's hands' or 'see with one's eyes'. As he declares:

> Every abstract concept therefore provides knowledge of a reality whose existence it reveals: an 'abstract concept' then means a formula which is apparently abstract but really terribly concrete, because of the object it designates. This object is terribly concrete in that it is infinitely more concrete, more effective than the objects one can 'touch with one's hands' or 'see with one's eyes' – and yet one cannot touch it with one's hands or see it with one's eyes. . . . Simply speaking: in order to be able to analyse these concrete capitalist societies (England, France, Russia, etc.), it is essential to know that they are dominated by that terribly concrete reality, the capitalist mode of production, which is 'invisible' (to the naked eye). 'Invisible', i.e. *abstract*.[47]

This, it seems to me, is the aesthetic and experiential – which is also to say representational and figural – problem at the heart of a materialism without matter, or, to shift the formulation somewhat, a realism of the abstract. It is a problem which, as I have tried to argue with regard to the aesthetic parameters of actor–network theory,[48] cannot even be posed in contemporary invocations of materiality that repudiate the ideas of social form and totality and insistently demand that all representations be if not reducible at least traceable to a transaction between the nodes of a network. Yet it is also a problem that remains daunting in its perilous under-determination: how are we to tell apart the negative from the positive absences, ideology from the structure of capital? How are we to posit that which the effects of this absence presuppose? It is here that a materialism without matter calls on a finer science of invisibilities – a metaphysics indeed, but one which is indexed to real abstractions and not merely cognitive protocols. Making the invisible visible and making the invisible known are not necessarily coterminous activities (science, for Althusser, is not an aesthetic). But the character of that invisibility varies – are we speaking of a form, a force, a structure? And could we not say that the problem of representing capital is much better framed as a problem about the representation of a metamorphosis, the sequence and syncopation of value *forms*, than it is in terms of *an* absent structure?[49]

But perhaps the thorniest problems that such a materialism without matter raises, which leads us back from abstraction towards praxis, is: *whom* is this visibility for? The preface to *Capital* is addressed at least in part to a proletarian audience, which it presumes to be better prepared to the apprenticeship in abstraction to the extent that it has felt the impact of these 'invisible' realities on its labouring, suffering bodies. Anticipating the autobiographical confession that theoretical anti-humanism was but a prelude to practical humanism, the essay on Cremonini stresses that the play of displacements, skewed reflections and determinate absences in the Italian painter's canvases is there to mark the distance between *knowledge* (which is a knowledge through the gaps in the false) and *recognition* (another 'aesthetic' thematic). Inserted into ideology in order to mark a distance from it, Cremonini's painting stands comparison with the great works of revolutionary anti-humanism (or, we could suggest, it allegorises them) to the extent that it embodies the conviction that

> the *freedom of men* is not achieved by the complacency of its *ideological* recognition, but by *knowledge* of the laws of their slavery, and that the 'realization' of their concrete individuality is achieved by the analysis and mastery of the abstract relations which govern them. ... This painter of the abstract, like the great revolutionary philosophers and scientists, would not paint, and would not paint the 'abstraction' of their world, if he did not paint for *concrete* men, for the only existing men, for us.[50]

It is this 'us' which forms a kind of third absence, after those of capital and man, an absence both practical and prophetic, that of a concreteness and collectivity to come. It over-determines a knowledge which here amounts to nothing but – but this nothing is all – showing the gaps or opening the distances within the order of abstract domination itself.

Goldsmiths, University of London

Notes

1 For further reflections on the relationship between materialism and partisan-ship, see my 'Partisan Thought', *Historical Materialism*, 17.3 (2009), pp. 175–91.

2 Étienne Balibar, *The Philosophy of Marx* (London: Verso, 1995), p. 23.

3 Friedrich Heinrich Jacobi, 'Open Letter to Fichte', in E. Behler (ed.), *Philosophy of German Idealism* (New York: Continuum, 1987), p. 123. Jacobi's concern was of course with the other side of this polemic, casting Fichte in the role of an inverted Spinoza.

4 *The Philosophy of Marx*, p. 25.

5 Christopher J. Arthur, *The New Dialectic and Marx's Capital* (Leiden: Brill, 2004), p. 167.

6 I have sketched out some of the sources and themes of this research programme in 'The Culture of Abstraction', *Theory, Culture & Society* 25.4 (2008), pp. 57–75; 'The Open Secret of Real Abstraction', *Rethinking Marxism*, 20.2 (2008), pp. 273–87.

7 Marc Shell, *The Economy of Literature* (Baltimore, MD: The Johns Hopkins University Press, 1993), p. 1.

8 Antonio Gramsci, *Quaderni del Carcere*, ed. V. Gerratana (Torino: Einaudi, 2007), p. 1442.

9 *Quaderni del Carcere*, p. 1402.

10 Walter Benjamin, *The Arcades Project*, ed. R. Tiedemann and trans. H. Eiland and K. McLaughlin (Cambridge, MA: The Belknap Press of Harvard University Press, 1999), p. 485.

11 Theodor W. Adorno, *Against Epistemology: A Metacritique*, ed. and trans. W. Domingo (Cambridge: Polity, 2013), p. 10.

12 We encounter here an unexpected convergence between Adorno and Althusser, who writes: 'the idea of an absolute point of departure (= of an essence) belongs to bourgeois philosophy'. Louis Althusser, *Essays in Self-Criticism*, ed. and trans. G. Lock (London: New Left Books, 1976), p. 52, quoted in Warren Montag, *Louis Althusser* (Basingstoke: Palgrave, 2003), p. 72. Or, as Adorno will later state:

> By no means will ideology always resemble the explicit idealistic philosophy. Ideology lies in the substruction of something primary, the content of which

hardly matters; it lies in the implicit identity of concept and thing, an identity justified by the world even when a doctrine summarily teaches that consciousness depends on being.

Theodor W. Adorno, *Negative Dialectics*, ed. and trans. E.B. Ashton (New York: Continuum, 1973), p. 40.
13 *Against Epistemology*, p. 7.
14 See Ch. 1 of his excellent *Louis Althusser*, 'Towards a New Reading of Althusser'. A fuller treatment of these questions would also need to explore Althusser's response to Foucault's *Birth of the Clinic*, and the latter's articulation of the visible and the invisible.
15 Karl Marx, *Grundrisse*, ed. and trans. M. Nicolaus (London: Penguin, 1973), p. 164.

These *objective* dependency relations also appear, in antithesis to those of *personal* dependence (the objective dependency relation is nothing more than social relations which have become independent and now enter into opposition to the seemingly independent individuals; i.e. the reciprocal relations of production separated from and autonomous of individuals) in such a way that individuals are now ruled by *abstractions*, whereas earlier they depended on one another. The abstraction, or idea, however, is nothing more than the theoretical expression of those material relations which are their lord and master.

16 See also 'The Culture of Abstraction'.
17 I have commented critically on Meillassoux's materialism in 'Against Speculation, or, a Critique of the Critique of Critique: A Remark on Quentin Meillassoux's *After Finitude* (After Colletti)', in Levi R. Bryant, Nick Srnicek & Graham Harman (eds.), *The Speculative Turn: Continental Materialism and Realism* (Melbourne: re. press, 2011).
18 Friedrich Albert Lange, *The History of Materialism and Criticism of its Present Importance*, ed. and trans. E.C. Thomas (New York: The Humanities Press, 1950 [1865]).
19 For an introduction to Sohn-Rethel's fundamental argument, which has the considerable merit of also laying out an incisive critique of his understanding of the commodity and value, see Anselm Jappe, 'Sohn-Rethel and the Origin of "Real Abstraction": A Critique of Production or a Critique of Circulation', *Historical Materialism* 21.1 (2013), pp. 3–14.
20 Alfred Sohn-Rethel, *Intellectual and Manual Labour: A Critique of Epistemology*, ed. and trans. M. Sohn-Rethel (London: Macmillan, 1978), p. 53.
21 Sohn-Rethel, *Intellectual and Manual Labour*, p. 25.
22 Ibid., pp. 44–5.
23 Ibid., p. 96.
24 Ibid., p. 65.
25 Ibid., p. 67.
26 Marx, *Grundrisse*, pp. 225–6.

27 For an influential exploration of this notion from Kant's *Critique of Judgment*, see Jean-François Lyotard, 'Sensus Communis', in A. Benjamin (ed.), *Judging Lyotard* (London: Routledge, 1992), pp. 1–25.

28 Horkheimer and Adorno encapsulated this feature of capitalist society in their analysis of the pseudo-individuality of the culture industry: 'The defiant reserve or elegant appearance of the individual on show is mass-produced like Yale-locks, whose only difference can be measured in fractions of milimeters'. Max Horkheimer and Theodor W. Adorno, *Dialectic of Enlightenment* (London: Verso, 1997), p. 154.

29 Sohn-Rethel, *Intellectual and Manual Labour*, p. 45.

30 Ibid., p. 130.

31 *Negative Dialectics*, p. 10. The key document for the Adorno/Sohn-Rethel relationship is their correspondence, currently being translated into English: Theodor W. Adorno and Alfred Sohn-Rethel, *Briefwechsel 1936–1969*, ed. C. Gödde (Munich: text + kritik, 1991).

32 Sohn-Rethel, *Intellectual and Manual Labour*, p. 45.

33 Isaak Illich Rubin, *Essays on Marx's Theory of Value*, ed. and trans. M. Samardzija and F. Perlman (Montréal-New York: Black Rose Books, 1973), p. 37. As an aside, though one crucial for a proper philological reconstruction of this materialism without matter, form-determination was a Hegelian term that Marx used repeatedly in his *Dissertation* on Epicurus and Democritus to account for the character of the former's atomist materialism.

34 Karl Marx, *Capital, Volume 1*, ed. and trans. S. Moore and E. Aveling (London: Lawrence & Wishart, 1983), p. 54.

35 Marx, *Grundrisse*, p. 304.

36 Ibid., p. 297.

37 Karl Marx, *Capital, Volume 2*, trans. D. Fernbach (London: Penguin, 1992), p. 241. And further:

> What is also brought to fulfilment here is the fetishism peculiar to bourgeois economics, which transforms the social, economic character that things are stamped with in the process of social production into a natural character arising from the material nature of these things. Means of labour, for instance, are fixed capital – a scholastic definition which leads to contradictions and confusion .... means of labour are fixed capital only where the production process is in fact a capitalist production process and the means of production are thus actually capital, i.e. possess the economic determination, the social character, of capital; secondly, they are fixed capital only if they transfer their value to the product in a particular way. ... What is at issue here is not a set of definitions under which things are to be subsumed. It is rather definite functions that are expressed in specific categories (p. 303).

38 Louis Althusser, 'A Letter on Art in Reply to André Daspré', in *Lenin and Philosophy and Other Essays*, ed. and trans. B. Brewster (New York: Monthly Review, 1971), p. 222.

39 Louis Althusser, 'Cremonini, Painter of the Abstract', in *Lenin and Philosophy and Other Essays*, p. 230.
40 Gilles Deleuze, *Francis Bacon: The Logics of Sensation*, ed. and trans. D.W. Smith (London: Continuum, 2003), pp. 56–7.
41 Althusser, 'Cremonini, Painter of the Abstract', p. 232.
42 Ibid., p. 234.
43 Ibid.
44 Here another contrast with Deleuze's Bacon, and his 'frames', would surely be instructive, as would an exploration of the resonances with Foucault's writings on Velázquez or Manet.
45 Althusser, 'Cremonini, Painter of the Abstract', pp. 236–7.
46 Ibid., p. 239.
47 Althusser, 'Preface to *Capital* Volume One', in *Lenin and Philosophy and Other Essays*, p. 77.
48 'Seeing It Whole: Staging Totality in Social Theory and Art', *Sociological Review* 60, supplement S1: *Live Methods* (2012), pp. 64–83.
49 See Fredric Jameson, *Representing* Capital: *A Commentary on Volume One* (London: Verso, 2011).
50 Althusser, 'Cremonini, Painter of the Abstract', p. 241. The link between the text on Cremonini and the preface to *Capital* is made explicit in one of the remarkable letters to Franca Madonia, Althusser's lover and Cremonini's sister-in-law, dated 9 February 1965:

> the painting is made to be seen, it is addressed to a living gaze: this presence is reflected in the work precisely by the *absence* of any painted subjectivity, or again in the fact that the work takes as its object objectivity itself in its abstraction. I think that this is profoundly the case not only for this painting, but above all for people like Spinoza and Marx: that the *address* [*destination*] of the (theoretical, painted, etc.) work figures in the very structure of the work, that this structure implies in itself, in the fashion in which it announces the presence of its addressee, the presence of its practical-human or historical *function*.

Louis Althusser, *Lettres à Franca (1961–1973)*, eds. F. Matheron and Y. Moulier Boutang (Paris: Stock/IMEC, 1998), p. 601.

Interview

Susan Stewart, Rebecca Colesworthy and Peter Nicholls

An exchange with Susan Stewart

TP: How do you conceive of the intersection of poetry and economics? How does poetry relate – or, perhaps, not relate – to our current economic conjuncture?

SS: Poems, like all art works, have their own economy: the circulation of images and metaphors, the reach of the work in time and space, the density of the syntax and specificity of the words – all appearing under a rule of the non-superfluous: there can be no waste in a poem – everything counts. To take away any part is to destroy the whole. Although most commodities are used up or worn down to worthlessness by their participation in exchange, the completed poem – a 'poetic', made, thing – lives on, renewed, in the gift economy of communication and interpretation.

Meanwhile, capitalism's 'real' economy imitates the meaningful forms of gift economy, especially through advertising: Master Card's 'priceless' campaign; notions of 'luck and skill in investing'; the consumer's language of 'choices' and 'finds'. The rush of gambling and risk is a – perhaps unknowing, perhaps calculated – parody of creativity.

All of our metaphors come from nature, including economic metaphors of margin, cycle, and surplus. Yet we tend to forget our own place in nature when we describe the global economy, a made system, driven by human desire, as a non-human force like weather. Framing the economy as a world of 'fortunes' beyond human volition represses the causal forces at work, including the brutal facts of human sacrifice that underlie our over-accumulation. At the same time, infinitely mutating nature is an infinite resource for thought and there is no reason why our frames for value cannot change.

TP: You speak of poetry, and art and communication more broadly, as a gift economy. How is this gift economy related to – or, rather, abstracted from – nature in a way that is different from contemporary capitalism or 'the economy'? Is there a specifically poetic mode or form of abstraction? How would poetic abstraction, or poetry as abstraction, differ from the abstraction of economics?

SS: Poetic abstraction is inherently bound up with concretising. Art works, including poems, can help us avoid binary thinking by truly instantiating the relation between abstractions and particulars. The classical philosophical examples of abstraction – infinity and freedom, for example – resist representation by definition. They are supersensible. And aesthetic objects, inherently objects made by and for the senses, by definition resist abstraction. But those who write on aesthetics, starting with Baumgarten, Kant, and Schiller, have long recognised that art objects involve, in both their production and reception, in their material forms and the speculation they inspire, concrete particulars and confused percepts and concepts, the sensible and the reasoned.

In contrast, when we talk about abstraction in economics, it seems to me we are dealing with ideology and, increasingly, the rationalisation of irrational practices. There is no economic relation that is not specifiable: everything comes from somewhere and goes somewhere and when we deal with economic realities abstractly it is because we either want to forget their particulars or hope our vagueness sounds like prognostication. A true free market would not involve items of calculable worth. Practices and things that increase the more they are spent seem to me to be the most valuable: making art, reading, learning, renewable and renewing relations to natural phenomena, most kinds of pleasure.

TP: How are we to explain the pleasure afforded by poetry? Does poetic pleasure have a relationship to the abstraction of the market and economics?

SS: Much of our pleasure in art and thought stems from the experience of transformation within a context of limited or reversible consequences; abstraction can be free of contingent need, an outcome of leisure, an everyday luxury of living elsewhere than in the real.

The dominant system of valuation in the culture – the economic system – is far more rigid than that: its outcomes are not reversible; they are indelible. Money is a collective fiction, but one with real consequences. In philosophy and art making we have the freedom to doubt, withdraw, control. But in our relation to the market, we are part of the 'confidence game' – even believing economists can predict the future. It seems to me that the ethical problem with the market economy is not its abstraction [i.e. the implicit sense of loss in Marx's notion that an abstract relation takes the place of a concrete one]; it is the self-deception involved in concealing the particulars of the process and confusing categories. From the factory owner who ignores safety rules, knowing there will always be replacement workers in a period of low employment, to the happy shopper convinced of his luck as he finds a 'bargain' produced in truth by slave labour, we fall into greed or narcissism or indifference – those sloughs of despond that keep us from pursuing the fundamental question of what human life is for.

TP: It seems like nature may function as an indispensable third term in your conceptualisation of the relation between poetry and economics. You suggest, 'Infinitely mutating nature is an infinite resource for thought', including economic thought, and 'all of our metaphors come from nature'. What if there were a *real* relation, as opposed to simply a metaphorical relation, between economics on the one hand and literature, philosophy, and other forms of intellectual production and communication on the other?

SS: Processes of abstraction, including the work of metaphor, seem to be inimical to terminological stability. Epistemological issues quickly turn into ontological issues. What is a 'real' relation? – and is a metaphorical one in some way 'simpl[er]'? If the literal is more real than the metaphorical, it is also, it seems to me, less complex, just as denotation is less complex than connotation in the sense that we spend less time on it. But I don't think we can parse out or distribute the real in this way. Marx reminds us that what may seem like a material relation [as the commodity may first strike us as an outcome of use value] is in fact a social relation – value arises in interaction with other human beings and every value is a social value. This is what is wrong with merely adding 'social' clauses to labour contracts or committing to a percentage of 'social' investments – such practices may ease someone's conscience, but the systems of exchange are social from the outset.

And of course the causal force driving intellectual and artistic practice is also a social one – art and ideas emerge in response and call for response; their value is overdetermined by their past contexts and underdetermined by their future contexts. As acts of communication they enter into social life and play their role in modifying and shaping social life. But I believe some practices, like making and receiving poetry, are not readily subject to predetermination. When and if they are, they are diminished in their range and possibilities.

It is intriguing, and somehow pathetic, that the financial sector imitates certain features of artistic practice: an attraction to serendipity, a sense of the macro and micro intersecting with personal fate, a theme of 'inspiration'. But art draws on nature without depleting it and whereas artistic practices are reversible, these financial sector practices are not. Such sublimated creativity makes the 'play' of one very small class the ruination of masses.

Poetry

Susan Stewart

Abstraction set

I *The Sea*

Drawn away and diverted, like the sea and
    the pebble at the edge of the sea,
aggregate wearing visibly, invisibly
    into grain, into
garnet, silica, atom – this
    and this and this, and yet
you cannot say this, not this,
    is the sea.
You had an intuition of an all
    without detail (and every thing
a part of it). Pocket of popped knot-
    wrack, wadded dulse,
nacreous chips from the lining
    of a shell, and here,
rubbed between your finger
    and thumb, the coin you found
(on one side, a queen's face)
    (on the other, a garland).
Lucky, you decide,
    worth keeping, like the others
(but there is only one face to the sea).
    The sailor hides a map
to hidden treasure,
    which leads him to believe
there will be land.
    The coin you hold is yours
for the trading. Your hand, waving.
    Your luck floats in luck like a wave.

II *Rule of the Margin*

horizon, fading, deferred   motion
to a line   geometric, inferred

                              how space takes up
                              its own part of space

unreal horizon, inferred   to a line
motion, geometric   deferred, fading

HOW ABSTRACT IS IT? THINKING CAPITAL NOW

III *time to do the numbers*

(For Gideon Rosen)

as the philosopher did,
    not as items to be counted like ducklings
        on the current, swinging out single
           file, a set of ones, and their setting out
               itself an instance. Their direction drifted
                  leeward, wobbling toward Spring,

and what it meant for me was not at all
    what it meant, I thought it meant,
        for them. A 'by the way' – swirling water
           and clouds, numerous, the water
               made of clouds and vice versa.

Still, numbers cannot live
    in your mind, or theirs. There was something
        I wanted to remember, driven
           by a 'felt need', like thoughts,
               inseparable. The possibility

of every possibility. Elated, then, later,
    terrified. Infinity, after-image, intruding,
        horizon as a wall as a horizon.
           The wind coming down
               from the north hard pressing
                  the rain now lifting from the south.

IV *the sky*

Absurd to say
the sky above
is your favorite

sky, a little less
to hold some
cirrus dearer

than mackerel,
but even more
to claim

that cloud
is my cloud:
possession

isn't nine-
tenths of
this law.

Susan Stewart
Princeton University

Stephen Shapiro

From capitalist to communist abstraction: *The Pale King*'s
cultural fix

David Foster Wallace's *The Pale King* achieves a new novelistic form that
narrates different capitalist temporalities simultaneously – in his case, the
classic logistic of capitalism and its particular contemporary form in neoliberalism. A reading of his novel suggests a solution to the goal of cultural
materialist theory. By rereading the second and third volumes of Marx's
Capital, we can perceive the absence of a term – *fixed labour-power* –
that ought to be present but is not. By providing this term, we can
resolve incompletely theorised techniques from Russian Formalism and
its later adaptation by Fredric Jameson. *The Pale King* thus creates a text
that suggests what a Western communist or left front novel in the post-
Cold War, post-9/11 period might look like.

With *The Pale King* (2011), David Foster Wallace realised the analytical possibilities of literary postmodernism's formal technique.[1] This incomplete (alas) novel marks a threshold for decades of artistic experiments involving metareflexive narration, flattened emplotment, typographical interventions and mixed media alienation-effects on the body text, scrambling of high-low cultural value distinctions, and jumbled or fantastic time sequences. *The Pale King* does not take leave of postmodernism so much as it makes postmodernism useful for socially progressive fiction. Wallace finally perceived that the narrative bifurcations of postmodern techniques do not merely lead to an illustrative critique of coherent individual subjectivity, exemplified by blank affect, or the voiding of grand historical narratives, but that these devices can be used to present something otherwise difficult to convey – capitalism's nested time cycles. Through numerated sections that often highlight one of a recurring cluster of individuals and their life trajectories leading to incorporation within a Midwestern branch of the Internal Revenue Service (IRS), *The Pale King* manages to convey the simultaneous, but heterogeneous temporalities within capitalism in ways that neither sequential social realism nor magic realism's relaxed attitude to historicity and empiricism could easily achieve within their generic conventions.

Capitalism's need to overcome its internalised contradictions, generated by the endless pursuit of accumulation through the exploitation of surplus-value, results in cyclical re-formations on an expanded scale. Most historically informed criticisms strive to define capitalist *periodisation* by seeking to nominate exemplary features that differentiate one temporal phase, and its associated cultural forms, from another. The political motivations for marking the dividing line between historical phases are self-evident, since knowledge about how one phase of capitalism separates itself from a prior one may also cast light onto clues for a way beyond dominant capitalism. Consequently, cultural materialist criticism has mined *Capital* volume 1, with its tale of revolutionary shifts through different 'eras' of capitalism, as well as Marx's arc-light comments tracing the transition into capitalism. Yet this emphasis on periodisation has often come at the expense of an analysis into what Marx calls *periodicity*, the recurring features of capitalism throughout multiple cycles of social reproduction and value refluxes.[2]

It has been difficult to develop a narrative form that conveys capitalist periodicity, since such a task requires learning how to handle simultaneously two different timescales: that of capitalism's longer-lasting, recurrent general features on the one hand, and the shorter, particular traits of specific phases of capitalism on the other. Because cultural materialist critics have not fully developed a means of discussing periodicity, we have left ourselves open to claims that we repeatedly seem to discover the 'first' arrival of capitalist traits (commodification, alienation, etc.) no matter what historical period we discuss, be it the early modern or the contemporary. Of course, these features are always present in capitalism, but their action and density vary within the circuit of capital turnover and the structurally variable ways these cycles appear over time. The problem lies initially with our lamentable lack of familiarity with *Capital*'s later published volumes, wherein Marx shifts perspective to discuss transformations within reiterative cyclicality, which he geometrically likens to an ellipse or spiral through time.[3]

The Pale King attempts this goal of describing periodicity and periodisation as Wallace deploys the devices of self-reflexive and auto-distractive narration and accounts of traffic-flow systems to create an aesthetic form for the synchronicity of two different layers of capitalist temporality and their social relations. On the one hand, the characters' memoirs and third-person narration consciously springboard from Tocqueville's *Democracy in America* (1835/1840), which analyses the states of psychic damage generated by the price-setting marketplace as a portrait of the general features of developed capitalism.[4] According to Tocqueville, the subject within bourgeois civil society is destined to experience new forms of internalised anxiety, depression, and ongoing rituals of humiliation generated by the power of what he famously called the tyranny of the majority. In *Oblivion*, the short story collection published just prior to *The Pale King*, Wallace relates how corporate and media interests come together to make individual abasement and self-hatred a structuring feature of capitalism.[5] Yet while these stories were often considered as possible chapters for the work-in-progress that became *The Pale King*, they do not fully apprehend the particular features of the most recent phase of capitalism within which they appear.

Unlike *Oblivion*, *The Pale King* charts a story about the post-1970s phase of capitalism, now called neoliberalism.[6] While we now have several synoptic scholarly accounts of neoliberalism's rise and its periodising features, Wallace's contribution is to describe how individuals panting after privatising incentives to speed the devaluation of public State service used the ever-present features of capitalism's psychological derangements. If Tocqueville felt that moody restlessness and the undertow of mental insecurity were the logical after-effects of modern societies' constitution, Wallace describes how contemporary capitalism *used* structurally generated affective disorders to facilitate neoliberalism's dissolution of the public welfare State. At the heart of *The Pale King* is the onset of what is known as the Spackman Initiative. This plan changed the IRS from being a public service apparatus that seeks to inculcate a non-charismatic ideal of tax revenue delivery as civic responsibility to one that internalises the incentivized search for the highest profit return as an ideal private business mentality.

Wallace uses *The Pale King*'s postmodern formal techniques to narrate the concurrent, but uneven temporalities of capitalism in general lasting centuries (Tocqueville) and that of the particular, shorter-term 'moment' lasting decades (Spackman/neoliberalism). Wallace's achievement in *The Pale King* has been difficult to recognise since Marx's expanded description of the multiple temporalities within the circuit of capital implies a term – *fixed labour-power* – that is nonetheless absent in his writing. If we provide this term, which ought to be present, some long-standing discussions about the operation of culture within capitalism become newly clear and mutually useful, even in ways gesturing to a larger general field theory of cultural materialism. To invoke an older Althusserian-school terminology, fixed labour-power is the 'object' for which the 'domain' of cultural materialism has been searching.

Once in place, the substance of Wallace's intervention into the capitalist abstraction of human relations also becomes clear. For the abstraction of human labour is not only a general process of capitalism's logic, but it also takes a specific form of appearance as the fictitious capital of credit, as a form of money that does not ever become mediated through a commodity. Credit is a chief tactic both within the circulation of capital and for the switching crises sparking the passage from one phase of capital accumulation to another. *The Pale King*, written amidst one such periodising crisis, marks this metamorphosis in the terms of literary tradition by staging a response to another exemplary American novelist of anti-capitalism, Herman Melville. Against Melville's transcendentalist concerns about the individual's erasure within obsessive goal-oriented, massifying directives, such as Ahab's reshaping the crew of the Pequod for his ends, Wallace defends a form of counter-hegemonic abstraction, the ideal of selfless dedication to unheroic, 'boring' service for the collective's well-being. If the communist hypothesis – from each according to their ability, to each according to their need – is to be established, these ethics of accepting an uncelebrated unnoteworthiness must be reinstated. We used to characterise such dedication to the collective commonwealth as communist party discipline, until such self-sacrifice was tainted as complicit with Stalinism and, more recently, refused by the neoanarchist celebration of the antinomian. *The Pale King* draws itself into comradely conversation with Melville, but also reorients what Wallace sees as Melville's misdirection. For Wallace, the 'paling' of the romantic self is not a mark of vulnerability to dominant capitalism, but a tactic for its destruction.

Tocqueville's *Democracy in America* simultaneously makes its author a key early figure in the theorisation of modernity, or the notion of a radical disjuncture from the past, and in theories of modernisation, the idea of the continuity of past elements in new social forms or modalities.[7] Tocqueville's core claim in *Democracy in America* and his later *The Old Regime and the Revolution* (1856) is that civil society has a tendency to return to the older spirit of hierarchical sovereignty, despite the intertwining of political and economic liberalism exemplified by the rise of individual liberty in market society. Tocqueville, however, marks a break from earlier theories of simply reiterative cyclical time (cf. Vico) or of lapsarian secular cycles, ranging from ideas of imperial decline (Gibbon) and cultural degeneration (Spengler) to Malthusian warnings about natural resource depletion as a result of demographic pressures. Tocqueville broaches the argument of continuity *within* change and thus looks to Marx's own claim for capitalist periodicity even within periodising revolutions in the mode of production.

In the first volume of *Democracy in America*, Tocqueville argued that modern democracies replace the tyranny of the absolutist state with a new form of control, the tyranny of the majority. In democratic societies, where decision-making is determined by popular will, the individual is made both sovereign and subaltern. The sole subject, newly liberated from the old regime's top-down regulation, soon realises that she or he is unexpectedly weak, unprotected, and helpless before a new anonymous and decentralised power, the force of mass opinion. Because the subject no longer has the social certainty of a centralised figure that is knowingly accountable for decisions, she or he feels a new kind of insecurity and anxiety, the fear, paradoxically, of being too much of an individual and thus easily targeted by the collective weight of majority opinion.[8]

Tocqueville argues that this modern vulnerability has three results. First, it establishes and fosters a new kind of affective, sociocultural subjectivity, which he calls individualism, and the rise of the public–private split. If the public is a capricious zone of unpredictable power, the subject will seek to retreat to smaller, more secure, and knowable zones of personalised comfort, such as the family, religious belief, or care for the self. Tocqueville calls this retreat from the public, apathy. The uncertainty of modern democracy also creates a sense of damaged interiority, an emotional realm where the fear of not attaining what others receive is turned outwards. This is because the emancipation from the old regime that civic *liberty* allows is immediately counterbalanced by the desire for enforced *equality* where no one can receive a greater piece of the pie. But revanchist egalitarianism is marked by entrenched self-doubt. As initial exemplars of democratic society, Americans 'normally look calm and possess a playful disposition ... yet ... a cloud usually darkened their features and they appeared serious and almost sad even when they were enjoying themselves.'[9] In more contemporary language, this moody restlessness can be renamed as structurally catalysed, socially conditioned depression and anxiety.

Second, the fear of social unpredictability stokes the swift consumption of material goods wherein bodily pleasures compensate for mental uneasiness. For if the future's shape is based on the chaotic whims of the mass, long-term planning is too great a risk. Individuals believe that it is better 'to snatch any [of the good things of this world] that come within their grasp' because people are 'frightened that they will stop living before being able to enjoy them.'[10] The desire for immediate use of commodities is most clear within the group that dominates democratic societies.

> The passion for material prosperity is fundamentally a middle-class affair; it expands and grows with that class and becomes important along with it. Starting there, it works upwards into the higher levels of society and downwards to the mass of the people.[11]

Finally, Tocqueville argues that subjects in a post-absolutist society desire a new kind of despotic State power to protect them.

> I see an innumerable crowd of men, all alike and equal, turned in upon themselves in a restless search for those petty, vulgar pleasures with which they fill their souls. Each of them, living apart, is almost unaware of the destiny of all the rest. His children and personal friends are for him the whole of the human race. . . .

> Above these men stands an immense and protective power which alone is responsible for looking after their enjoyments, and watching over their destiny . . . It would be like a fatherly authority, if, father-like, its aims were to prepare men for manhood, but it seeks only to keep them in perpetual childhood; it prefers its citizens to enjoy themselves provided they have only enjoyment in mind. It works readily for their happiness but it wishes to be the only provider in judge of it . . .

> Thus, the ruling power, having taken each citizen one by one into its powerful grasp and having molded him to its own liking, spreads its arms over the whole of society, covering the surface of social life with a network of petty, complicated, detailed, and uniform rules to which even the most original minds and the most energetic of spirits cannot reach the light in order to rise above the crowd. It does not break men's wills but it does soften, bend, and control them; rarely does it force men to act but it constantly opposes what actions they perform; it does not destroy the start of anything

but it stands in its way; it does not tyrannize but inhibits, represses, drains, snuffs out, dulls so much effort that finally reduces each nation to nothing more than a flock of timid and hard-working animals with the government as shepherd.[12]

With this critique of political and economic liberalism, Tocqueville stands in a spectrum of thought that links social regulation and interiority, running from Rousseau ('man is born free, but he is everywhere in chains') to Foucault's account of social control through disciplinary regulation of normal–abnormal boundaries of mental and physical behaviour. Tocqueville escapes demophobia and the nihilism of nostalgic conservatism as his solution for liberalism's ills comes through what he calls *administration*, or what today might be labelled participatory democracy. Individuals should be encouraged to engage with civic governance to grant them a sense of belonging to the political system by assuming responsibility for the well-being of other citizens, rather than retreating from the public sphere and relegating paternalist duties to the State. If subjects are active in tending the gears of government, they learn to acquire a sobering maturity and long-sightedness and become less inclined to pursue manic consumption driven by childish fear, envy, and hatred.

In his short story collection *Oblivion*, Wallace took up Tocqueville's insights about the fragility of the modern individual to describe the psychic derangement of mass society contoured by corporate and media spectacle culture. The collection's last story, 'The Suffering Channel', combines a glossy lifestyle magazine journalist's pursuit of a shy Midwesterner, who excretes perfectly formed sculptures of the West's iconic art and architecture, with the post-facto context that many of the magazine's editorial staff will shortly die on September 11, 2001, in the attacks on the World Trade Center. That story's organising statement is that the 'core of American experience' revolves around

> the single great informing conflict of the American psyche. The management of insignificance. It was the great syncretic bond of US monoculture. It was everywhere, at the root of everything-of impatience in long lines, of cheating on taxes, of movements in fashion and music and art, of marketing.

This is 'the deeper, more tragic and universal conflict of which the celebrity paradox was a part. The conflict between the subjective centrality of our lives versus our awareness of its objective insignificance'.[13] Wallace's reformulation of Tocqueville is that the individual subject today does not look to the paternal State for protection, but the perceived benefits of celebrity and individuation solely through consumer choice, rather than the now obsolete forms of family allegiance or religious faith. The management of this insignificance is thus described in *Oblivion* as having particularly contemporary features.

The power of this personal frustration is deployed by corporations, which amplify domestic insecurity for their own profit. In Wallace's riposte to the War on Terror, the first story in *Oblivion*, 'Mister Squishy', involves an advertising focus group shadowed by a vaguely terroristic presence climbing the corporate towers outside. The actual threat, though, is within this consumer Green Zone as the story relates the ceaseless production of 'stressors' or strategic games invented and enacted by corporate executives as they compete for prestige and authority. The collection's ensuing story, 'The Soul is Not a Smithy', presents the viewpoint of an attention deficit youth who is told that he is traumatised by the police emergency response team's assassination of a substitute teacher who writes 'Kill them all' on the chalkboard during a civics class. Yet this instructor's Kurtzian *cri de coeur* refers perhaps less to the students than the agents who will shape their future. This is because the narrator's real trauma is not his incomplete understanding of the school tragedy, but his elliptical realisation that the classroom's gridded seating simply prepares him to fit into his father's place in another corporate grid of workdesks. For the 'nightmare about the reality of adult life' was the image of his father in an 'utterly silent room full of men immersed in rote work', a room that 'was death' as the 'men in the room appeared as both individuals and a great anonymous mass'.[14] Welcome to democracy in America.

Oblivion's themes run into *The Pale King*, as one of its characters states that if you continue to ask any American what is wrong with their lives, everyone will ultimately confess some unhappiness.[15] The source of this misery is individualism and apathy, as DeWitt Glendenning, Director of the Midwest Regional Examination Center, nicknamed 'The Pale King', explains. Citing Tocqueville, Glendenning highlights Tocqueville's paradox that as citizens become more equal, they also become 'so individualistic and self absorbed they end up as solipsists, navel-gazers'.[16]

But Glendenning goes beyond *Oblivion*'s arguments to make three additional points on the Tocquevillian paradox. First, he sees the contradictory sense of self-interest and self-doubt as historically mutable. For while he links it with 'the manic US obsession with production, produce, produce, impact the world, contribution, shape things, to help distract us from how little and totally insignificant and temporary we are', he also sees that the corrosion of civicism was amplified by the advent of 1960s ideals of spontaneity and anti-institutionalism.[17] The politics of personal liberation occurred alongside 'some transition in the economy and society between the age of industrial democracy and the stage that comes after', marking the shift from production to consumption.

Second, these two social trends were then appropriated by corporations, which sought to diminish social responsibility for their own benefit.

> Corporations are getting better and better at seducing us into thinking the way they think — of profits as the *telos* and responsibility as something to be enshrined in symbol and evaded in reality. Cleverness is opposed to wisdom. Wanting and having instead of thinking and making.[18]

Corporations were able to craft a new form of 'incredible political consensus' where liberty became defined not as a political feature but as the freedom to consume, even if this was ultimately the consumption of what corporations wanted us to buy in the first place, and the purchasing of these commodities was thought of as a form of rebellion against authority.[19] Consequently, 'the American nation today is [not so much] infantile . . . as adolescent — but is ambivalent in its twin desire for both authoritarian structure and the end of parental hegemony'.[20]

He, thus, bemoans the rise of socially apathetic, privately enshrining consumerism as enabling the retreat from public service, which offers neither thrills nor celebration because of its longer-term, more abstract nature. Contrasting the nation's Founding Fathers, 'modest men', who 'didn't regard themselves as all that exceptional', to modern individuals, who seek self-defining fun even as they adopt a 'corporate attitude', Glendenning defends the ideal of patient labour for the collective as that which guarantees actual freedom. In contrast to the corporate siren songs that tell us liberty lies with retail therapy and the immediacy of purchasing, he says, 'sometimes what's important is dull. Sometimes it's work. Sometimes the important things aren't works of art for your entertainment'.[21] That the IRS's dull administrative labour protects the revenue streams necessary to finance the welfare and civic infrastructure projects means that he sees 'paying taxes' as 'one of the places where a man's civic sense gets revealed in the starkest set of terms', where a subject's dedication to the social contract of wealth redistribution overcomes the desire for a personal consumption reserve.[22]

Finally, these older values of mundane commitment are now coming under attack not only from the corporate reengineering of consumer desire, but also from the complicity of the State in reinforcing the goals of private business. *The Pale King* charts out the traces of an internecine conflict, due to an 'enormous internal struggle and soul-searching' resulting in 'what's come to be known among tax professionals as the New IRS', called by its defining policy, 'the Spackman Initiative'.[23] The 'whole "New IRS" thing was an increasing anti-or post-bureaucratic mentality', which represents a deeper conflict over the very mission and *raison* of the Service ... the struggle here was between traditional or 'conservative' officials who sought tax and its administration as an arena of social justice and civic virtue, on the one hand, and those more progressive, 'pragmatic' policy-makers who prized the market model, efficiency, and a maximum return of the investment of the Service's annual budget, on the other hand. Distilled to its essence, the question was whether and to what extent the IRS should be operated like a for-profit business.[24]

This reengineering of the State's motive looks to shift the governmental agency's focus away from malfeasance detection of tax returns as an ethic of collective fairness to the IRS's pursuit of infractions based on the profitability of the time spent, so as to hit performance targets. As the IRS agents accept these private corporate-like goals, the proper noun Spackman should be replaced with the more abstract one of *neoliberalism*, since the Initiative is contemporaneous and congruent with the post-1970s move towards State deregulation; the privatisation of public resources; punitive legislation and policing of collective organisations, like labour unions; and the dismantling of the post-war corporate-labour compact that traded lower strike activity for social welfare schemes.

While signalling these features, *The Pale King* also narrates a less widely understood attribute of neoliberalism, involving the de- and re-composition of the American middle class as it shows how neoliberal advocates manipulated the general psychopathology of capitalism to their own particular ends. Wallace uses the varied individual characters' life-changes to show how their youthful personal stress was reshaped, first by their entry into the IRS and then by the Spackman Initiative, so as to bend them incrementally, small conversation by small conversation, to new profit-oriented detection strategies. *The Pale King* documents the life passages of its characters according to both the general derangements of capitalism and the more period-specific one involving the neoliberal liquidation of the State. In so doing, Wallace gestures towards the truth lodged within the lesser-discussed expanded form of the circulation of capital that Marx presents in *Capital*'s second and third volumes.

In volume 1 of *Capital*, Marx examines the sphere of production to detail the conditions of class struggle by means of a simple model of capital's circuit: M-C-M', money is used to purchase commodities to be sold for resulting profit. On the one hand, a single turnover circuit, M-C-M' is treated in abstraction. On the other, Marx uses the confrontation within this single circuit to layer expanding phases of relatively homogenised history (the era of handicrafts, the era of manufacture, etc.). Marx's handling of history here is in discrete time-sections, but it is also mobile, since, as Jakobson notes, 'the synchronic is not the same as static'.[25] *Capital*'s second and third volumes switch perspectives to concentrate instead on the conditions of infracapitalist competition, and these books have less thrilling history and fewer literary references, and are notoriously dry, if not outright boring, for long stretches.

To illustrate the texture of capitalist competition, rather than bourgeois-proletarian conflict, Marx invokes an expanded version of capital's circuit, which treats value's transformation through its movement through three distinguishable spheres involving the productive labour process, commodity circulation, and money-dealing capital. The formula for this circuit, using money capital as the starting point, is M—C ... P ... C'—M', or money for the commodities of labour power (LP) and means of production (MP) that are used as 'productive consumption by the capitalist of the commodities purchased' to make a different commodity that will be sold for the profit of the enterprise.[26] He treats these three figures or subcircuits as configuring three kinds of capital: money capital, productive capital (the focus of volume 1), and commodity capital. The agents for each roughly correspond to bankers, lenders, and investors for money capital, known today as the financial services; merchants, retailers, and wholesalers, for commodity capital, those who do not produce commodities for traffic between markets; and the actual bosses of production capital.

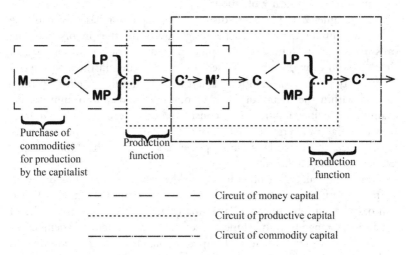

Purchase of commodities for production by the capitalist

Production function

Production function

— — — — — Circuit of money capital

· · · · · · · · · · · · Circuit of productive capital

— — — — — — Circuit of commodity capital

The Three Circuits of the Expanded Form of Capital Circulation[27]

These later volumes examine space and time from a different viewpoint than in the first volume, since they address the manner in which the tensions between capitals create mismatches between one circuit's ability to consume what another produces in order to produce what a third needs to consume and complete the turnover circuit. Capitalist crisis is not considered in the second and third volumes as strictly a matter of class struggle, which is volume 1's theme, but as one of infraca-pitalist competition and the devaluations resulting from the disarticulation of one circuit from the others, a disjointedness propelled by the agents of every circuit's desire for autonomy and drive to leapfrog ahead. Yet each particular capitalist's search for independence from the web of social capital is destructive of the overall capitalist system as it creates value-destroying gaps of time and space. Consequently, Marx argues that while the form of appearance (for instance, on the two-dimensional page) makes it seem as if the circuits work sequentially (*nacheinander*), one after another, one metamorphosing into the other, the reality is that they must also exist simultaneously (*nebeneinander*).[28] While individual capitalists seek to limit these value-inactive synaptic overlays, capital, as a system, requires the constant presence of reserves to suture gaps between the different circuits' need for inputs. For money capital, there must be a financial reserve that can be borrowed from to facilitate exchange; for commodity capital, excess stock (including raw materials or energy inputs) to overcome supply shortages; and productive capitalists require a 'labor fund' through surpluses, usually achieved by the creation of an unemployed reserve army of labour.[29]

In volumes 2 and 3, Marx distinguishes these purchases as involving different temporal durations, depending on whether they involve what he calls fixed or fluid (circulating) capital. The distinction is simply one of time.[30] Fluid capital is entirely used up or consumed in the single act of commodity production. Nothing is left over as its value is entirely trans-formed within the metamorphosis of one commodity into another, for example linen into a suit. Marx considers both the *means of production* (raw materials or energy inputs) and *labour power* as fluid capital, as capi-talists conceptualise workers' labour power as simply another kind of object necessary to be purchased.

Fixed capital, on the other hand, trickles value, decongealing bit by bit as fractions of it are made incrementally fluid, circuit by circuit, so that it will only be entirely consumed after many turnover circuits. Examples of fixed capital range from machinery, used many times before it depreciates or falls apart, to rented land and implantations in the built environment, mainly involving transportation and communication networks. The fluid has a temporality of present-ness, while the fixed binds the past and future as it extends through multiple cycles of value movements. Conse-quently, the fluid is analogous to periodisation and the fixed to periodicity, since both pairs are distinct but interdependent.

David Harvey has used the distinction between fluid and fixed *means of production* for his concept of the *spatial fix*. For Harvey, the spatial fix is a tactic for capital to prevent a complete devalorisation of capital from potential inactivity by allocating it to lower profit, but longer-term fixed capital by switching from one circuit to another, often by sinking into the fixed capital of land, the built environment, and foreign geographies.[31] This tactic is both a response to the overproduction of excess capital by lowering a possibly overheating system and a means to restore surplus-value through investment into technology. When the working class uses its newfound class subjectivity to demand more rights, capital overcomes its reluctance and invests in the fixed capital of new technology to create unemployment as a means of forcing wage reductions. Hence one kind of reserve creates another, and fixed capital generates a reserve army of labour. In this way, capitalism has its own regulating invisible hand that seeks to transfer risk onto the backs of the working class and to transform infracapitalist competition back into class struggle. The spatial fixing of capital has a second, but equally important feature, as new geographies are appropriated so that the marketplace can expand to relieve the pressures of the build-up of underused commodities or loan money. As Ernest Mandel insists, spending on military equipment and personnel for imperialist adventures should be understood as a form of originating ('primitive') accumulation that is also the search to create fixed capital in new territories.[32]

Yet because Marx constantly works through binary oppositions (formal versus real, absolute versus relative, constant versus variable), we can expect a fourth term to appear, but which remains unmentioned by Marx, alongside fluid means of production, fluid labour power, and fixed means of production: fixed labour-power. What might the category of fixed labour-power entail? In one sense, this must be what Marx calls the consumption fund, all the materials that labour needs, but which capitalists do not provide, to ensure their human survival long enough to sell their labour power again and initiate a new circuit of capital: food, clothing, shelter, healthcare, and educational training. The magnitude of this consumption fund matters since it effects the socially necessary labour time, beyond which stands surplus-value. The elements and magnitude of the consumption fund vary historically and socially, but it can be considered 'absolute' fixed labour-power in the same way that Marx defines 'absolute surplus-power' as the external force of overwork that does not alter the internal relations of the production process that delivers 'relative surplus-value'. 'Relative' fixed labour-power goes beyond the consumption fund to include everything that shapes class subjectivity, such as the social infrastructures responsible for durability of class solidarity and subordination. This is the realm of Gramscian hegemony, and merely to call it the sphere of social reproduction incompletely captures its constant reformulations as it is made fluid and ultimately becomes used up in relation to emerging historical pressures. The utility of fixed labour-power as a term consists in the way that it illuminates and links together several notable materialist arguments and their textual practices.[33]

Given the links between the fluid and the fixed, the presence of a spatial fix in the category of means of production suggests an analogous one in the category of labour power, a cultural fix. Just as the special fix ensures the continued production of social capital by creating a longer-lasting reserve, so, too, is a cultural fix necessary to establish durable class relations and a longer-lasting reserve of identities and subjectivities wherein capitalism can ensure that subjects will present themselves as proletarians beyond the isolated moment of the exchange of labour power for wages. Just as the spatial fix involves opening new geographies, the cultural fix, likewise, looks to establish new identities for control. As fixed formations create the reserves that will be consumed over time, they function as what might be called the archives of capitalism, the sources awaiting circulation. Hence a study of the historical formation and use of these reserves might be called an archaeology of capitalism and would involve the truth claims now inherent in these institutional reserves as well. If Foucault's call for an archaeology of knowledge is considered as the study of how truth formations operate within the dynamic environment of class struggle, then his use of archaeology (the study of fixtures) and genealogy (the study of fluidities) can be read as a complement to Marx's dual temporalities of capital.

Similarly, Fredric Jameson's often difficult to implement use of Greimas's semiotic rectangles for literary studies can be refreshed. The semiotic rectangle is drawn up through the 'binary opposition ... of two contraries (S and − S), along with the simple negations or contradictories of both terms', that, in turn, produces an additional 'complex term' and a 'neutral one'.[34]

Complex term

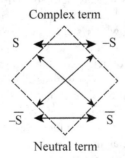

Neutral term

Yet the difficulty of this abstraction vanishes when the real forces of the rectangle are read as Marx's stereogenic torus of fixed and fluid relations.

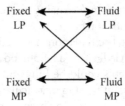

Furthermore, the complex and neutral terms do not need to be delivered through critical ingenuity when they are read as holders for positions in the expanded circuit of capital, where the commodity form is the literary text as commodity itself. Once this is done, the 'complex' form is seen as class struggle for labour power and the 'neutral' as the non-value-producing term for infracapitalist competition, which lacks the confrontation between the two molar classes.

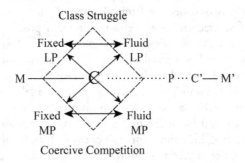

The 'complexity' of the class tension between the synchrony of fluid capital and the diachrony of fixed capital is manifested even in language itself, as Voloshinov intimated. Voloshinov claims that even a single 'word has the capacity to register all the transitory, delicate, momentous phases of social changes' because 'production relations and the sociopolitical order shaped by those relations determine the full range of verbal contacts between people, all the forms and means of the verbal communication'.[35] Yet if 'existence reflected in the sign is not merely reflected but refracted ... By an intersecting of differently oriented social interests within one, in the same sign community, i.e. *by the class* struggle', the operation of this interaction was often left implied, rather than illustrated as the locale for fixed labour-power relations.[36] With the notion of the fixed labour-power of social infrastructure, ranging from capital investments into education and other cultural mores to notions of consensus and coercion, we might have a better means to explain why certain words, genres, or methods of narration arise and fall over long waves of aggregated capital turnover cycles. While Raymond Williams' concept of a 'structure of feeling' remains resonant, along with his terms of residual, dominant, and emergent, it was not immediately linked to Marx's analysis of capital circulation and crisis. But this was only because the object of knowledge (fixed labour-power) was necessary to pronounce before these concepts could be fully apprehended.

Just as there is a constant tension of articulation between the fluid and the fixed (the *parole* and *langue* of socio-economic relations), so, too, is there a constant centripetal and centrifugal tension between the circuits. Although Marx never completed his proposed volume on credit and money-dealing capital, enough commentary exists to indicate its role in rearticulating the spheres by providing capitalists with loan capital to purchase necessary commodities for the next round of trade, even in advance of the realisation of profit through the sale of their own wares. Credit creates a dual temporality within capitalism as it separates out the time of loan repayment from the time of the commodity's turnover completion cycle, the time of debt collection from the time of sale. The former amplifies the role of abstraction as an extra-materialised process and lever for labour alienation as Marx calls credit the most irrational form of capitalism, since money-dealing capital operates as if material commodities are unnecessary. Money capital trades money for money (M—M') without the mediation of commodity production. This 'insane' activity becomes amplified when 'debts appear as commodities in the mind of the banker', so that credit becomes itself a derivative commodity as credit is treated itself as a tradable commodity rather than a loan for an actual one.[37]

The general use of credit as a horizontal 'fix' to allow a disaggregating system to maintain forward movement has a particular knock-on effect. Money-dealing capitalists are conventionally allowed to hive off profit from productive capitalists, through the paid interest on loans, because they act as systemic regulators and guardians of social capital, the totality of capital within the system. Bankers are meant to deliver fiscal aid for distressed capitalists or be authorised to cut off the life support for those capitalists whose continued presence might catalyse a larger crisis. Bankers' regulation is usually also tightly interlaced with the State, which legitimises the use of financial violence, to paraphrase Weber. Yet what happens when the administrators of irrational capital become tired of providing collective oversight and use their privileged place over capital for their own singular benefit? What happens when the State abets this retraction of supervision, and abstracts itself from the same as well? Such a gesture of the verticalisation of the previously horizontal, when credit is used for private hoarding rather than as social capital, might well characterise what we call neoliberalism, which combines the loss of a spatial fix through the removal of statist capital flow controls, often highlighted as 'postmodernism', with the erosion of the existing cultural fix, here simplified as the vastly amplified dissolution of civic engagement in favour of Tocquevillian apathetic individualism and competitive selfishness.

To return therefore to Wallace: cultural fixlessness is the tale Wallace relates with the history of the Spackman Initiative, and he argues that it occurs less through dramatic changes than through trickling alterations. Just as Foucault argues that power operates through decentralised institutional details that seem superficially non-objectionable, the character 'David Foster Wallace' confirms that social transformation need not be hidden, made covert, or enacted through repressive coercion, since it can be effectuated entirely in the open by leveraging the subject's fear of insignificance as a form of the tyranny of the majority. '1985 was a critical year for American taxation' (one year beyond the sign of '1984's' feared repression), since

> the birth agonies of the new IRS lead to one of the great and terrible PR discoveries in modern democracy, which is that if sensitive issues of governance can be made sufficiently dull and arcane, there will be no need for officials to hide or dissemble, because no one not directly involved will pay attention to cause trouble.[38]

For

> we recoil from the dull [since] dullness is associated with psychic pain because something that's dull or opaque fails to provide enough stimulation to distract people from some other, deeper type of pain that is always there, if only in an ambient low-level way, in which most of us spend nearly all our time and energy trying to distract ourselves from feeling directly or with our full attention.[39]

In this light, all the forms of the spectacle, of the nervous use of media as a means of self-distraction, the ubiquity of television in public spaces, our constant checking of email, manual fiddling with mobile phones, and aimless Internet surfing, exist to protect the individual from 'the terror of silence with nothing diverting to do'. As the character 'David Foster Wallace' says, 'I can't believe everyone really believes that today's so-called "information society" is just about information. Everybody knows that is about something else, way down'.[40] The need for constant distraction emerges as a protective, distracting buffer against the spirit of concentration, which might not only be used to waken a mindful awareness of our fragility, but could also be directed to detect social and financial fraud. The devil certainly lies in the details, but he is safe there, since no one in modern societies will explore these to discover the demon.

The 'old' IRS tried to counter this apathy with an ethics of professional focus on rote tasks. One agent relates the story of a Jesuit accounting teacher giving a homily to his students as he says that they are 'called to account'.[41] The instructor means this in both senses of turning to accountancy as a vocational servitude, much like the priesthood, and in the meaning of facing a moral examination not unlike the scrutiny by the divine in the immediate moments of the afterlife. The ethics of service belongs to an old-school dedication to craft's requirement that actual, rather than virtualised, labour time stands as the index of real value. 'Enduring tedium over real time in a confined space is what real courage is. Such endurance is . . . Heroism', as action without audience or applause.[42]

> Effacement. Sacrifice. Service. To give oneself to the care of others' money – this is effacement, perdurance, sacrifice, honor, doughtiness, valor. Hear this or not, as you will. Learn it now, or later – the world has time. Routine, repetition, tedium, monotony, ephemeracy, inconsequence, abstraction, disorder, boredom, angst, ennui – these are the true hero's enemies, and make no mistake, they are fearsome indeed. For they are real.[43]

The new IRS refuses these values of fixed, patient concentration that requires one to face the dragon of personal insignificance for the sake of collective welfare, and instead it seeks to recruit damaged individuals who obsessively engage in auto-distractive, obsessive–compulsive rituals that prevent them from concentrating on their individual traumas. Rather than seeking agents who can concentrate, the neoliberalised IRS wants ones with extrasensory perception, so that they can simply 'feel' profit in a file rather than hunker down to the forensic labour of deductive reading for the small signs of omission in income reporting by individuals.

The Pale King Glendenning cites Tocqueville to hearken back to the older service ethics as he celebrates the necessity of non-charismatic regulation for freedom. While Tocqueville presented a glass half-empty by indicating the demand for equality as a fear of liberty, Wallace's Glendenning suggests that equality is not the containment of liberty, but its enabling foundation. With this claim, *The Pale King* echoes the older communist ideal of self-control and party discipline as empowering the soviet State's institutional struggle for survival in a capitalist-dominated world system. The opposition to capitalism's abstraction of value from humans will be a replacement communist abstraction that empties out selfish lack of concentration for the less than amusing focus on the details of dirty deeds done by men in clean business suits. This seeks to restore a cultural fix to neoliberalism's celebration of liquidity. Wallace sees individual insouciance, exemplified by the novel's staging of jaunty, Mamet-like, aggressive dialogue, as part of the problem, as its twitchiness removes infrastructural works from the individual passions of the bourgeois interiorised self. *The Pale King*'s turn against individual singularity belongs to this suspicion of the liberal subject's motivations running from Tocqueville through Foucault, and it forms the heart of Wallace's collegial disagreement with Melville.

Melville is, of course, the magisterial figure who helped inaugurate American literature's critique of nineteenth-century capitalism. *The Pale King*, considered as the twenty-first century *Moby Dick*, uses its own post-modern heritage to critique Melville's deviation from the task. Melville's anti-capitalist fiction – mainly 'Bartleby the Scrivener: A Story of Wall-Street', *Moby-Dick*, and *Pierre; or the Ambiguities* – are intertexts for *The Pale King*. The ghostly Bartleby, who challenges the fiction of consensual capitalism by passive-aggressively goading his employer to command him to work against his preferences, and then haunts the workplace, is echoed by *The Pale King*'s IRS agents who remain dead at their desk for days until being noticed or the actual ghosts hovering round the bureaucrats' desks. By naming the eponymous pale king DeWitt Glendenning, Wallace references Melville's own metareflexive *Pierre*, about a novelist, Pierre Glendinning, who ultimately commits suicide to 'neuter' his mind after attempting to achieve renown as an American writer from within a Wall Street coldwater studio. Glendenning's first name also recalls New York Governor DeWitt Clinton (1769–1828), who was the main advocate for the Erie Canal, America's first large public project in the built environment, a spatial fix par excellence. *Pierre* is also the American novel fascinated with competing, but simultaneous modes of time as Glendinning becomes mesmerised by a mystical, Transcendentalist tract that argues for the tension and linkage between 'horological' time of the 'terrestrial' calendar and 'chronometrical' time of celestial design.[44] *Pierre*'s tragic end, which effectively destroyed Melville's public standing, stands as a self-reflexive cautionary tale about the dedication to the Romantic, antinomian self as a mechanism for simultaneously unleashing a demotic collective identity, a move championed by populist Transcendentalism, such as Whitman's poetry.

Wallace uses non-narrative postmodern techniques to void out this subservience to the royal bourgeois subject of complex interior emotions, in favour of a flat ('pale') sovereign of selfless dedication to public service and lists of details, in order to encourage careful examination of what seems insignificant or overly abstracted from the drama of emotive biography. Consequently, *The Pale King* draws parallels to *Moby Dick* to

form a kind of literary gam, those scenes in *Moby-Dick* when two ship cap-
tains meet for a dialogue that usually ends with their dissociation. Most of
Moby Dick's readers suffer through the middle 'cetology' chapters dedicated to whale anatomy and ship construction, but Melville finally releases
his grip of tedium to reward the reader with the Pequod's final pursuit of
the whale. Wallace is reluctant to move beyond banal descriptions of
bureaucratic procedural language and protocols, as he wants to train the
reader to be *in* abstraction, rather than flee from it. *The Pale King* wants
the reader to be 'called to account' and focused on details as training for
a similar civic action.

The edited novel begins with a description of the stereotypical American landscape and ends with the admonition to 'read these'.[45] This is a
metareflexive call to examine the Midwest, as that which usually lacks interest to the bicoastal cultural elites. It is a truism that Henry James' novels
not only illustrate his dedication to aesthetic ideals, but they also train
the reader into the means for appreciating aestheticism. James' novels are
performative in so far as the reader learns how to read a (James) novel
through the process of consuming it, so long as she or he allows her or
himself to let go, to abandon resistance to the Jamesian prose style.
Wallace is decidedly anti-aesthetic, as *The Pale King*'s anti-style seeks to
replace readerly pleasure with readerly attention. For instance, the
novel's section 25, typeset in double column like a bureaucratic form,
simply lists the names of IRS agents as she or he 'turns a page'.[46] Of
course, it is not simply the IRS agents steadily turning pages in search of
the fudges, imperfections, or noteworthy details of potential crime, but
we, the readers, as well, turning the pages of Wallace's non-narrative text
in hopes of somehow finding perhaps interesting or narratively gripping
details to read. Wallace's point is that readerly pleasure is not the agent
for discovering historical transformation, the details of which are found
in a different kind of abstraction, the 'bore-ing' in on the unremarkable
process of capital, be it found in *The Pale King* or the uncompelling
pages of *Capital* volumes 2 and 3.

By refusing the lure of entertainment, we can notice the minutiae of
capitalist abstraction and then replace the individual liberty of selfishness in
favour of a selflessness in service of collective emancipation. Here, David
Foster Wallace joins a lineage that insists that learning how to read, learning how to do an observant textual practice, belongs to a left ethics in
service of real emancipation. His achievement with *The Pale King* is to
have created what an American communist or left front novel in the
post-Cold War, post-9/11 period might look like.

University of Warwick

Notes

1 David Foster Wallace, *The Pale King* (London: Penguin, 2011). For a useful discussion of literary postmodernism's fate, see the special issue 'After Postmodernism: Form and History in Contemporary American Fiction', ed. Andrew Hoberek, *Twentieth Century Literature* 53 (3), 2007. For commentary on David Foster Wallace and *The Pale King*, see: *A Companion to David Foster Wallace Studies*, eds. Marshall Boswell and Stephen J. Burn (London: Palgrave Macmillan, 2013); *David Foster Wallace and 'The Long Thing': New Essays on the Novels*, ed. Marshall Boswell (London: Bloomsbury Academic, 2014); Paul Giles, 'All Swallowed Up: David Foster Wallace and American Literature' in Samuel Cohen and Lee Konstantinou (ed.), *The Legacy of David Foster Wallace* (Iowa City: University of Iowa Press, 2012), pp. 3–22; and two pieces by Adam Kelly, 'David Foster Wallace: the Death of the Author and the Birth of a Discipline' *Irish Journal of American Studies*, 2 (2010). Online: http://www.ijasonline.com/Adam-Kelly.html; and 'David Foster Wallace and the New Sincerity in American Fiction' in David Hering (ed.), *Consider David Foster Wallace: Critical Essays* (Austin, TX: SSMG Press, 2010), pp. 131–46.
2 Karl Marx, *Capital I* (New York: Vintage, 1977), p. 786. See also: 'the repeated turnover of industrial capital expresses the periodicity and renewal of the entire reproduction process (including the process of consumption).' Karl Marx, *Capital III* (London: Penguin, 1981), p. 418.

Just as the heavenly bodies always repeat a certain movement, once they have been flung into it, so also does social production, once it has been flung into this movement of alternate expansion and contraction. Effects become causes in their turn, and the various vicissitudes of the whole process, which always reproduces its own conditions, take on the form of periodicity.

3 Marx, *Capital I*, pp. 198, 727.
4 Alexis Tocqueville, *Democracy in America and Two Essays on America*, trans. Gerald E. Bevan (London: Penguin, 2003).
5 David Foster Wallace, *Oblivion* (New York: Little, Brown and Company, 2004).
6 Synoptic accounts of neoliberalism include Gérard Duménil and Lévy Dominique, *The Crisis of Neoliberalism* (Cambridge, MA: Harvard University Press, 2011); David Harvey, *A Brief History of Neoliberalism* (New York: Oxford University Press, 2005); Naomi Klein, *The Shock Doctrine: The Rise of Disaster Capitalism* (London: Allen Lane, 2007); and Philip Mirowski, *Never Let a Serious Crisis Go to Waste: How Neoliberalism Survived the Financial Meltdown* (London: Verso, 2013).
7 David Harvey, *Paris, Capital of Modernity* (London: Routledge, 2003), p. 1.
8 Tocqueville, *Democracy*, pp. 19–20.
9 Tocqueville, *Democracy*, pp. 622–3.

10 Tocqueville, *Democracy*, p. 623.
11 Tocqueville, *Democracy*, p. 617.
12 Tocqueville, *Democracy*, pp. 805–6.
13 Wallace, *Oblivion*, p. 284.
14 Wallace, *Oblivion*, pp. 103, 108.
15 Wallace, *Pale King*, p. 19.
16 Wallace, *Pale King*, p. 143.
17 Wallace, *Pale King*, pp. 145–6.
18 Wallace, *Pale King*, pp. 132–3.
19 Wallace, *Pale King*, pp. 144, 148.
20 Wallace, *Pale King*, p. 149.
21 Wallace, *Pale King*, pp. 136, 139, 140.
22 Wallace, *Pale King*, p. 143.
23 Wallace, *Pale King*, p. 72.
24 Wallace, *Pale King*, pp. 81fn, 85.
25 Quoted from Pierre Macherey, *A Theory of Literary Production* (London: Routledge, 1978), p. 9.
26 Karl Marx, *Capital II* (London: Penguin, 1978), p. 110.
27 Modified from Meghnad Dessai, *Marxian Economics* (Oxford: Blackwell, 1979), p. 33. The original chart reappears in David Harvey, *The Limits to Capital* (London: Verso, 1982), p. 70.
28 Marx, *Capital II*, p. 183.
29 Karl Marx, *Grundrisse* (London: Penguin, 1973), pp. 454–5.
30 Marx, *Capital II*, pp. 237–8.
31 Harvey, *Limits*, pp. 431–8.
32 Ernest Mandel, *Late Capitalism* (London: NLR Books, 1972).
33 Marx says that the 'inner relation' of capital relations has the capitalist place the worker in a condition of 'indifference, externality, and alienation' in that the capitalist does not need to support a worker's human existence as a slave would require, removes the means of labor and access to raw materials and energy sources from the worker, and considers the commodity as the source of value. Most cultural materialist criticisms beyond 1900 see Marx's claim of 'indifference' to workers' lives as contradictory to the need to reestablish class relations over time. Marx, *Capital III*, p. 178.
34 Fredric Jameson, *The Political Unconscious* (Ithaca: Cornell University Press, 1981), pp. 166fn, 167.
35 V. N. Vološinov, *Marxism and the Philosophy of Language* (New York: Seminar Press, 1973), p. 19.
36 Vološinov, *Marxism*, p. 23.
37 Marx, *Capital III*, p. 596.
38 Wallace, *Pale King*, p. 85.
39 Wallace, *Pale King*, p. 87.
40 Wallace, *Pale King*, p. 87.
41 Wallace, *Pale King*, p. 235.
42 Wallace, *Pale King*, p. 231.

43 Wallace, *Pale King*, p. 233.
44 Herman Melville, *Pierre or the Ambiguities* (New York: Penguin, 1996), pp. 214–5.
45 Wallace, *Pale King*, p. 5.
46 Wallace, *Pale King*, pp. 312–5.

Richard Godden and Michael Szalay

The bodies in the bubble: David Foster Wallace's
The Pale King

While predominantly concerned with the transformation of the Internal Revenue Service (IRS) during the 1980s, David Foster Wallace's *The Pale King* (2011) represents signal contradictions in the nature of money, from 1971 (when Richard Nixon ended the convertibility of the dollar into gold) to the events of the 2008 financial crisis (when derivative trading dominated global financial markets). As unstable admixtures of abstraction and concreteness, Wallace's fictional IRS workers embody the changing nature of these contradictions and the uneasy convergence between corporate and corporeal persons caught within the particular processes of abstraction associated with financialisation.

'The most important week in American financial history since the Great Depression', writes James B. Stewart in *The New Yorker*, 'began at 8 A.M. on a Friday in the middle of September.' That day was 12 September 2008. On 7 September, the Federal Housing Finance Agency had placed Fannie Mae and Freddy Mac in government conservatorship and began a preferred stock purchase agreement with those companies to ensure their positive net worth. On 11 September, a Thursday, Timothy Geithner, head of the New York Fed, had told Henry Paulson, the Treasury Secretary, and Ben Bernanke, the Chairman of the Fed, that Lehman Brothers would not open for business on the coming Monday. And so, on 12 September, 'as Bernanke hurried to the Department of the Treasury for his weekly breakfast with Secretary Paulson, crisis loomed'.[1] Paulson was initially reluctant to involve the federal government, and preferred a private sector solution to the upcoming crisis. But he relented, and over the next days, the two met with Wall Street CEOs and engineered what would become the Emergency Economic Stabilization Act. On 18 September, Bernanke and Paulson met with Congressional legislators and proposed their rescue plan. Bernanke reportedly told the legislators, 'If we don't do this, we may not have an economy on Monday.'[2]

12 September 2008 is also the day that David Foster Wallace, arguably the most important American novelist of his generation, hanged himself in his home in Claremont, California. We offer no account of why Wallace killed himself. But we read the novel on which he was then at work, the novel whose writing had consumed him for the better part of the previous decade, as preoccupied with economic contradiction and the failure of financial liquidity. We read Wallace's suicide as in some sense entailed or at least anticipated by the problems of corporeality and abstraction with which that novel, published posthumously as *The Pale King* (2011), associates finance capitalism.

Wallace sets *The Pale King* in the mid-1980s, when Ronald Reagan's trickle-down 'voodoo science' resulted in 'an era of business deregulation' and 'the death of civics'.[3] A study in the neoliberal transformation of American governance, the novel's central drama involves a conflict within the Internal Revenue Service (IRS) brought on by the agency's new mandate to increase its collection efficiency in the face of mounting military budgets and the declining revenues attendant upon Reagan's decision to lower tax rates on corporations and the wealthy. Wallace fictionalises efforts to 'deregulate the IRS' (p. 113) and turn it into 'a business – a going, for-profit concern type of thing' (p. 112). *The Pale King*, then, questions the ostensibly public nature of the bailout that took place days after the death of its author: for Wallace, the US Treasury, the financial arm of the state, undergoes effective privatisation during the 1980s. It

follows for Wallace that tax dollars cease to be public monies, and that the
state, in its efforts to secure the integrity of money during a turn to global
finance, does so as one corporation (albeit a large one) among many.

John Maynard Keynes drew from G. Knapp's *The State Theory of
Money* (1924) in arguing that the state alone had the right to decree
what could be used for the payment of taxes and what could count as
money. For Keynes, money devolved from the nation state, for purposes
of nation building.[4] After the Second World War, a Keynesian view of
money was to underpin welfare state capitalism by means that ranged
from a system of fixed exchange rates, through schemes for the stabilising
of commodity prices, to industry protections and national capital controls.
Many of these means were designed to absorb or otherwise socialise the
risks of future volatility among commodity prices and exchange rates. In
the words of Antonio Negri, 'Keynes's first imperative is to remove fear
of the future. The future must be fixed as present.'[5] Organised by its
own fear of the future, and its own distension of the present, *The Pale
King* demonstrates how global financial processes might themselves select
what will function as money in the wake of Keynesian state policy,
especially in light of the development within global finance of new mechanisms for stabilising prices across space and time.

Put in only slightly different terms, Wallace's novel dramatises the
manner in which state monies give way not simply to market-determined
commodity monies (as advocated by marginalists like Carl Menger and
libertarians like Friedrich Hayek), but to monies derived from 'commodities whose primary function is the commensuration of other commodities' – that is to say, to financial derivatives. We are guided in our
reading of Wallace by Dick Bryan and Michael Rafferty's claim that
derivatives are 'meta-commodities' that, particularly since the 1980s,
have come to work as 'market-created money without formal nation-
state guarantees', by 'anchoring the global money system in a way that
bears some key parallels with the role played by gold in the nineteenth
century'.[6] It will be our contention that *The Pale King*, rather than
simply addressing an historical transformation in the nature of money
and the state, itself functions as a meta-commodity, performing an analogue of the work that derivatives do, and in the process accentuating
contradictions in that work, in order to stand as a text that embodies
the state of a troubled nation. Wallace offers something more than the
generic postmodern reflexivity that preoccupies his essay on television.
His IRS workers read tax forms that are representations of money. At
a second remove, his readers read not simply accounts of workers who
read representations of money, but a representation that itself assumes
the form of its content, becoming in the process a literary version of
derivative money.

Abstract equivalence: blowing bubbles

Wallace's more immediate subject is the unstable relation between corpore-ality and the forms of abstraction inherent in finance capital. In his novel, Reagan's minions 'want everything quantified' (p. 303), an imperative that, for Wallace, occludes the difference between human and corporate bodies, even as it changes the nature of each. As one IRS employee puts it, 'the term corporation' comes 'from body, like "made into a body"' (p. 140). Accordingly, and during 'the couple of years in question here', watching the IRS become a corporation was 'like watching an enormous machine come to consciousness and start trying to think and feel like a real human' (p. 80). But, even as the IRS comes to life, so the 'real' humans in its employ lose their bodies; their once solid forms melt into systems designed for the processing of tax monies.

Wallace's own body proves central. The character 'David Foster Wallace' about whom we read, it would seem, is not fictional at all, but a representation of the actual author. In the novel's 'Author's Preface' placed on page 66, Wallace addresses us directly ('Author here') and sets the record straight. 'The book's legal disclaimer', he tells us, the one situ-ated on the copyright page, 'defines everything that follows it as a fiction, including this Foreword.' But that is misleading, he says, because 'the whole thing is really nonfiction' (p. 67). He needs the 'special legal protec-tion' afforded by the disclaimer so that he can more safely describe his brief employment by the IRS at the start of the 1980s – neither he nor the pub-lisher wants to be sued. The events that he describes are, nevertheless, 'sub-stantially true and accurate' (p. 67); at its core, he writes, *The Pale King* is a memoir. However familiar the literary devices that follow may seem, they 'are not meant to be decoded or "read" so much as merely acquiesced to as part of the cost of our doing business together, so to speak, in today's com-mercial climate' (p. 73).

That commercial climate animates our understanding of Wallace's ostensibly real life (just as it does, ultimately, the reader's understanding of what she 'reads'). His declared choice of genre, for example, seems as motivated by the prospect of financial gain as by the more basic fact that its events are 'substantially true and accurate'. He points out that,

> in 2003, the average author's advance for a memoir was almost 2.5 times that paid for a work of fiction. The simple truth is that I, like so many other Americans, have suffered reverses in the volatile economy of the last few years, and these reverses have occurred at the same time that my financial obligations have increased along with my age and responsibilities ... . I would be a rank hypocrite

if I pretended that I was less than attuned and receptive to market forces than anyone else. (p. 81)

The influence of market forces on Wallace is near absolute. He grows up in a corporate home ('It was a bit like a for-profit company, my family, in that you were pretty much only as good as your last sales quarter' [p. 257]), and a corporate state ('we as individual citizens have adopted a corporate attitude' [p. 137]). The events that propel him into the IRS reflect this fact. At college, he ghostwrites papers for other students. We are told that, 'The chief motivation behind this little enterprise (plagiarism) was, as it so often is in the real world, financial' (p. 74). He adds,

> You can probably also see why these sorts of exercises would be good apprentice training for someone interested in so-called 'creative writing.' The enterprise's proceeds were invested in a high-yield money market account; and interest rates at that time were high, whereas student loans don't even start accruing interest until one leaves school. The overall strategy was conservative, both fiscally and academically. (p. 75)

His decision to seek employment within the IRS is motivated by similarly conservative fiscal principles. So long as he works for a federal agency, his student loans do not accrue interest.

Wallace thus epitomises the manner in which, by 1985, US citizens 'without capital were, more generally, being asked to think like capitalists'. Randy Martin's claim, regarding what he calls, 'the financialization of daily life' during the 1980s and 1990s, speaks to the cultural creation of 'a shareholder/stockholder model of the "investor nation" ... [as it] renders the corporation the ideal citizen held to the highest standard of being an ethical subject'; ethical, presumably, in the degree to which those citizens who aspire to corporate personhood 'self-manage', 'taking responsibility', by way of 'investment' and 'risk stratagem', for the home, health, education and aging of their households. The financial crisis of 2008 reflected this new form of self-management: self-articulation through corporate finance may extend, at times of asset bubbles in stocks and real estate, to a 'responsible' decision on refinancing: where the home becomes an ATM, the home can be cast as the 'security' from which the ethical coherence of the corporate subject takes substance structurally inseparable from deficit and risk. By 2002, 50 per cent of the US population partook, more and less directly, in stock speculation.[7]

David Foster Wallace ('Author here') aims to capture how the corporate citizen, or responsible shareholder in his own life, begins to lose solidity – begins to become, in effect, more like the kind of abstract person that corporations are understood to be. One version of this process takes shape in the novel's relatively straightforward drama of mechanisation. When the character David Foster Wallace (allegedly based on the actual author of that name) arrives in Peoria, the IRS is in the grips of a conflict between two factions. One, led by Merrill Lehrl, advocates automating the human labour of IRS examiners; another, led by DeWitt Glendenning, advocates the continued use of human tax examiners. Glendenning understands taxes as a civic sacrament; citizens return their money to the state and thereby enter the *corpus mysticum* of the nation – becoming, in the process, its lifeblood. That said, the overall tendency is towards mechanisation, and Glendenning's acolytes become like the machines that threaten their obsolescence. Glendenning, 'a Mozart of production', contrives to have his human team, produce at an '*exactly* average' (p. 367) rate, such that their output conforms to a computer's, to a mathematically improbable degree; he thinks of his subordinates 'both as human beings and as parts of a larger mechanism whose efficient function was his responsibility' (p. 434).

The character David Foster Wallace (henceforth, 'Foster Wallace') becomes part of a larger mechanism (as the actual author becomes a literary character within the larger mechanism of his novel) in a much more interesting and pointed fashion.[8] Upon first arriving at the Peoria office of the IRS, he is mistaken for one David Francis Wallace (henceforth, 'Francis Wallace'), a more senior employee who works for the service. He is treated with deference undue a person of his rank, and it takes him some time to realise that he has been confused for another and removed from the agency's database. After Foster Wallace arrives at the IRS, 'the two employees became, so far as the Service's computer system was concerned, the same person' (p. 413). Subsequently, our narrator 'did not exist; his file had been deleted, or absorbed into, that of David F. Wallace' (p. 411). Foster Wallace vanishes into Francis Wallace, and the IRS computer system more generally; thus Foster Wallace 'disappears – becomes a creature of the system' (p. 546).

The two F. Wallaces each become what the IRS considers 'ghost redundancies' (p. 411) of one another, redundancies whose supposed equivalence mirrors the slippage between author and character. Foster Wallace disappears into Francis Wallace and the IRS just as David Foster Wallace, the ostensibly 'real' author, disappears into Foster Wallace and, more generally, the body of *The Pale King*. The IRS's 'ghost conflation problem' leads Foster Wallace to consider himself 'The "unreal" David Wallace [i.e. the author]' (p. 414). Conflated, deleted, and rendered spectral, this 'unreal' Foster Wallace disappears within Francis Wallace, 'an older, high value' (p. 413) version of himself (in just the way that David Foster Wallace [the author] becomes a ghostwriter for Foster Wallace). It makes sense, then, that Foster Wallace will be accused, by those within the IRS who eventually learn of this conflation, of having committed against the agency a version of the ghostwriting fraud that leads to his expulsion from college.

It also makes sense that Foster Wallace's authorial disappearance, engineered through redundancy, should change our understanding of what kind of 'creative writing' we are reading. In its author's preface, *The Pale King* distinguishes between its 'real author, the living human holding the pencil', and its 'abstract narrative persona', which is something like a 'pro forma, an entity that exists just for legal and commercial purposes, rather like a corporation' (p. 66). 'Pro forma' echoes 'persona' (even as persona contains person), and refers to an accounting document that records a firm's financial activities. The author David Foster Wallace writes of Foster Wallace as an accountant might write of a company, and the 'persona' that he creates, in its 'abstraction', reduces and occludes what it 'incorporates'. But since, in his 'Author's Preface', Wallace (author) confesses to write for 'legal and commercial ends', we doubt his capacity to distinguish between persons and personas. The logic here begs two questions: who swallows whom and who is whose ghost? In the statutory construct of what we take to be a novel (here analogous to the 'system' into which Wallace vanishes), the 'real' author's doubled body disappears, and takes a spectral form inseparable from the imperatives of corporate finance.

Wallace's disappearance, his dissolution into the accounting document that is his novel, confirms a central conceit: the author's blood, no less than the blood of his characters, is made of money. This is no less true of the nation's *corpus mysticum*, the abstract if fractured and disorganised body Wallace's *Pale King* would personify. A promotional documentary produced by Wallace's fictional IRS observes that

> In the body politic of the United States of America, many have likened your IRS to the nation's beating heart, receiving and distributing the resources which allow your federal government to operate effectively in the service and defence of all Americans.

The simile suggests that these resources are the monies that flow in and out of the Treasury's coffers, under the supervision of the IRS. But the same PR material also claims that 'the men and women of today's IRS' are 'the lifeblood of this heart', just moments before noting that these men and women 'keep the lifeblood of government healthy and circulating' (pp. 101–2). Being the 'lifeblood' of a heart might mean, alternately, being the substance of which that heart is made or being the substance that circulates through it, an alternation that allows the extrinsic (blood) to become the intrinsic (heart), even as the state becomes those monies that flow through it. IRS workers might then be the blood that makes up 'the muscle of the heart, the stuff of it, the thing that squeezes and relaxes' (p. 467), and/or the blood that courses through the heart's two atriums and ventricles. Wallace casts IRS employees both as agents who facilitate the circulation of money (understood as a measure of value), and as instances of money (understood as the physical medium of circulation itself). Wallace's IRS workers are preoccupied with the exteriors of their bodies; 'in reality', one of them declares, 'everything was the surface' (p. 499). Effectively hollow, they channel financial 'throughput' (p. 368). But in so doing, their bodies become indistinguishable from that throughput. Wallace's self-referential author, his figure for the contemporary literary novelist, possesses a similarly doubled body: he is a channel or conduit through which money moves, just as he is himself a species of currency. In fact, as we will argue throughout this essay, Wallace's characters possess two bodies, one abstract and one concrete, in ways that vividly recall Marx's account of money.

For Marx, concrete acts and kinds of labour become abstract when they are said to be equal to each other and then exchanged. As with labour, so with the commodities made from labour: they possess use values even as they come to express a more abstract form of value in and through a given act of exchange. If the market stipulates that 20 yards of linen are equal in value to one coat, then we say that the coat, here the 'equivalent form of value', expresses the value of the linen, here the 'relative form of value'. While Marx allows that these positions are reversible (we might say that one coat equals 20 yards of linen), he insists that in any given instance of exchange, one commodity must be relative and one equivalent:

> Since a commodity cannot be related to itself as equivalent, and therefore cannot make its own physical shape into the expression of its own value, it must be related to another commodity as equivalent, and therefore must make the physical shape of another commodity into its own value-form.[9]

If 20 yards of linen are said to be equal to one coat, then the coat serves as the value-form of the linen. As a consequence, the coat possesses a double body: it is a 'sensuous extrasensory thing' (*sinnlich übersinnliches Ding*) endowed with a 'spectral objectivity', because it is possessed of concrete qualities even as it functions as the abstract quantitative expression of a value not its own.[10]

In a very mundane way, experiencing one aspect of the commodity's body requires overlooking the other; wearing the coat, for instance, we do not think of it as the value-form of linen. More importantly, however, Marx asks us to understand the tension in the commodity's two bodies as itself an expression of the tension in the labour equated in their exchange. As he writes in a letter to Engels, 'if the commodity is a duality of use value and exchange value, the labour represented in the commodity must also possess a double character ... . This is in fact the whole secret of the critical conception'.[11] The double character of labour is itself twofold, because in the above act of exchange, two parties implicitly agree to understand the linen as an expression of 'the socially necessary labour time' generally required to make it, as opposed to the concrete labour expended by x workers over y hours while making *this* particular linen. They also agree that the socially necessary labour embodied by the linen can be rendered commensurate with the socially necessary labour embodied by the coat. For Marx, 'the secret of the expression of value' is 'the equality and equivalence of all kinds of labour because and insofar as they are human labour in general' (I:152).

These agreements are implicit in exchange but, importantly, unacknowledged by those involved: people do not exchange commodities because they think those commodities require equivalent amounts of abstract labour. The commodity owner, Marx claims, has 'already acted before thinking', insofar as he participates in conventions the direct apprehension of which must be disavowed. When we experience the double body of the commodity – or, better, when we fail to perceive the tensions in its 'extrasensory sensuousness' – we experience the displacement at the heart of 'commodity fetishism', in which 'the commodity reflects the social characteristics of men's own labour as objective characteristics of the products of labour themselves' (I:164). That displacement removes contradiction from our sight. This is what Theodor Adorno means when, following Georg Lukács, he claims that 'all reification is forgetting: objects become purely thing-like the moment they are retained for us without the continued presence of their other aspects: when something of them has been forgotten'.[12]

Put in only slightly different terms, when we perceive commodities only as things, we forget the divisions of labour responsible for their production and exchange; more specifically, we forget the constitutive tensions within and between the valuation of concrete labour in the realm of production and the valuation of abstract labour in the realm of circulation. Commodities do not themselves induce this amnesia. An exchange is a social agreement in which one commodity is said to embody the 'value-objectivity' (*Wertgegenständlichkeit*) of another. But we are predisposed, Marx says, to perceive this agreement as the result of a natural relation between what is most concrete and sensuous in commodities. That predisposition is social and not psychological in origin. Individuals have no immediate control over the social relations that govern their lives, and perceive the contours of these relations only obliquely, in acts of exchange, as imaginary social relations between sensuous commodities: 'Their own movement within society has for them the form of a movement made by things, which far from being under their control, in fact control them' (I:169–70). This is what it means for Marx to claim that individuals matter only as 'personifications of economic categories' (I:92).

Marx will describe 'the complete metamorphosis of a commodity' – as linen is sold for money and as that money is in turn used to purchase a coat, for example – as a process that requires 'denouements and … dramatis personae' (I:206). The linen requires the intervention of human agents to change its form, but those people are expressive vehicles, stage actors playing out a script whose author is a specific stage of capitalism. Wallace's characters are personifications and *dramatis personae* of just this kind. Their invariably double bodies capture the simultaneously abstract and concrete processes of finance capitalism, and thereby recall us to something we might otherwise forget about that capitalism.

Thus, for instance, blood specifies for Wallace tensions within money's double body that became exacerbated by Richard Nixon's decision to end the convertibility of the dollar into gold (1971). Marx's value theory – or, what Michael Heinrich calls a 'monetary theory of value' – insists that the same forgetting described above obtains when money mediates the exchange of one commodity for another – when price expresses the magnitude of value in a given commodity.[13] When we imagine that identically priced linen and a coat have the same value as a function of having the same price, a 'money commodity' like gold, for instance, serves as a 'universal equivalent' through which two parties (unthinkingly) equate abstract quantities of labour. 'Gold confronts the other commodities as money', Marx says, 'only because it previously confronted them as a commodity' (I:162). And like other commodities, gold possesses a double body: it has an 'extrasensory sensuousness' because it functions, concretely, as an instrument of hoarding (an 'independent embodiment of value' possessed of desirable qualities) and, abstractly, as a (quantitative) measure of a value not its own.[14] Wallace assumes that, with the failure of the gold standard, it would seem more than it yet had that money must perforce index a form of value that it could not itself contain (a paradoxical venture replicated by *The Pale King* itself, which pretends to the kind of indexical truth promised by a memoir, even as it acknowledges that it is, in fact, a fiction).

Personifications of a new kind of money, Wallace's characters reference forms of value that they cannot contain. As one IRS employee, Chris Fogel, tells us,

> Sometimes I'd be sitting there in a room and become aware of how
> much effort it was to pay attention to just your own heartbeat for
> more than a minute or so – it's almost as though your heartbeat
> wants to stay out of awareness, like a rock star avoiding the limelight.

Wallace's 'rock star' bespeaks a particular kind of 'rock', gold, gone to
spectacle and light, receding in concreteness and yet sequestered. Fogel
thinks that his heart encourages a deficit in his attention – even as he
senses a deficit within the blood that moves through that heart. He com-
pares listening to his heart to listening to the Beatles' 'Fixing a Hole',
basing his analogy on the perception that attending to each admits him
to, 'an emptiness at the center of the warmth ... as though right at the
center of this safe, enclosed feeling is the seed of emptiness' (p. 183).
His 'heart' as a 'hole' amounts to a 'safe' that stores not bullion, but a
vacancy: Fogel's 'seed of emptiness' expresses the deficit at the core of
his own and of the national economy, signalling ultimately (as we shall
argue), the contradictory nature of the debt-structured derivative monies
beginning to move through the IRS during the Reaganite 1980s.

IRS accountants are 'today's cowboys', declares one of Fogel's
accounting professors; they are trained in 'riding herd on the unending
torrent of financial data' (p. 233). Financial data might represent cash
money, but also functions, for Wallace and financiers alike, as the particular form that value takes in an era of declining industrial production and
profits. 'In today's world', argues the professor, 'boundaries are fixed,
and the most significant facts have been generated.' It follows that 'the
heroic frontier now lies in the ordering and deployment of those facts.
Classification, organization, presentation. To put it another way, the pie
has been made – the contest is now in the slicing' (p. 232). In the age
of the 'post-production capitalist' (p. 144), in which the pursuit of profit
requires trading and re-trading finite amounts of extant value, 'financial
data' specifies not just data about money, but a form of money whose
value specifies a deficit: the 'pie' having already been made, and presumably
sold, profits must come from slicing that pie and selling it, as slices, a
second time – or as many times as needs be. As with pies, so with derivatives, tradable forms of 'financial data' that, in the case of mortgage-backed
securities, for example, sell and resell the finite amount of labour required
of homeowners to pay off a given bundle of residential mortgages.

Understood in this context, the author who disappears into the IRS is
an author whose body is made up of the 'abstract money' that Randy
Martin claims had, 'by millennium's end ... [become] concrete', as 'the
world of bonds and promissory notes between firms, that Marx had
described as "fictitious capital", was becoming a master tale of economic
life'.[15] Wendy Brown adds that neoliberalism, the political face of the

financial turn, should be understood as 'a constructivist project', insofar as 'it does not presume the ontological givenness of a thoroughgoing economic rationality for domains of society, but rather takes as its task the development, dissemination and institutionalization of such a rationality'.[16] We would add that since an economy – for all its apparent abstraction – may best be understood as a mask worn by social relations, where said economy takes finance as its model (rather than merely as its means), the social relations of finance (to lever, to short, to securitise) become the basis of social practice and thus of personhood.[17] In such times, the citizen mimes the financialised corporation, and personifies the deficit at the heart of finance. The exemplary corporate citizen, Wallace can and must be both 'unreal' and a 'living human holding the pencil', because the blood that guarantees his doubled life proves simultaneously abstract and concrete in the contradictory way that derivative monies are.

In the heart of the heart of the financial state

Wallace's characters, most of them employed by Glendenning, suffer from all manner of bodily anxiety. They sweat uncontrollably; manifest varieties of 'blister, scab and lesion' (p. 298); if beautiful, cut their skin, for fear that beauty is skin deep, or unconsciously use their front teeth 'to peel tiny fragments of dead skin' from lip to tongue-tip (p. 352). Aptly, the generic term for Wallace's co-workers is 'wiggler': wigglers examine tax forms at 'tingles', where the desk (or 'tingle') nominally extracts sensation from its user. For subjects who pass into a proximate object, 'wiggling' or irritation of the skin would seem par for the professional task. Moreover, we are assured that the collective and incorporated body of the IRS exhibits a cardiomyopathy – or disease of the heart muscle – among whose significant symptoms are arrhythmia (associated with circulatory failure), retention of fluid and a conspicuous pallor of the skin.

In mid May 1985, expelled from college, and seeking employment in the IRS as 'a way to defer the mechanisms of Guaranteed Student Loan collection' (p. 283), Foster Wallace joins new recruits for an intake and orientation day conducted by the Mid-West REC (Revenue Examination Center) in Peoria, Illinois. Chapter 24 details the compound *dis*orientations by way of which the IRS takes in or ingests Foster Wallace and his co-workers – those more than 3000 Peoria employees who process and examine 'the math and veracity of some 4.5 million tax returns per year' (p. 266). 'Veracity', the recruits are assured during induction, matters less than 'returns on audit' (p. 332); files, it would seem, in the new IRS should be read for 'substantial gains' (p. 333) and not merely for 'throughput' (a criterion of 'the bad old days' [p. 332]).

Since Foster Wallace journeys from Philo, and his 'for-profit' family, to join an institution as it transforms itself into a 'for-profit' concern, the manner of his ingress speaks to the state of the nation's profitability, circa 1985, as seen from the perspective of 2005, the year during which Foster Wallace composes his memoir. In this, Wallace's invention and timing of the 'Spackman Memo' proves crucial. The memo, composed in 1969 (though ignored at that point) dates from what the economic historian Robert Brenner describes as the early days of 'the long stagnation'[18]; from which stagnancy, Reagan and Thatcher would rise to office, equipped with a trinity of neoliberal imperatives: to deregulate, to curb labour, and to release finance. Between 1965 and 1979, returns on US capital at pre-tax levels (for non-financial corporations) fell by 35 per cent.[19] The Spackman Memo presumably responds to an associated fall in tax revenue. Applied in 1981, and yielding the enlarged Peoria intake of 1985, the Memo, as fabricated by Wallace, represents part of a more general turn to finance, or to the making of money directly from money.

As a child of Spackman, in employment terms, Foster Wallace embodies financialisation: he enters IRS Post 047 in debt and seeking to defer debt repayment, true to national economic imperatives. Over the course of the last two decades of the American century, the economy of the world's largest debtor had depended on deficit finance; nor had the problem lessened in the early twenty-first century. Giovanni Arrighi claims that by the early 2000s, deficits in the current account of the US balance of payments had grown steadily to nearly $3 trillion since 1982; he notes that they were being added to at a rate of one and a half billion dollars a day at the time of the invasion of Iraq.[20] Between 1947 and 1981, total countrywide debt (federal, corporate, domestic) had remained largely stable; in the 1980s, however, indebtedness (expressed as a per cent of GDP) rose abruptly from 150 per cent to 200 per cent; its subsequent rise has been almost continuous.[21] Robert Brenner explains the figures, arguing that, despite its long decline in manufacture, the USA (after 1980) saved itself 'by its own debility', insofar as it operated as 'a market of last resort', a site for deficit spending (federal, corporate, domestic), funded by 'vast inflows of private and public monies from abroad'.[22] Federal debt, held by foreign and international investors, rose from below $200 trillion in 1985, to just under $2000 trillion in 2005.[23] The purchase of American debt, or sale of credit, allowed S.E. Asian governments to maintain their own 'export dependent, manufacturing growth machines', while stimulating various 'wealth effects' in the US Dot.Com booms, consumption highs, asset-price run-ups in stocks and real estate – each bubble realised though credit, each burst a revelation of deficit.[24] It follows that, viewed from the perspective of 2005, credit (or liquidity) during the 1980s and 1990s masked abyssal and deepening debt.

The IRS, during this phase of sustained and sustaining national deficit, may best be understood as a factory for debt processing, on behalf of a nation that had become 'an industrial producer of debt'.[25] The issue is not simply that tax is owed retrospectively; additionally, the monies with which persons, whether individual or corporate, paid at the close of the twentieth century and beyond were in large part 'fictitious'. We borrow Marx's term: money made from rents on money, or 'money that expands its own value independently of production', insofar as it proves to be 'pregnant' only with itself, amounts to 'fictitious capital'.[26] Rents take various forms: for example, at the domestic level, consumption has become synonymous with 'the ability to shoulder debt' and its attendant uncertainty.[27] Given that by 2004, 43 per cent of US households were spending more than they earned – spending via mortgage, car loan and credit card – those households had effectively invited debt into their homes and interiors; homes and interiors which, in turn, viewed financially, proved increasingly to be debt-effects, volatile rather than secure, in direct relation to their exposure to risk through owner indebtedness. In such a household, a tax bill might join other bills (many of them interest payments extending towards perpetuity) as just one more rent to be set against wages not yet paid, for work not yet done. Consumer loans, whether for house, health, car or education, during a phase of financialisation, enter the market as assets. Because a borrower promises to pay due sums at due dates until a designated time, her loan functions as an income stream or saleable debt, available to the banking sector for repackaging with other and diverse streams (of greater and lesser probity) prior to resale as credit. After 1973 – the year in which US 'financial assets surpassed those of production' – this process of 'securitisation' often led to investment in a bond market that ballooned during the 1980s, in large part due to deficit finance.[28] From rent comes rent; or, in Marx's terms, 'fictitious capital ... doubles and trebles everything into a mere phantom of the imagination'.[29] We trace this debt trail in part to characterise a curious concreteness inherent in debt, understanding its phantonomic absences to be filled with fees and transactions pertinent to the raw materials that pass through the hands of Wallace's tax inspectors.

A relatively new species of financial instruments, derivatives structure these absences. Even as the culturally hegemonic factory, emerging from the nineteenth century to hold court for much of the century that followed, apparently recedes in significance, to be replaced by flows of information from the core (which, extending along supply chains, effectively outsource production to the peripheries), so financial instruments, derivatives especially (most typically deficit funded), began to cover the American earth. Under conditions of global finance – during what Braudel calls the system's 'Autumn' – the process of 'equivalence' organised by these instruments seems to shed those elements between which its relations form.[30] If middle- and working-class Americans without capital were encouraged to act like capitalists, then financiers behaved like capitalists without capital, insofar as they dealt with a form of capital defined by its absence. Take, for example, the person who 'shorts': a representative dealer in 'fictitious capital', the short trader handles the curious concreteness specific to speculative goods in a culture where being in debt to debt, via leverage, amounts to cash in hand. To short is first to lever. The short sell involves an investor borrowing a stock, for a fee to its lender, in the expectation that its price will fall. Prior to that fall, the borrower sells the stock. When the market drops, as anticipated, he re-buys that which he has sold, confident that its value will subsequently rise to levels that allow him to sell at a price that covers both his fee and the initial value of the borrowed stock (repaid to its lender) while leaving him substantially in profit. The borrowed stock amounts to the lever, or other people's money used to make the investor's lack of money pregnant with more money. The fee amounts to rent. The person who shorts, whether successfully or unsuccessfully, trades in an asset that is no more than a locus of price variation, or of money made or lost through volatility from borrowed money. The referent for the short trade might be figured either as $M\text{-}M^1$ or as $M\text{-}M^{-1}$, where M equates with money (less or more) and the dash denotes risk, which emerges from a conjunction of anxiety and exuberance, mediated through stockprice.[31] The trader trades less in 'substance', than in a peculiar materialisation of euphoria, panic and liquidity generated through the rhythm of market movement.

Stated algebraically, Marx's equation for commodity production $(M\text{-}C\text{-}M^1)$ gives way to $M\text{-}M^1\text{-}M^2$, his formula for fictitious capital. We should note the content of the missing term: 'C', the moment of production, contains a complex of elements (mp [means of production] + L [labour power]), whose conjunction yields surplus value (if valorised through exchange), 'C' becoming 'M^1' by means of circulation.[32] But, during a financial phase (under the hegemony of $M\text{-}M^1\text{-}M^2$) and with 'C' gone to the peripheries, it might seem at the core – or in the heart of the heart of a financial state – that M generates more of itself from its own circuits. In 1990, having exhaustively analysed a structural change from Full to Flexible Fordism, en route anatomising developments within production, labour markets and consumption, David Harvey suspected that innovative primacy lay with 'the search for financial solutions to . . . crisis tendencies'. Concluding that 'the financial system [had] . . . achieved a degree of autonomy from real production unprecedented in capitalism's history', he recommended, in response, that we 'concentrate our gaze on the role of credit'.[33] In 1997, having done as much, Fredric Jameson argued that finance capital (that locus of credit spun from deficit), 'brings into being ... a play of monetary entities that need neither producers (as capital does) nor consumption (as money does) [but] which supremely ... can live on their own internal metabolisms and circulate without any reference to an older type of context'.[34]

Expressed theoretically, the shift in emphasis, inherent in the financial turn, might run as follows: we borrow from Žižek who borrows from Karatani, both of whom focus on the moment of sale (C-M^1) and in so doing reconceive production. Žižek, having acknowledged that 'value is created in the production process', adds the rider that,

> it is created there, as it were, only potentially, since it is actualized as value only when the produced commodity is sold, and the circle M-C-M^1 is thus completed ... In capitalism, the production process is only a detour in the speculative process of money engendering more money – that is to say, the profiteering logic is ultimately also what sustains the incessant drive to revolutionize and expand production.[35]

In practical terms, speculation (finance) trumps production (factory) because, from the viewpoint of the former, production is always in debt to an anticipation of future sale. As industries, seeking to ensure competitiveness, invest in a range of fixes – spatial, technological and managerial innovations which cost borrowed money – so 'the incessant drive to ... expand' sets debt at the heart of their production, debt dedicated to 'the wager that the cycle of circulation will be accomplished'. Consequently, from the perspective of finance, value no longer inheres in the commodity as congealed labour power, but rather takes shape, 'retroactively actualized [and] performatively enacted', as the work of credit. Where labour once stood, money or equivalency now stands ('equivalency' because 'money occupies the formal place of the general equivalent of all commodities'). Having stressed 'how capitalism lives and thrives on future credit', Žižek claims that 'the essence of credit is the being credited of the essence of itself'. By such lights, 'value', the 'essence' of capital, lies in the capacity of those forms which it assumes and casts off (labour, commodity, money) to attract or 'be' credit.[36] So inflected, credit suffuses production with its 'as if' and 'will have been', inducing industry to live in the future perfect anticipation of circulatory success. Such logic gives all credit to credit, and in monetary terms, privileges liquidity among the threefold functions of money, while simultaneously modifying the body of the commodity itself, so that 'use value' shall be perceived as merely a means to exchange (or what Wolfgang Haug calls 'promise of use'), even as deficit circulation displaces production as the life blood of accumulation (for 'modifying' read 'mortifying').[37] In effect, Žižek all but declares money productive of money without the intervention of labour. Whereas, for Žižek emphasis within the phrase, the 'real abstraction' of capitalist value, falls on 'abstraction', value under capital (as we earlier argued) must be understood, after Moishe Postone, as possessed of a 'twofold nature', both abstract *and* real.[38]

With this methodological interlude completed, we return to the monies that pass – care of 1040 forms – through the hands (as well as circulatory and digestive systems) of Wallace's double-bodied wigglers. In Chapter 29, one page after a chapter that concludes Wallace's account of the Peoria intake and orientation day, a group of IRS employees, during their surveillance of a business suspected of falsifying tax returns, exchange 'real' stories 'about shit' (p. 347). But, as one of the surveillance team immediately asks, 'Why Shit?' (p. 347). For Wallace, shit and blood both figure circulatory monetary flows; but shit further specifies the deficit, noted above, that Fogel feels in his blood. As an IRS Examiner puts it, 'the system kicks us mostly shit' (p. 106), and that shit is unmistakably money emptied of value (here, money made from rent on debt). The faecal images shared by the IRS surveillance team amount to a critique of 'flow and output' (p. 35). Bondurant initiates general discussion of a shared childhood preoccupation with stepping in dog waste. The group grants that 'whoever had it on [his] ... shoe' gained 'some kind of terrible power' (p. 348). The extent of ontological transmutation requires that discussants drift from becoming 'instant butt', via 'toilet training', to she who trains and the shared insulting of mothers by boys at puberty, 'saying you'd had sex with their mom and how she wasn't any good and couldn't get enough' (p. 349). To 'become shit', the 'shit monster' needs must confuse 'mum's' vagina and anus, in order to relocate his birth as an act of defecation. Reconceived, the anecdotalists graduate from mediated to immediate contact with their subject. Bondurant recalls tripping at twilight during a game of hide-and-seek, 'both hands ... into a big new yellow steamer. Which I can still almost smell' (p. 349). His insistence on retained phenomenological acuity ('The feeling, the colour, the dispersal, the rising smell' [p. 349]) maximises 'horror', inseparable from a joint and specific sense of mutation:

> Jesus not even on the shoes but the hands. The personal skin ... The hands being especially close to your idea of your identity of who you are, adding to the horror. Exceeded only by the face in terms of closeness, maybe. (pp. 349–50)

Hands, generally associated with labour, but here recast, displace the face as the primary index of identity; a shift in the signatory element which commands a compensatory iteration of the possessive pronoun ('your').

Where 'skin', befouled, elicits the tautological modifier 'personal', the capacity of said skin to retain possession over the 'person' contained might be questioned. An oddity of phrasing ('The personal skin') initiates a corrosive tension between the definite article deployed and an antonymically present, though receding, possessive ('your'). Bondurant emphasises that his 'hands didn't look like my hands anymore', and that he 'held them as far away from me as was humanly possible' (p. 350); initiating a gap between 'me', 'mine', and what is 'human', the shit upon his hands exerts a fascination inextricable from its capacity to induce panic:

> I howled, screamed, and everyone of course comes running, and as soon as they see it *they're* screaming and 180ing and running from me, and I'm both crying and roaring like some kind of horrible shit-monster and chasing after them, horrified and repulsed but also somehow underneath it all glorious in my role of monster. (p. 249)

As Frankenstein (p. 350), care of fresh 'yellow' excrement, Bodurant (whose Francophone name not only contains 'bond' [a means to elicit credit, one therefore necessarily adjunctive to debt] but 'bonde' [Fr.] or 'bung' and 'bunghole'), glories in his ability to alarm.

John Maynard Keynes once likened the proceedings of stock market traders – deficit dealers in risk – to those engaged in musical chairs. In each game, as chairs are withdrawn, excitement and panic mount. Likewise, Bondurant's hide-and-seek turns into tag, a serial game in which those tagged become parties to the duplication of monsters by tactile contagion. Keynes's analogy allows him to address market affect: those who deal, whether swept by euphoria or anxiety, buy and sell less in relation to the supposed value of the asset, than according to the behaviour of others. Christian Marazzi, in his study *Capital and Language*, makes a similar point: 'financialization depends upon mimic rationality … [or] imitative behaviour, [itself] based on the structural information deficits of … investors'. Subject to double deficit – of information as of capital – whether he buys or sells, the dealer behaves as another, and becomes another for yet another, *ad infinitum*. Moreover, his deficits, serially accruing towards a collective judgement, 'take on the status of a reference value', whereby the value of the asset amounts to a materialisation of its attendant affect – or so much shit, whether golden (as with euphorics) or faecal (as with panic).[39]

This is to understand Bondurant's yellow excrement as a form of 'flexible gold'.[40] Too much, here, might seem to depend on Wallace's choice of faecal colour ('yellow'), yet the story that follows – that of Fat Marcus the Moneylender – refines the link between money and human waste. Where

Bondurant's initial anecdote recasts 'money in the hand' as 'crap on the hand', his follow-up modifies a second financial commonplace, 'put your money where your mouth is'. Bondurant recounts how, at college, he and five or six others would burst into freshmen dorms so that while a student victim was held to his bed, 'Fat Marcus the Moneylender [might] take his pants down and sit on his face' (p. 351). The listeners are assured that Fat Marcus, a 'careful bookkeeper', able to 'compound daily without a calculator', 'always had cash and lent it out' (p. 351). 'Ass-imprint' and usury (or money made from rent on money) conjoin in the figure of the obese Jew, only for their conjunction to be distanced from racial slur, '[n]ever even just Fat Marcus, it was always "The Money Lender". He was a Jew but I don't think that had anything to do with it' (p. 351). One might argue that the Semitic cast of the student financier derives less from his ethnicity than from the nature of finance itself: notoriously difficult to trace – hedge funds, for example, are not subject to regulation, while off shore exists specifically to disguise assets and their exchange – financial movements call for a figure apt to their illicit flows.[41] The conceptual Jew fits Wallace's scheme. Long associated with hidden power; at once conspiratorial and contagious; both of the Left and Right (Socialist and Capitalist) – the Jew, everywhere and nowhere, proves coterminous with what Zygmunt Bauman has called 'liquid modernity'. Indeed, Bauman specifically links his category to Europe's Jewry.[42] We would recall Marx's account of the elusiveness of value in process; he notes that, in circulation, value 'suddenly presents itself as a self-moving substance which passes through a process of its own, and for which commodities and money are both mere forms'. Where 'forms' fail him in his representation of 'value ... itself', Marx reaches for the Jew. He insists that however 'tattered a commodity may look', and however 'badly' the money made from it 'may smell', its value, from the viewpoint of the capitalist, resides not in its 'mere forms', but, like the 'circumcised Jews', in its 'wonderful' capacity for making 'still more money out of money' (I:256). Money made from money, or 'pregnant with itself', amounts to finance capital and takes form, for Marx as for Wallace, through the figure of the swollen Jew, Semitic via economic abstraction rather than simply by way of race.[43]

That Marcus sits on faces, anus to mouth, compounds the acuity of the tale as financial commentary. For Marazzi, finance in process depends upon 'linguification'. To explain, we return to the short trader, who is uninterested in the underlying commodities or concerns to which his trades nominally refer, and interested only in anticipated prices and the possible sale and resale of contracts (options and futures) concerning them. Financial instruments like options and futures set what Brenner calls the 'real economy' in abeyance, or so Marazzi claims. The language of 'the financial performative ... does not describe a state of things'; rather, 'taking as its institutional ballast the behaviour of others', the financial contract becomes 'an instrument' for the 'production of real facts'. Ergo, in finance 'facts are created by speaking them'. The process is both linguistic and performative. Put crudely, speculators find themselves immersed in 'the productive force of financial language', and lacking time to absorb it look to their peers (also linguistically immersed and also suffering from a lack of attention time induced by information excess).[44] Financial language induces serial behaviour, which in turn attributes value to the instrument. Such a value, or referent, may be said to be immanent within linguistic excess since it materialises through the iteration and citation of moneyed talk. It is apt, then, that Marcus puts his anus where someone else's mouth is. Anus (metaphoric fount of deficit finance) and mouth (means of production of the financial class); their conjunction creates a circuit as perfect as Marx's equation for the flows of finance capital $(M\text{-}M^1\text{-}M^2)$, in which everything 'doubles and trebles ... expanding its own value' without reference to anything but M, and in which finance capital's appetite for itself may be satisfied without recourse even to mediation through language.

Bondurant supplies an unhappy ending to his tale, in which Marcus's last victim, one Diablo, 'the Left-Handed Surrealist', 'Doberman'-like, bites the ass that would feed him (pp. 353–4). Copious faecal and arterial flows result, and the perpetrators are expelled and sent to Vietnam, where they serve as G2 bookkeepers for the US military then occupying Saigon (p. 352). Wallace thus resituates Marcus's coprophragia-interruptus within the larger history of US debt. Diablo may be devilish, but his violent resistance provides Bondurant with state training in accountancy and his subsequent entry into the IRS, where his surveillance skills result in the recovery of deficits owed by delinquent tax payers. Bondurant's career path tracks the global path of US debt, for which both 1971 (the year of Fat Marcus's exploits) and Vietnam proved crucial. Throughout the late 1960s, America's fluctuating fortunes in Southeast Asia had prompted foreign central banks to convert their dollar inflows into gold, thereby drawing heavily on US Treasury gold stocks. In 1971, faced with bankruptcy, Nixon broke the link between the dollar and the market price of gold. Unable subsequently to recover gold from paper, foreign bankers learned that American paper enabled them primarily to purchase further American paper, in the form of US Treasury obligations (or promises eventually to pay). Levels of US spending abroad precluded a withdrawal of support for the dollar, since any attendant dollar devaluation might simultaneously devalue prior IOUs and extensive foreign dollar holdings. In effect, after 1971 and care of Vietnam, the US government chose to fund guns, butter and 'a new form of imperialism' by running a balance of payments deficit. Since the circuit whereby the USA used its national debt to drain the financial resources of creditor nations amounted to 'a tax on foreigners' by way of their central banks, Bondurant's training in 1971 Vietnam makes sense: he 'spend[s] a fucking year in Saigon learning requisition write-up accounting' (p. 354).[45] To extend the point: for Bondurant read America, whose 'requisition[ing]' of monies from the world's credit nations, in support of its deficit, served not only to pay for its wars (from Korea through Afghanistan) but also to flood the global market with dollar denominated liquidity – post 1971, the new global currency and mainstay of the nation's hegemonic bid. 'Bondurant' links 'bond' and 'bung' (in this instance, presumably removed), but also refers to Matt Bondurant's fictional account of his grandfather, Jack Bondurant's moonshine empire in West Virginia (*The Wettest County in the World* [2008]). Liquidity calls to liquidity within a name, identifying the national typicality of its bearer's practices.

Debt workers and deficit doppelgangers

Confronted with the question, '"What do you think of when you masturbate?" ... A very interior time', Claude Sylvanshine replies 'Tits', to which his questioner responds, 'Just abstract tits?' (pp. 24–6). Abstraction necessarily attends bodies (and the presumed interiority of their desires) caught within the incremental flow of the deficit dollar. Given that, as Marx had long since noted, money 'obliterates' and renders 'invisible' the 'specific attributes' and 'real elements' of the production that it represents, those deficit funds typically deployed by finance, in passing through the secrecy of its circuits, obtain an opacity akin to abstraction-squared.[46] And yet, as we have been suggesting, Wallace personifies these circuits – his characters process representations of money (tax forms) and are themselves representations of what is most contradictory about money in an age of debt and finance. Constitutive of that contradiction is the manner in which his double-bodied wigglers, industrial processors of debt, render concrete that which seems abstract (financial flows) and abstract that which seems most concrete: 'shit', 'urine', 'blood', 'sweat', 'tit', and (we anticipate) semen. The contradiction that holds these wigglers together, even as it tears them apart, extending through their most intimate bodily functions, as a lived abstraction, might also be understood as a metaphoric conjunction between the abstract and the concrete, meeting in their persons. The internalised metaphor ('real abstraction') takes physical form as a double body produced by the passage of each term (abstract and concrete) through the other, by way of social practices. As each subsumes the other – becoming what it is not – so each leaves residues of its prior state in that which subsumes it; those residues irritate insofar as they recall alternate processes and experiences, lost but not gone.

Wallace's wigglers, mirroring the Foster Wallace/Francis Wallace conflation, most typically practise doubling, and consequent abstraction, as a form of self-equivalency. Take Fogle, a colleague of Foster Wallace, who attributes his accountancy skills and capacity to concentrate to 'Obetrolling' (p. 180). Fogle's use of the anti-obesity drug Obetrol, initiated in experiments with Ritalin during a World Cultures Class (p. 158), results in what Fogle 'used privately' and repeatedly 'to call "doubling"' (pp. 180, 181, 187, *passim*). Elsewhere in his monologue, Fogle likens 'doubling' to 'an explosion in a hall of mirrors' (p. 188). Indeed, he stumbles mistakenly into an Advanced Tax Review class (a mistake that will lead to his entry into the Service in 1979), rather than into a seminar on American Political Thought, because the buildings and rooms in which the respective classes were located 'were literally almost mirror images of one another' (p. 189). In an economic refinement of Lewis Carroll's Alice, Fogle 'doubles himself', so that as his own 'mirror image', he may pass through a mirroring room into the IRS, where his putative possession of a number, access to which supposedly triggers absolute concentration (p. 539), promises not only to maximise revenue drawn by examiners from future deficit flows, but also to obviate Lehrl's planned replacement of examiners with computers (since an examiner in possession of Fogle's number would, presumably, be a computer's equivalent in productivity terms), thereby saving the IRS and the nation considerable expenditure on information technology.[47]

Fogle assures a video crew preparing footage for an IRS promotional film that on Obetrol, 'if you really look at something, you can almost always tell what type of wage structure the person who made it was on' (p. 182). More seems to be involved than retrospectively pricing a paint-job by staring at a beige surface in a student room. Feeling the need to elaborate, Fogle adds that if he really looked at

> the shadow of the sign and the way the placement and height of the sun at the time affected the shape of the shadow ... I knew I was ... aware of the awareness. It may be sounds abstract or stoned, but it isn't. To me, it felt alive. (pp. 182–3)

The sign in question is 'a huge neon ... foot' (p. 163), advertising a podiatric clinic across from Fogle's dorm window at University of Illinois at Chicago. From house painter's hand to podiatrist's foot, Fogle on Obetrol finds in his exemplars not paint or price but 'wage structure', not 'shadow' but 'time' and 'height of the sun'. Concentration yields a totalising imperative that enables him to recover from the items of everyday (significantly, here, as they attach to the body's extremities – hands and feet) the structural source, be it wage system or solar movement, from which they derive their form. Seeking to sum up his lengthy discourse on Obetrol use, Fogle notes, 'I felt like I actually *owned* myself. Instead of renting' (p. 186): that is to say, 'double[d] up' (p. 183) and standing outside himself, he sees himself not as the renter might see him – as a property to be rented for a time at a price – but as his own proprietor: either way, intrinsic selfhood proves inextricable from price, whether retail or rental. Aptly, even as he constructs his analogy for Obetrolling, Fogle twice deems his comparison 'cheap' (p. 186), thereby owning up to the underpricing of what he 'owns'. The depth of Wallace's play on 'own' (a pun whose lateral skid yields a dense superficiality) leaves the possessive term possessive only in and through its dispossession by the price mechanism.

Fogle doubles towards a more revenue productive version of himself, in a progress that might usefully be glossed via Marx's equation for the work of fictitious capitals (M-M^1-M^2). Fogle's equation proves more complex: F + Obetrol (concentration) allows F^1, but F^1 + Fogle's secret number exponentially extends the equation (F^1-F^2-F^3 ...), where dashes indicate maximised rents drawn from national deficits. We augment Wallace's abstraction in order to make more concrete the 'heart' and 'soul' so important to what Randy Martin and Wendy Brown call neoliberalism's 'constructivist project': 'Economics are the method', declared Margaret Thatcher. 'The object is to change the heart and soul.' In his scrupulous attention to Fogle's phenomenology, Wallace locates the financial logic 'internal' to his efforts at self-modification, efforts whereby (adapting Fogle) he may 'feel alive' through abstraction.

In another instance of doubling and abstraction, in Chapter 36, an anonymous six-year-old initiates a project 'to press his lips to every square inch of his own body' (p. 394). The narrator notes that 'the boy had no conscious wish to "transcend" anything .... He was, after all, just a little boy' (p. 401), for whom progressively extreme areas of his own skin become the focus of meditative concentration and physical adaptation, over a five-year period. Marking each anticipated point of contact with soluble ink, the boy, having made contact, follows procedure:

> These areas had been touched, tagged on the four-sided chart inside his personal ledger, then washed clean of ink and forgotten. The boy's tendency was to forget each site once he had pressed his lips to it, as if the establishment of its accessibility made the site henceforth unreal, for him and the site now in some sense 'existed' only on the four-faced chart. (p. 401)

The boy transfers his skin, ink mark by ink mark, onto a ledger, 'fashioned
... [as a] free standing four-sided cardboard chart ... [from] copies of
B. R. Faucet's famous neuromuscular diagrams (@ 1961, Los Angeles
College of Chiropractic)' (p. 404): this concern for bibliographic accuracy
in a chapter where musculoskeletal references abound – each of them
checkable against anatomical reference works – proves intriguing. The
boy renders his body 'unreal' to himself in the degree to which he
records its 'existence' on a 'four-faced chart', the probity of whose
source, checked, proves fictitious. The child seems in no simple sense
motivated by desire. To 'press' or 'touch' skin with lip is not 'to kiss':
Wallace uses the verb 'to kiss' only twice in the 13 pages of Chapter 36;
first, with reference to a cartoon's 'exaggerated pucker' (p. 395); second,
in noting that 'the upper portion of his [the boy's] genitals ... were protru-
sively kissed and passed over' in favour of 'plans for the Ilium' (p. 397); the
speed of passage towards the 'uppermost and largest bone of the pelvis',
accompanied by its latinate nomenclature, keeps 'kiss' and 'genitals'
apart, thereby curtailing any but the merest smidgen of early eroticism.

Our aggregation of the novel's self-abstracting characters moves from
Fogle to the boy to Shane Drinion. In Chapter 46, Drinion, a Utility
Examiner is subject to seduction by Meredith Rand, a GS10, during a
Friday Happy Hour at Meibeyer's Bar, at the close of an IRS shift.
Rand, 'wrist-bitingly attractive' (p. 447), seeks to interest Drinion who,
though capable of exhibiting 'complete attention' (and consequently a
highly revenue productive examiner [p. 458]), lacks all affect. Drinion's
nick name, 'Mr. X, short for Mr. Excitement' (p. 448), where 'X', standing
not simply as the classic mark of excision, but also as a recurrent boxed
entry on any 1040 form, serves to catch the general sense, among his
peers, of Drinion's absence. Directed by 'X' to the 1040s (primary raw
material of Drinion's work), we recall the novel's epigraph, 'We fill pre-
existing forms and when we fill them we change them and are changed.'
The 'X' against Drinion's name speaks to death only insofar as we
ignore the 'changed' life that results from his labour. The body of any
labouring class – whether manual or cognitive – will adapt to that
mode of production to which it contributes its labour power. The life of
its body will, accordingly, be particular to the 'pre-existing forms' of its
work, 'forms' which change but cannot afford to excise the collective
body of the worker, not least because surplus value and the continued
health and accumulation of capital derive from that body. Neither person-
ally nor structurally, therefore, can Drinion be absent; rather, 'he's there
but in an unusual way; he becomes part of the table's environment like
the air or ambient light' (p. 448), 'air' and 'light' being obviously essential
to the life of the bar. 'Ambient', however, evidences the degree to which
there is no 'there' there, in Drinion's case, since the directional imperative

('there'), lacking a specified location, imperiously points towards a subject available only in diffusion. 'Ambient' recurs with the narrator's observation, 'there is a kind of ambient unsonic hum about him' (p. 453).

To focus 'intently', indeed perhaps with Drinion's 'attention', on the sound of this account of absent sound, is to recognise that 'hum' and 'him' share an acoustic that absorbs 'un': but the 'i' ('h*i*m') that emits two 'u's ('*u*nsonic' and 'h*u*m'), only to deny one of them ('*u*n'), cannot pass into even a single 'u' without residue, albeit graphemic. '[U]nsonic' in itself suggest a need to shift from the phonic to the graphic. As phonemes accordingly cease to speak to us, the text begins to text us, in units that having disrupted syntactical contiguity further disrupt lexical and graphemic integrity. The passage of 'i' into 'u' yields as its remainder a single, though shortened, graphemic perpendicular, plus a floating point; all of which makes a certain sense when located within the Examiner's reading experience. Examiners, of whom Drinion is exemplary (seeming to live only to examine), do not presumably read either somatically or semantically. Were they to read somatically, even to themselves, attention to the body (diaphragm, throat, tongue, and palate) might distract.[48] Moreover, for IRS employees, the semantics of a 1040 must be minimal: to the practised Examiner, having a semi-automatic knowledge of the forms, instructions tend to numbers, and numbers tend to positions on a page, any intrusion of the semantic into the numeric serving to impede the process of reading as scanning. We recall that as a child, Fogle would count rather than read words, a habit preserved into adulthood, 'the counting goes on when I'm reading or talking, as a sort of background noise.... For instance, I've said 2,752 words right now since I started' (p. 161). It seems plausible that his supposed possession of a number that triggers absolute concentration relates to the subset of his reading practice. Fogle initiates his monologue (Chapter 22) with the comment, 'it may be that this kind of work changes you. Even just rote exams. It might actually change your brain' (p. 154). Rand observes that upon occasion, in response to her questions, Drinion will engage in 'very brief moment[s] of inward scanning' (p. 481); we would question her use of the word 'inward', arguing that Wallace's attentiveness to the labour of page-turning ensures that for Drinion, as for his co-page-turners (Chapter 25), 'intrinsic value', growing from the outside in, 'bears the extrinsic at its heart'.[49] Yet they who scan are not machines: note how the 'i' – 'u' distinction (a faulty equivalence) never quite loses a pronominal inclination (I, you, 'him'), through which it retains links, however tenuous, to the body, or more properly, to the body ('u' plural) of a particular work force. Let us suppose that each of those who 'turn a page', as listed in the twin-columned pages of Chapter 25, emit, at variant levels, an 'unsonic hum' (as index to their industrially required concentration), what would that 'unsonic hum', so close to Drinion's 'him', sound like?

The narrator tries again: 'if he [Drinion] gave off a sound it would be like a long single tone from a tuning fork or an EKG flat line instead of anything that varies' (p. 450). The EKG analogy joins Drinion's nickname in seeming to nominate extinction, but like the nickname, the high-pitched whine of the line that evidences a stopped heart necessarily retains, by way of compelling rhythmic contrast ('blip', 'blip'), the life whose cessation it proposes. Similarly, a 'tuning fork' establishes its 'single tone' only for as long as each of its tongs minutely shifts position or vibrates. Paid sufficient 'attention', the proffered and invariant 'lines' vary, even as their linear analogies combine, going to the heart of Drinion's heart by way of the ear. Neither analogy permits the simple deduction that Drinion is undividedly machinic or dead, though both suggestions hover 'about him' as the text strives towards new terms.

Chapter 46, at 60 pages, the second longest in the novel, reads like the transcript of a sustained conversational effort to come to terms with Drinion's 'whole different type of intensity' – for Rand, 'an intensity that had nothing to do with flirting or anything romantic' (p. 473). She stresses that, 'it isn't excitement, but it is intense, a little like standing near the high-voltage transformer park south of Joliet Street' (p. 502). We return to a 'hum' (that of transformers), to electric lines ('high voltage') and to an energy basic to the system; each of them proximate to Drinion's singular capacity for 'attention' (the essence of his 'form' of labour). Yet it will be noted that our account of Drinion makes no mention of equivalency, doubling or mirrors, thereby seeming to differentiate him from the very group into which we seek to set him. Indeed, asked by Rand, 'you don't ever compare anything to anything?' (p. 463), he responds that he has 'no way to compare'. He adds, 'I have a hard time paying attention to more than one thing at a time,' by which logic Drinion becomes that 'one thing' to which he attends, be it Rand or a tax form. So, for example, he most typically meets Rand's inquiries with paraphrase (variants of, 'You're asking me to . . . ?' [p. 451]): dialogue would imply that Drinion occupies a position; exegesis indicates, rather, that he speaks only as the exegete of his interlocutor, since as he points out, 'I don't think I'm really anything' (p. 462). Drinion needs no mirror or double; his capacity to become the object of his attention makes him the equivalent of Obetrol, or the boy's chart, or, better, of Fogle's 'string of numbers' leading to 'total concentration' (p. 539) . . . which would explain why Drinion levitates. During the exchange with Rand, Drinion's bottom gradually and almost imperceptibly leaves his chair; the narrator measures the final gap at 'almost 1.75 inches', adding:

> One night someone comes into the office and sees Drinion floating
> upside down with his eyes glued to a complex return, Drinion
> himself unaware of the levitating thing by definition, since it is
> only when his attention is completely on something else that the levi-
> tation happens. (p. 485)

To return to terms offered by Randy Martin at the start, we understand
Drinion, levitant, to be 'abstract money made concrete': as money which
'obliterates' the process of its making, while subordinating, by way of
price, that to which it refers, Drinion has all but no body, yet remains as
'intently' alive as that 'real abstraction' (the monetary form) through
which we all live, but the fullness of whose experience we most typically
ignore. Drinion exemplifies, in its purest form, the delight of concentrated
cognitive labour as it extracts revenue from numerical information. But we
should remember that Rand links his 'hum' to the Joliet Street transformers, where 'Joliet' identifies both a seventeenth-century French Canadian
explorer, responsible for discoveries along the upper reaches of the Missis-
sippi, and a file system commonly used to store information on CD-ROM
computer disks. The sound of which name, even allowing for the Midwestern pronunciation familiar to Wallace, residually stores both 'joy' (as in
'joie' or 'jolly') and an inference of a faecal vessel, aptly containing its
own 'small story about shit'.

Drinion's levitation does not derive from introspection – he is
'himself unaware of the levitating thing'. Rather it originates in the form
of his labour, or more exactly from the concentration required by a specific
process of production. Drinion 'turns a page'; in turning it repeatedly on
behalf of the extraction of revenue from deficit, he becomes a man without
qualities: as Alfred Sohn-Rethel puts it, in his pursuit of the historical
origins of abstract thought within commodity exchange, 'abstraction in
its precise literal sense [means] ... complete absence of quality'.[50]
Drinion seems to have gone missing. Where has he gone? The answer –
through the marks on 1040 forms towards the state of perfect concentration enabled by knowledge of Fogle's number – though attractive in
terms of our pursuit of the logic of equivalency (as it tends towards a
supreme equivalence and at absolute measure) lacks an historical dimension, which we will eventually supply by considering the financial turn
undertaken by the state, as Foster Wallace enters the Peoria Branch of
the IRS in 1985.

Throughout *The Pale King*, Wallace's bodies, though doubled, tend
towards the abstraction required of them by the form of their labour; we
experience them dissolving into equivalency, historically misconceived by
way of the financial turn, as abstract and therefore single-bodied. And
yet, the very bodily functions that figure this movement towards deficit-

backed liquidity confront us with a graphic concreteness that resists the abstraction at its heart. 'Pecunia non olet', the Roman Emperor Vespasian is reported to have said to his son, who complained that his father was taxing the public lavatories: money does not stink. And yet it does. For Wallace as for Marx, liquidity remains a material affair. Money, Marx writes, always 'leaves behind a precipitate' as it facilitates the metamorphosis of commodities. 'When one commodity replaces another, the money commodity always sticks to the hands of some third person. Circulation sweats money from every pore' (I:208). Not fully water, even the abstract sweat of circulation contains the residue of contradiction – its minerals, lactate, and urea (products of work) yield the trace elements that will not reduce to some fully transparent common denominator. Wallace's common denominator, the flow of deficit finance, is still more abstract than the general equivalence according to Marx, and Wallace's fictional sweat figures the correspondingly recalcitrant precipitate left behind by the circulation of 'financial data'.

We encounter that sweat as Foster Wallace and Cusk travel, in a packed IRS transport, towards the Peoria REC in May 1985. Cusk sweats copiously; on disembarkation, Foster Wallace finds 'the whole left side' of his corduroy suit 'wet from … ambient perspiration' (p. 285). Partial immersion in liquidity stands as an apt baptism for one seeking orientation in the nation's deficit flows. Elsewhere, Wallace annotates the unguent:

> It was in public high school that this boy [Cusk] learned the terrible power of attention and what you pay attention to. He learned it in a way whose very ridiculousness was part of what made it so terrible. And terrible it was. (p. 91)

Aged sixteen, in a World Cultures Class, he experiences 'a shattering public sweat' (p. 94). Subsequently, every element in his life exists for him in relation to future sweating: each thing, from the position of a desk (p. 97) to the sound of a woman's legs 'crossing and recrossing' in 'sheer hose' (p. 330) (pun on 'hose' intended) operates as an indexical sign, causally linked to 'internal heat' (p. 94) and its effusions. Sweat, therefore, functions as an abstraction, and becomes Cusk's supreme equivalence: that which allows him to compare and quantify all items encountered in terms of risk. 'Dating from that day in World Cultures … his attempts to avert or avoid or control his fear, began to inform almost every moment of his day' (p. 94). Control consists in paying 'close and sustained attention to whatever was going on outside him' (p. 318), in order that 'his true self' (p. 99), 'a winged thing breathing fire' (p. 92, n1) might not 'literally leak out' (p. 99). But leak he invariably does, and Cusk's interior and exterior each serves as the other's measure, the degree of their equivalency finding expression in specific quantities of sweat. He learns that concentration on selected externals reduces 'emissions of perspiration' (p. 330), a discovery that apprentices him to a cognitive labour akin to accountancy. As a tax examiner, he concentrates on files. For Cusk, a flow of sweat abated amounts to a flow of 1040s maximised, along with an accompanying hike in 'the District's net profit' (p. 346). Like Fogle, Cusk doubles towards a more revenue productive version of himself, in a progress that recalls Marx's equation for the work of fictitious capitals $(M-M^1-M^2)$. For M (money) read C (Cusk); for '-' read state deficit flows: C, care of managed sweat, becomes C^1, where $(^1)$ equals 'substantial gains' $(C-C^1)$.

Wallace monetises perspiration, and produces 'abstract sweat' at a moment (circa 1985) when neoliberal financialisation sought to collapse 'society' into 'economy' by requiring workers to express all aspects of their lives in what Max Haiven has called, 'an economic vernacular'.[51] For Randy Martin, such an idiom pervades 'a culture of financialized individualism, in which full economic subjectivity means the transformation of personal horizons into economic investments'.[52] In tracing Cusk's 'self-management', we have argued that his phenomenology amounts to an equivalency mechanism, whereby experience (A) becomes sweat (B), so that sweat or sweat controlled may become money (C). But A, B and C are not equivalents; money may link them, in and through its insistence on equivalence, but each contains within that abstraction its particular concreteness. Another way of putting this would be to say that equivalency – or the presumption that A is B – necessarily leaves a residue as A passes into B. Money, a prevalent expression of the commensurability assumed by equivalence, proposes an eventually metaphoric relation, but would deny it. To repeat a point made earlier, where metaphor retains a tension between its terms, what Paul Ricoeur calls a 'semantic impertinence' yielding a split referent, money (or metaphor in denial) substitutes itself for that which it prices, inviting us to forget its second term – the sweat that went into the priced good, be that commodity labour time or a marketable deficit.[53] As Fredric Jameson argues:

> If radically distinct objects can be grasped as equivalents of one another then the door is wide open for ideological theories of the just price (and the just wage), along with ... projections of equilibrium theory (where prices somehow become 'the same' as values) ... and aesthetic conceptions of reflection, whether in self-consciousness or in art, in which that historical invention called the mirror is called on to justify a whole ideological program.[54]

Where equivalence proves synonymous with 'reflection', allowing money to pose as a just replication of that which it prices, time will 'mirror' money and wage subsume sweat.[55] In contradistinction, Wallace's attentiveness to Cusk's discomfort brings to visibility the body's resistance to economic subsumption and to the progress of equivalency; consequently, his sweat remains double-bodied (or inconclusively abstract), both deficit monies *and* a 'cheesy' smell on Wallace's corduroys.

When Foster Wallace finally gains admission to the Peoria REC, he does so soaked in Cusk's sweat, and by way of an entrance that is at once a tax form, a mirror, and an anus. The entrance serves three purposes: it architecturally simulates a report on financial data; its mirror glass serves as an equivalency device, while its situation at the rear of the building infers the persistence of what we have called the recalcitrant precipitate, or olfactory residue of labour within the supposedly non-olfactory (because abstracted) deficits that he will be paid to process. Wallace assures us that 'the main building's rear, itself turned out to actually be the REC's front' (p. 276), which 'entrance ... behind' (p. 277), or 'front' at the 'back', or 'face' at the 'rear', seen from the stream of 'brown, orange, yellow' Service Gremlins, takes form as the exact replica of a 1040 form (p. 282). The Examiners will examine 1040s in the 'REC Annex' whose 'mirrored exterior' (p. 282) reflects the main building. Perhaps to compound equivalency, Wallace identifies the building as previously occupied by Midwest Mirror Works (p. 265); he adds, while describing how exactly examiners duplicate one another's page-turning, that 'one square acre of mirror' (p. 312) remains hidden in its walls.

Moreover, on entry, Foster Wallace is mistaken for Francis Wallace, in a 'ghost redundancy' that doubles his as a prelude to his 'disappearance'. Like Drinion, he will ascend into the form of himself best able to maximise 'eventuated revenue' or 'ER' (p. 117). We note that the initials ER, in their abstraction from that to which they refer, inform their referent – state revenues – with an alternate outcome, doing so residually, as through from below, in the whisper of a pun. Similarly, 'ghost redundancies' conjoins antithetical terms: 'ghost', in this usage, retains an allusion to the ghost-writing that propelled Foster Wallace to Peoria in the first place, a genre whereby two persons become one in a script. 'Redundancy' cannot avoid implying that where a government employee enters a higher form of himself, discarded labour will result from revenue maximisation. Symptomatically, for the brief period during which Foster Wallace (unbeknown to himself) doubles successfully as Francis Wallace, he is required, during an upper-level presentation, to absorb financial data pitched at a level of abstraction that proves entirely beyond him. In response, he reverts to skills learned as a ghostwriter, rote transcription, or 'automizing himself' (p. 337) by transcribing. His skills prove inadequate; 'his writing hand' cramps, 'assum[ing] a sort of automatic writerly claw shape' (p. 366) to be hidden in his pocket. Ergo, the effective doubling of Foster as Francis results in an industrial injury to the hand, even as that manual extension of cognitive labour had sought subordination to the dictates of the head. More is involved: a human 'transcription machine' (p. 336) breaks. Marx notes that when a thread snaps, or when a knife fails to cut, its user thinks of the weaver or the cutler, that is of the system that produced the fault. Transcription, or in this instance the successful circulation of information on behalf of the extraction of tax revenues from prior tax loopholes, falters. In the absence of loom or grindstone, we must surely question circulation itself, vaunted and data-dependent key to the production of nominal value during a financial phase.

Risk and volatile bodies

The extraction of money from money in Peoria would seem fraught with a breakage of circulation at whose heart lies risk. As in Peoria, so on a global scale. During and after the 1970s, the outsourcing of production along globally extended supply chains required new forms of financial connection and guarantee, since each link in the chain generated risk. Put simply: connectivity increases volatility, which increases risk, which promotes the derivative, an instrument for the translation of volatility into security. Suppose a corporation, calculating its revenues in US dollars, signs a contract to provide ten million cellular phones a year at a fixed price for five years to a Brazilian subsidiary of a South African corporation, and if those phones feature casings made in Mexico, components from Japan, and an interior architecture designed by a German–Italian concern, then the assemblage of said cell phones will be possible only if the corporation signing the contract has priced the risk of volatility into the rate of exchange between the dollar and the rand, yen, peso, and euro. Furthermore, and pertinent to the contracted price and consequent health of the company, the value of capital borrowed to finance licence, labour, and component costs must be made to fluctuate minimally (thus, variable rates on loans must be swapped for fixed rates). We would stress that risk appraisal necessitates the dismantling of any underlier (here a quantity of cellular phones) into its constitutive elements, and the trading of those elements in terms of contracts as to risk, without the trading of the underliers as a whole. The pricing of the various elements of our example, several of them already estimates of monetised relations between monetised relations (as in exchange or interest rate variables) takes place not against assets (and accordingly in the relevant commodity markets), but in options and futures markets, where prices will be

negotiated as indices of risk. It would follow that risk amalgams – genera-
tive of prices as anticipated prices – become the underlier to which derivatives refer, even as that underlier (long gone to price) is reassembled in
abstract form as a body of prices. Randy Martin characterises derivatives
as 'principles of assembly and disassembly'.[56]

Though the derivative, so described, 'has no concrete form', its monetary form has consequences both for assets and for the corporate bodies
that contain those assets.[57] Whereas asset, care of the derivative reconsti-
tuted through risk, exists primarily as the outlier for a contract concerning
its anticipated price, that price (believed to express the asset) will prove
constantly open to re-evaluation and resale. The asset therefore concretises
through the volatile and abstract form of itself lodged in its price and
subject to re-pricing through speculation. A corporation dealing in such
assets by logical extension includes within itself those 'principle[s] of
assembly and disassembly' that characterise its parts. In that derivatives
'involve the reimagining of seemingly all events as calculable and imagin-
able' they offer the corporation a means 'continually to verify the market
value of component pieces of capital', or to compare asset with asset,
event with event, within and beyond its own corporate structure.[58] With
the derivative at its core, and thereby acting on the presumption that
risk may be evaluated, the corporation becomes, through a built in compu-
tational mechanism, internally competitive to a degree that abnegates its
own rationale for corporate integrity. If the corporation were a person,
that person might experience epidural failure, while suffering in the
matter of its heart.

It follows that managers of corporations rich in risk, assuming the corporation to be a financial entity, whose identity lies in its pool of finance
rather than its productive activities, will attend primarily to the managing
of 'direct competition among [the] cohesive sums of self-expanding finance
that dominate the economic process for which they are responsible'.[59]
Witness Leonard Stecyk, Deputy Director of Personnel at the Peoria
branch of Wallace's IRS: Stecyk does to people what the derivative does
to assets – he treats them as price points to be maximised through risk
appraisal. (Our point here is not just that human resource managers
treat people as financial managers treat financial assets, but that for
Wallace, they must do so, since people are embodiments of finance.) We
would stress that the motor for the exponential expansion of the derivative
market over the last three decades has been debt. The indebted, whether as
persons or corporations, anticipate hazard and accordingly insure, where
insurance may take the form of personal-cover (life, health, home ...)
or of options, futures, and the various modes of swap and hedge
through which the risk inherent in derivative trading will (at a fee) be
offset to another. Citizens in a credit-driven economy live at risk, against

which risk they typically borrow. At the national level, debt-financing deficit in the cause of artificial stimulus, or the papering over of bad debt with further debt, amounts to what Andrew Kliman describes as more fire next time: which fire, as anticipated accident, fans the derivative market.[60]

Even as Foster Wallace joins the IRS to defer debt repayment, so Leonard Stecyk sits at its debt-driven heart as the apotheosis of risk, epiphenomenon of deficit. Stecyk, who does much of the work of his superiors in effectively directing a national debt-processing plant (p. 257, n3), lives in the expectation of accident, and has done so from his childhood. Age 10, noticing his father's 'facial tick', young Leonard, referring to the chart on the back of his bedroom door, links the tick to a three-month delayed doctor's visit and an eight-month overdue tetanus booster (p. 30). Presumably, his chart failed to anticipate his mother's 'terrible accident while cleaning the oven' (p. 31), an accident leaving her hospitalised and having 'to be turned and her limbs manipulated twice a day' (p. 35). To live with a child who sees persons as accidents about to happen and gas ovens as mechanical anthologies of risk (requiring memorised emergency telephone numbers [p. 31]) is to be subject to levels of anxiety at which bodies, parental and otherwise, may falter or seek extinction. The paternal tick and the maternal paralysis, expressions of exposure to pervasive, anticipated, and announced risk, join those symptoms of epidermal and coronary failure consequent upon interpellation by debt and, in these instances, its risk function.

A single episode may serve to sketch the implications of Stecyk's preoccupation. Faced with arterial blood, fanning at systolic pressure from the all-but severed thumb of his Voc. Ed. Instructor, during a tenth-grade Industrial Arts Class, young Leonard, inept in matters of wood but thoroughly versed as to equipment handbooks, safety procedures and arterial maps, saves Ingle's life. Leaving aside the novel's more generic concern with blood and the administration of circulation, much of relevance to risk stems from the incident. Ingle, after suitable convalescence, returns to teaching, though his manual impairment requires that he forgo Industrial Arts for Driver Ed. By implication, circulation, circa Autumn 1969 (the accident's identified date), displaces production for Ingle even as it does so for the US economy. Stecyk's handling of Ingle's hand, resulting in its eventual redeployment to vehicular risk limitation, has a further physical effect. Stecyk grows less visible; the 'hard boys' from Industrial Arts, 'ceased to see him or single him out' for 'daily cruelty' (p. 421). We would surmise that, apprenticed to risk, and insofar as he accordingly deals in hypotheticals (events that may or may not occur), Stecyk takes the form of his chosen raw material, becoming more inference than entity, more postulate than person. Nonetheless, the incident with the band saw springs as 'a clear and conscious memory' into the mind's eye of one 'hard boy' witness, 'twenty months later' in Vietnam (p. 421). Wallace compounds specificity as to time and place with particularity as to detail: the hard boy 'had thought of Stecyk in his little apron and paisley bow tie (the latter and distortion of memory)' (p. 422) while a 'fat-boy draftee' took charge of his squad – lost for its corporal – and led them between North Vietnamese Army platoons to safety. Season and location (summer of 1971, Plaines des Joncs, Indochina [p. 421]) link the memory to Bondurant's military training in requisition accountancy (also 1971), also Vietnam, also the result of '*arterially* shooting blood' [p. 354]), but perhaps more significantly to Nixon's severing of the direct convertibility of the US dollar to gold (August 1971). Nixon, as we have argued, faced with a run on federal gold holdings by the nation's creditors, creditors rendered panicky by levels of US expenditure in Indochina, floated the dollar free of its metallic tie. Since America's withdrawal from the Bretton Woods agreement effectively broke the global gold standard, it may be said to have paved the way for the emergence of risk mitigation and its instruments as the new 'precious' or 'flexible gold', but just as Stecyk's commitment to risk causes him to recede from visibility, so 'flexible gold' proves elusive in terms of its representation.

Gold has heft; it summons bank vaults and casts the precious (or the supreme equivalent) as that which can be brought shining to sight from paper, plastic or electronic impulse. Risk, in contradistinction, proves both ontologically problematic and less subject to figuration. Indeed, the term 'flexible gold', borrowed from Bryan and Rafferty's account of derivatives, is itself an attempt to image the alternate supreme equivalent hidden within the stochastic evaluations obscurely enacted by the market in derivative contracts. As noted above, Bryan and Rafferty describe derivatives as 'anchor[ing] the global financial system in a way somewhat analogous to the role of gold in the nineteenth century', adding that, in an era of floating exchange rates, some concept of 'fundamental value' must exist if 'perceived equivalencies' are to be underpinned, and risk measured.[61] Given that derivative contracts 'establish price relations between bits of capital',[62] the exponential expansion of the derivatives market over the last three decades constitutes a global alternative to the gold standard – a new metal whose 'flexibility' proves apt to the volatility consequent upon expanded economic interconnection. Arguably, the need for exchange rate stability, 'has led the demands for each part of capital (not just each firm or corporation) to justify its value (and contribution to profitability) in an on-going and perpetual process'.[63] Under such mutable conditions, risk measurement yields perceived rather than fixed asset equivalencies, doing so via a measure that proves flexible to the point of evanescence. As our theoretical guides note:

derivatives are crucially the link between money, price and fundamental value not because they actually determine the fundamental values (for there are no truths here) but because they are the way the market judges or perceives fundamental value. Derivatives turn the contestability of fundamental value into a tradable commodity. In so doing, they provide a market benchmark for an unknowable value,

unknowable, not least because 'there has to be some theory of value even though we are in full knowledge of its contingency'.[64] Contingency, so known, risks setting risk at the heart of those very instruments designed for its annulment.

The above detour glosses the hard boy's false memory: Stecyk's recalled but non-existent bow tie exists (like the archaic turn in Bryan and Rafferty's 'flexible gold') to reassure, suggesting that Stecyk, rendered barely visible by his mastery over risk, may none the less be drawn from hiding towards visibility as a figure for 'actual value'. Wallace comments that 'a strange unease came over the hard boys when they ... thought of Stecyk' since 'for the brightest among them, their idea of what toughness was, of the relation between coolness and actual value, had now been somewhat fucked with' (p. 421), 'fucked with' perhaps because in tying his 'deft two-knot tourniquet' at 'the crucial branch[ing]' of the 'ulnar and radial arteries' in Mr Ingle's forearm, Stecyk did so '(w/just a hint of Edwardian flourish to the top's four-loop bow ...)' (p. 420). One parenthetical bow (Wallace's) calls to another (the hard boy's); each archaic, the accessories emerge from an earlier epoch. We are reminded that for Karl Polanyi, historian of the gold standard, the Edwardian age of haute finance stood as the apogee of that instrument's application.[65] Stecyk's 'bow[s]', actual and misremembered, are 'Edwardian'. The 'new gold' is not the old gold, though a touch of nostalgia may yet persuade otherwise – 'hint[ing]', through 'distortion', that gilded risk, for all its risks, may yet be good as gold in serving as a sufficient standard in a neoliberal market gone notionally global.

To rehearse the risky logic of risk and Stecyk's place within it: if, care of deficits, all assets are perceived as tradable risk, risk becomes the preferred form of equivalence, through which persons and things must pass if they are to achieve financial apotheosis as commensurable assets in a deficit-driven marketplace. Entirely aptly, therefore, Foster Wallace, having passed through the suppressions of equivalency into the higher form of himself (Francis Wallace) has an appointment with the new supreme equivalent, Stecyk. Failing to meet in person they will meet in significantly phantasmal form. Much delayed in accessing the REC as Foster (though rushed through induction as Francis) Wallace, doubled and abstracted and yet still managing to miss his meeting with the Deputy Director of Personnel, finds himself not in Stecyk's office but, at alternate risk, in an 'electrical closet ... backed up against a warm series of circuit boxes' (p. 308, n67), being orally serviced by his escort, Miss Neti Neti.

Just as Cusk and Fogle experience their initiation into doubling during World Cultures classes, so Foster Wallace enters his apogee care of she who – under 'the sobriquet "Iranian Crisis"' (p. 308, n67) – further evidences the reach of equivalency from core to periphery. She who fellates does so, we are told, because to one who came of 'economic age' in the 'euphemism intensive culture' of pre-revolutionary Iran, the instruction that she 'extend every courtesy' to the incoming recruit recalls the necessity that those who sought to leave Iran, during the last days of the Shah's regime, should 'barter' sexual for political favours (p. 308). Enlarging the context, even as Neti Neti's names enlarge the implications of her mouth-work, we would note, on the basis of Wallace's annotations (pp. 307–8, n67), that Carter's Iranian Crisis involved more than the release or non-release of hostages. The USA funded the Shah's regime, returns on which deficit-based investment required the extraction not simply of the Shah and his supporters, but of their capital accumulations. We are told only that Neti Neti's oral service to 'high-level functionaries' enabled her to 'get herself and two or three other members of her family out of Iran' (p. 308); no mention of property occurs. Likewise in the cases of Bondurant and Ingle, Wallace's insistence that the implication of local arterial flows has global provenance may well stop short of full economic extrapolation. Bondurant learns 'requisition write-up accounting' in Vietnam: 'to requisition' typically means, 'to require that a thing (good or service) be furnished for military purpose', though in the offered context of 1971, accounting for US military requisitions readily extends those bids to new forms of imperial demand – a reach surely exhibited by the angle of Ingle's severed thumb, 'hung by a flap of dermis ... [and] pointed straight down in a parody of imperial judgement' (p. 420). That Wallace does not fully articulate the 'judgement' – re. Bondurant, Ingle or Neti Neti – reflects the seriousness of his commitment both to the phenomenology of the new abstraction and to its historicity.[66]

Yet even as Neti Neti's nickname winds the world around Foster Wallace's member, her proper name (duplicating the doubling of his) catches with exactitude the quality of the orgasm she administers. Translated from the Sanskrit, 'Neti Neti' means 'not this ... not this', or alternatively, 'neither this nor that': within Hinduism (and more particularly the Vedic tradition) the 'neti neti search' involves a systematic negation of body and concept in the achievement of a true 'I', at one with the Brahman or Absolute. Transposed to Peorian imperatives, the goal of such a search might be seen as exemplified by Drinion's union with the

1040 form. Both translations of the phrase apply to Foster Wallace's pleasure in the place of circuitry: although his physical body manifestly remains, it does so as a function of his abstract body; both bodies, therefore, emerge and recede, each 'not this', yet each equally 'neither this nor that'. On leaving the cupboard, Foster Wallace observes Neti Neti's 'breasts' shapes against the damp corduroy of [his] upper legs' (p. 308, n67). Sylvanshine's 'abstract tits', registered in Cusk's abstract sweat, would seem to lend abstraction to Foster Wallace's semen as it hangs – necessarily non-seminal and non-nutritive – in the air before Neti Neti's face, withdrawn 'to a receptive distance that seemed, in that charged instant, much farther away than it really could have been, realistically speaking' (p. 309) at the close of section 24.

'Realistically speaking', in terms of a realism sensitive to financial imperatives, Wallace does not come in or near Neti Neti's mouth. Rather, he reaches orgasm care of the meeting of two faces in one. While closeted and subject to Neti Neti's attentions, Foster Wallace recalls a glance exchanged earlier with Stecyk, the extended circumstances of which glance replicate his own circumstances in the closet: 'the soft, bureaucratically mod face [of Stecyk] ... kept obtruding on ... [Foster Wallace's] mind's eye in the darkness of the electrical closet as the Iranian Crisis's forehead impacted ... [his] abdomen' (p. 309). We receive an account of Neti Neti's ministration only as a footnote (note 67) to a 'highly charged glance', passing between Foster Wallace and Stecyk. As the former waits to meet the Deputy Director of Personnel, Stecyk's office door being briefly and 'partly open', Foster Wallace sees what he should not, a sight that Stecyk's 'loathsome secretary' censors by emphatically shutting the door (p. 308). We would stress that the reading that follows results from our tracing of a sustained network of innuendo, whose connotative evidence can only and ever strain, through accumulation, towards a denotative moment of literal sight, which sight (the event in the room) such connotation may only and equally defer.[67] Accordingly, Foster Wallace prefaces his glance diagrammatically, as occurring while he looked past two 'turdnagels' (or low-grade IRS Support staff [p. 305, n63]), as though, that is, 'looking past them at something else', and therefore 'at an extension of the angle over the shoulder of the nagel who denied having been obtuse' (p. 306). The turdnagels in question engage in a dispute over which of them is the more 'obtuse': 'nagel', released from 'turd' and prompted by 'obtuse', takes anagramic form as 'angle', only for the 'turd' in the REC to haunt its abbreviation, though not for long ... given where the look leads. Foster Wallace sees Stecyk, seemingly 'squatting on his haunches', fellating 'another' and 'weeping' man, seated and 'hunched forward with his face in his hands' (p. 307). The event is not clear;

identities are occluded. Given what perhaps happens in the Deputy Director of Personnel's office, and since Stecyk's nickname is Sir John Feelgood (p. 304), while that of his Director, Richard Tate (whose work he largely does), is 'dicktation' (note 31, p. 279), we might assume – in accord with the passage's pervasive spirit of innuendo – that even as Stecyk takes 'dicktation' into his mouth in the main text, so Neti Neti takes Foster Wallace into her mouth among the notes, doing so exactly as her subject, waiting at the conjunction of 'three narrow hallways' (n67), recalls glancing into the Deputy Director of Personnel's (DDP's) office.

The lengthy note 67 offers the first glimpse of Neti Neti's oral generosity. Set within Foster Wallace's account of his glance, exchanged with Stecyk as Stecyk ministers to Tate, the note effects a double interruption, or species of jump-cut, serving to make literal what Foster Wallace calls, at the note's close, 'the "cluster-fuck" of my first several days as an IRS immersive' (p. 308). Given our claim that Stecyk fellates Tate, it is worth further noticing that Sir John Feelgood refers to a Muppet. Supposedly modelled on Sir John Gielgud, the Muppet teaches the delights of grandiloquence; which is to say, he delivers by mouth. Oral satisfaction, whether rhetorical or erotic, carries a homosexual inference in the suggestion that a male puppet and DDP gratifies (hand up the back of ...) his male puppet-Director of Personnel by taking his words (dick/dictation) into his mouth, prior to recasting them. We belabour a pun to catch how Wallace's innuendo renders semen inextricable from verbiage. Indeed, one might argue that the run of his puns towards dirty talk puts such talk (a species of critical Tourettes) in the place of semen: an apt displacement, given that the mouths that suck belong to a financial manager and to one of his workers, both presumably adept in the medium of their labour, deficit finance or capital as in no small part an exercise in rhetorical excess. Christian Marazzi argues that, in the post-Fordist workings of financial markets, underlier-absence grants financial language a 'bodiless self-referentiality', whereby the collective force of a data-based assumption 'create[s] facts by speaking them'.[68]

Who or what, 'realistically speaking' satisfies Foster Wallace? His satisfaction, whether occurring in the closet, the DDP's office, or both, is to say the least 'risky', a quality that lodges it securely within Stecyk's purview. But why should an orally delivered pleasure conclude Foster Wallace's induction into the alternate body of a newly embodied IRS? 'Receptive distance' measures the degree of Neti Neti's withdrawal: announced as the focal point of a memory, identified by Foster Wallace as 'one of the most vivid [and] sensuous' of his induction day (p. 308, n67), the designated distance at which Foster Wallace spends himself might be read as what is known in the pornography industry as a 'money'.

The money shot, tennis, and suicide

Because Stecyk manages workers whose bodies Wallace likens to money, he manages something like a portfolio of financial assets. But it also makes sense to think of this director of personnel as a director of pornography, one who – as feminists from Gayle Rubin to Leopoldina Fortunati and Maria Mies point out in the context of sex work – extracts value from women's bodies by, in effect, converting those bodies into money. Seen this way, Stecyk is a pornographer when converting his employees into money, and a financier when managing the money those employees have become.

D. T. Max tells us that *The Pale King* began as a novel about pornography. That book was to be called 'Sir John Feelgood', and it was to have chronicled the adventures of an IRS agent, also named Drinion, who acts in X-rated films:

> The conceit is that Drinion is so slight, so ethereal, that, by using overlay technology, other men can superimpose their image on his. The only thing more erotic than watching another man having sex with a porn star, supposes Wallace, reasonably enough, is watching yourself do it. It seems a lonely kind of ecstasy, to be sure, pleasuring oneself as one's image does the same on a TV screen. And for Drinion, watching his own sexual act be erased by another man's, it's even lonelier. But, as Wallace notes, 'every love story is a ghost story'.[69]

Here we find another version of the self-doubling so important to *The Pale King*, in which characters engender abstract equivalents of themselves, and become thereby objects of exchange. And yet, as we have insisted throughout, Wallace's bodies are never fully abstract – they are a form of money that, to recall Marx, invariably 'leaves behind a precipitate'. The semen elicited from Foster Wallace by Neti Neti (in a moment of sex work initiated by Stecyk) is 'neither this nor that' (just as Wallace's fictional bodies, 'both flesh and not', are neither simply concrete nor simply abstract). Moreover, it is neither this nor that in a particular way: like the blood, urine, sweat, and shit that courses through Stecyk's workers (likened by Wallace to financial flows), Foster Wallace's semen figures the contradictory structure of personhood called forth by a system of derivatives.

Let us then freeze that semen, in mid-flight, to learn what Wallace himself wrote about derivatives, about what it means to live with them inside, and even by extension, what it means to think of pornography and finance as closely related endeavours. We leave Foster Wallace's semen suspended for a moment in air, just as Wallace leaves Drinion levitating. We do so to make a leap of our own; the leap, though tasteless, is, we believe, required by the logic of the novel. For Drinion suspended in the air, read David Foster Wallace hanged. The hanged man, rendered weightless by his literary correlate (having himself 'disappeared' into the 'system' that is *The Pale King*, in the guise of Foster Wallace) floats, suspended. Thus arrested, these buoyant physical forms (semen, Drinion, Wallace doubled) seem to lose their mass and, no longer solid, melt into air, or float upon it, within a financial bubble (about to burst).

As Wallace might have pointed out, capturing bodies in motion, and ascertaining the rate and trajectory of their movement, requires derivatives, mathematical functions that appear with frequency in his fiction and non-fiction, typically in their capacity to measure rates of change. Derivatives are implicit in the short story 'Good Old Neon', for example – in which the narrator asks, 'if time is passing, how fast is it going? At what rate does the present change?' They are explicit in Wallace's effort to explain, in *Everything and More*, 'motion at an instant', and the 'precise velocity at an instant, not to mention rate-of-change-in-velocity at an instant (= acceleration, 2nd derivative), rate-of-change-in-acceleration at an instant (= 3rd derivative), etc.' Determining 'motion at an instant', Wallace further informs us, requires determining 'the rate of change of a function w/r/t an independent variable'.[70] A serviceable definition of the derivative, to be sure, but we do not read Wallace for the mathematics alone.

Even here, in his treatise on mathematics, Wallace gives the derivative a sexual inflection, describing it as 'The McGuffin of differential calc. In sexual terms, it's an expression of the rate of change of a function with respect to the function's independent variable' (p. 116). A McGuffin is an often-elusive object of desire that catalyses narrative. The Rosebud sled in *Citizen Kane*, the glowing briefcase in *Pulp Fiction*: these objects do not resolve plot so much as they propel characters into dynamic relations with other characters. Perhaps, in some future and fully rationalised literary criticism, derivatives will quantify that propulsion. Derivatives measure how much one quantity is changing in response to changes in some other quantity; perhaps some day they will calculate how much a given fictional character changes in response to changes in another, or in the objects desired by that character. Financiers use mathematical derivatives to measure and place bets (with financial derivatives) on how much the price of, say, widgets changes or might change as currency conversion rates change. Might a pornographer use derivatives in an analogous fashion, to mitigate the risk of audience boredom? Might he quantify the changes produced in one body by changes in another, and thereby securitise his cast of characters? Since capital markets seem keen to apply derivatives to an ever-expanding array of relationships, with an eagerness that has made those instruments famously difficult to define or delimit, we might fairly assume the future emergence of exchanges for trading pornography contracts.[71] Indeed, for Matthew Goldstein, writing for *Reuters* in 2009, financial derivatives are finally only definable in relation to pornography. Sceptical about the Obama Administration's plans to regulate derivative trading, and about Geithner's promise to 'propose a broad definition of a standard derivative that will be difficult for banks to "evade" by putting so many bells and whistles on a transaction that it becomes a non-standard derivative', Goldstein suggests that 'even the bankers who create these exotic financial instruments often can't come to an agreement on what separates a plain vanilla derivative from a more unique transaction'. It is near impossible, he thinks, to do better than Supreme Court Justice Potter Stewart's 1964 definition of pornography: 'I know it when I see it.'[72]

Equal parts pornographer and financier, Wallace would render that object of sight strange and unfamiliar. At moments, he asks us to see bodies in the graphs and equations that represent mathematical derivatives. In *Infinite Jest*, Mikey tutors Inc in preparation for an exam. 'The derivative's the slope of the tangent at some point along the function,' he says. 'Derivatives're just trig with some imagination. You imagine the points moving inexorably towards each other until for all practical purposes they're the same point. The slope of a defined line becomes the slope of a tangent to one point.' If one can picture these converging lines, understanding derivatives would be, Mikey concludes, 'a big pink titty', by which he means no problem at all.[73] His colourful metaphor recalls Sylvanshine's 'abstract tits': it likens sloping lines on a graph to those that might define a woman's breast, even as it locates that now deracinated and abstract tit in an imagination subject to mathematical manipulation. At other moments, Wallace asks us to grasp the more contradictory manner in which three-dimensional and concrete bodies live within the forms of calculation proper to derivatives. Indeed, in one of his most accomplished essays, he asks us to see his own body as defined by that calculation – as suspended in the air, though only briefly, and for a moment, in an almost imaginary mathematical space.

'Derivative Sport in Tornado Alley' (1990) describes the effects on Wallace of having 'grown up inside vectors, lines and lines athwart lines, grids'.[74] Raised in a part of the Midwest 'informed and deformed by wind', an area referred to by scientists as a 'Thermal Anomaly' (p. 5), the mathematically inclined Wallace learns to master the wind, and becomes, between the ages of 12 and 15, a 'near great' (p. 3) tennis player. Playing tennis in his wind-defined environment

> requires geometric thinking, the ability to calculate not merely your own angles but the angles of responses to your angles. Because the expansion of response-possibilities is quadratic, you are required to think n shots ahead, where n is a hyperbolic function limited by the sinh of opponent's talent and the cosh of the number of shots in the rally so far (roughly). (p. 9)

Playing in Tornado Alley thus requires 'a jones for mathematics' (p. 3), but as the slang term 'jones' suggests, it also requires, he insists, 'imagination' (p. 10), of an implicitly sexual kind.

The erratic winds that buffet Wallace recall him to a conflicted adolescent body, both real and abstract. As Wallace and his competition get older, he loses his edge to bigger and stronger players; he is left behind in the onrush of puberty, for which the tumultuous windstorms and tornados of his region provide an objective correlative. 'This was the time,' Wallace recalls, 'when I discovered definite integrals and antiderivatives and found my identity shifting from jock to math-wienie' (p. 14). No longer able to master the wind with calculation, his body atrophies relative to those around him: his sexual diminution, from jock to wienie, accompanies the transition from court to classroom, even as it enforces a new distinction between physical and mental space. Wallace figures this transition in the final pages of his essay, during which he recalls the one time he experienced something like a tornado. Playing tennis, he and a companion feel the shockwave of an onrushing wind, and become akin to tennis balls. 'The big, heavy swings on the industrial swing sets took off, wrapping themselves in their chains around and around the top crossbar.' Wallace takes off as well; he tries to run, and is instead launched into the air, his feet 'not once touching the ground over fifty-odd feet, a cartoon' (p. 19). In flight, he becomes, again, a character who lives within imaginary lines, a cartoon, until he is thrown violently against a cyclone fence. Brought down to earth, he has made a different kind of cartoon, branded with the grid-like markings that define his region of the Midwest, the fence's 'quadrangular lines impressed' (p. 20) on his face, torso, and legs. The abstract has become concrete, as his body is exiled from theoretical space. His brief moment of flight, he perceives in retrospect, represents the apogee of his tennis career, before he is made to feel the full force of his body's limits.

The Midwestern terrain towards which Wallace falls reminds him, at an earlier moment in 'Derivative Sport', of the board game 'Monopoly' (p. 6). Seventeen years after the publication of that essay, the 2007 financial crisis just getting underway, it would seem that the buying and selling of real estate in the USA had become a game of Monopoly writ large, transacted with cartoon-like paper money whose ostensible worth bore no clear relation to underlying values. At the onset of that crisis, to the very day, David Foster Wallace climbed onto a chair in his suburban home and, like his namesake in 'Derivative Sport', fell through the air. Wallace had struggled for years with depression exacerbated by his inability to finish an unfinishable novel. We might understand that depression over and beyond its biochemical origins. Many of the novel's IRS agents, argues D.T. Max, 'contained identifiable parts of the real Wallace'.[75] *The Pale King* breaks Wallace into fragments, each character a refraction of the novelist who presents himself to us as the 'real author, the living human holding the pencil', not to be confused with its 'abstract narrative persona', the 'pro forma ... entity that exists just for legal and commercial purposes, rather like a corporation'. The editorial prospect of gathering these fragments together and assembling them against or in the face of Wallace's ruin was no doubt daunting, suggesting as it must have the need for an egoic literary form, possessed of great binding power.

Then again, perhaps Wallace wanted, instead, a mathematical literary form, powerful enough to calculate the intangible excess that attaches to unity, the value beyond simple addition that makes a whole greater than the sum of its parts. But, understood on its own terms, the novel's model for integration is financial more than psychoanalytic; it addresses the attenuation of the psychological via equivalency, even as it concerns itself with how to represent or itself approximate a mechanism capable of transforming people – and, ultimately, the novel and the novelist himself – into fungible financial data. All we can know for sure is that the 'real' author having passed into the pro forma entity that became *The Pale King* (abstracted thereby into some more purely exchangeable form), Marx's precipitate remained: a no longer 'living' or 'human' body. Wallace printed out the manuscript of his novel just before he hanged himself, and left it another room, a light shining upon it.[76] His gesture at least implies a conscious analogy, a mirroring of the body in the air and the body in the text. Put bluntly, the positioning of the body in relation to the text anticipates the body's annotation by way of the text. To suggest as much is potentially tasteless; not to suggest so sets aside the eleven years of authorial labour during which David Foster Wallace worked at issues of corporeality within a changing corporate state dedicated to the principles of risk inherent in the derivative. Whether critics who imagine it their business to adjudicate aesthetic merit deem the resulting work a living thing or a corporate entity hardly matters. Readers might doubt our inclination to view the published manuscript, in conjunction with the typescript, as 'a temporary and flexible coalescence of assets', to be scrutinised for alternate combinations by an editor acting in the manner of a derivative trader, the better to realise 'the value of its component pieces' through the price of the new edition.[77] Whatever the verdict, we would insist that *The Pale King* was not simply difficult but impossible to finish – its volatile contradictions belonging both to Wallace and to the phase of finance capitalism that he sought to anatomise.

University of California, Irvine

Notes

1 http://www.newyorker.com/reporting/2009/09/21/090921fa_fact_stewart#ix zz2Pd03p6GA [Date accessed: 14 October 2013].
2 http://www.nytimes.com/2008/10/02/business/02crisis.html?pagewanted=all &_r=0 [Date accessed: 14 October 2013].
3 David Foster Wallace, *The Pale King: An Unfinished Novel* (New York: Little, Brown and Company, 2011), pp. 107, 113, 144; hereafter cited in text. On Wallace and the Reagan tax code, see Marshall Boswell, 'Trickle Down Citizenship: Taxes and Civic Responsibility in Wallace's *The Pale King*', *Studies in the Novel*, 44.4 (Winter 2012), pp. 464–9.
4 For an elaboration of this position in relation to 'chartalist' thought, see Stephanie Bell, 'The Role of the State and the Hierarchy of Money', *Cambridge Journal of Economics* 25 (2001):

> Only the state, through its power to make and enforce tax laws, can make promises that its constituents must accept if they are to avoid penalties. The general acceptability of both state and bank money derives from their usefulness in settling tax and other liabilities to the state. This ... enables them to circulate widely as means of payment and media of exchange. The debts ['money'] of households and businesses are accepted because of their convertibility (at least potentially) into relatively more acceptable promises. These debts are not accepted at state payment offices and, thus, are not likely to become widely accepted means of payment. (p. 161)

5 Cited in Dick Bryan and Michael Rafferty, *Capitalism with Derivatives: A Political Economy of Financial Derivatives, Capital and Class* (London: Palgrave, 2006), p. 7.
6 Ibid., p. 133.
7 Randy Martin, *The Financialization of Daily Life* (Philadelphia: Temple University Press, 2002), pp. 3, 130. As Martin puts it, 'fixed debt ... [could be turned] into a promissory note of credit that could be turned over and reinvested as infinitely exchangeable bonds, futures ... and other financial niceties '. Martin, *An Empire of Indifference: American War and the Financial Logic of Risk Management* (Durham, NC: Duke University Press, 2007), p. 28.

8 From this point on, we will refer to the character as 'Foster Wallace' and to the author as 'Wallace', using the full authorial name 'David Foster Wallace' only where the distinction between author/character is otherwise unclear.

9 Karl Marx, *Capital*, Vol. 1, trans. Ben Fowkes (London: Penguin, 1990), p. 149. Hereafter cited in text.

10 The translation is Michael Heinrich's, and more accurate than the commonly accepted 'transcends sensuousness'; see Heinrich, *An Introduction to the Three Volumes of Marx's Capital*, trans. Alexander Locascio (New York: Monthly Review Press, 2004), p. 72.

11 Cited in Moishe Postone, *Time, Labor, and Social Domination: A Reinterpretation of Marx's Critical Theory* (Cambridge: Cambridge University Press, 1993), p. 56, n63.

12 Theodor Adorno and Walter Benjamin, *The Complete Correspondence, 1928–1940*, ed. Henri Lonitz, trans. Nicholas Walker (Cambridge, MA: Harvard University Press, 2001), p. 321.

13 Heinrich, *Introduction*, p. 63.

14 Ibid., p. 68.

15 Martin, *Empire of Indifference*, p. 24.

16 Quoted in Martin, *Empire of Indifference*, p. 20.

17 The regulation-school economist Michel Aglietta insists that without 'the social content of economic relations', we cannot interpret the forces and conflicts at work in the economic process. He adds that, 'production is always the production of social relations as well as material objects', a homily that applies equally to the production of less apparently material objects, such as futures, options, swaps or derivatives. See Aglietta, *A Theory of Capitalist Regulation: The U.S. Experience*, trans. David Fernbach (London: Verso, 1979), pp. 4, 24.

18 Robert Brenner, *The Boom and the Bubble: The U.S. in the World Economy* (London: Verso, 2002), see particularly, ch. 1, 'Persistent Stagnation: 1973–1993'.

19 Robert Brenner, 'Structure Vs Conjuncture: The 2006 Elections and the Rightward Shift', *New Left Review*, 43 (Jan–Feb 2007), pp. 41–2.

20 Giovanni Arrighi, *Adam Smith in Beijing: Lineages of the Twenty-First Century* (London: Verso, 2007), pp. 191–3.

21 Andrew Kliman, *The Failure of Capitalist Production: Underlying Causes for the Great Recession* (London: Pluto, 2012), p. 51.

22 Robert Brenner, *What Is Good for Goldman Sachs Is Good for America: The Origins of the Current Crisis*, Center for Social Theory and Comparative History (UCLA), 18 April 2009. (The text appears as the Prologue to the Spanish translation of the author's *Economics of Global Turbulence* [Verso, 2006], published by Akal, May 2009), pp. 12, 14, 36.

23 David Graeber, *Debt: The First 5,000 Years* (New York: Melville House, 2011), p. 369. See also Martin, *Empire of Indifference*, p. 28. In 2005, David Harvey noted the foreign ownership of nearly one third of stock assets on Wall Street, and one half of US Treasury bonds; he added, 'much of neoliberal financialization has become fragile and fictitious', *A Brief History of Neoliberalism* (Oxford: Oxford University Press, 2005), p. 193.

24 Brenner, *What Is Good for Goldman Sachs*, pp. 24, 38.
25 Martin, *Empire of Indifference*, p. 31.
26 Karl Marx, *Capital*, Vol. 3 (New York: Cosimo, 2007), pp. 460–2.
27 Martin, *Empire of Indifference*, p. 57.
28 Martin, *Financialization*, p. 23.
29 Karl Marx quoted by David Harvey, *The Limits to Capital* (Oxford: Blackwell, 1982), p. 269.
30 Ferdinand Braudel, *Civilization and Capitalism, 15th-18th Century, Volume Three (The Perspective of the World)*, trans. Sian Reynolds (New York: Harper and Rowe, 1984), p. 246.
31 We adapt Marx's formula for the movement of 'fictitious capital' $(M-M^1-M^2)$. See *Capital*, Vol. 3, pp. 460–2.
32 See Kojin Karatani, *Transcritique: On Kant and Marx* (Cambridge: MIT Press, 2003), p. 154.
33 David Harvey, *The Condition of Postmodernity* (Oxford: Blackwell, 1997), p. 194.
34 Fredric Jameson, 'Culture and Finance Capital', *Critical Inquiry*, 24 (1997), p. 265.
35 Slovoj Žižek, *The Parallax View* (Cambridge: MIT Press, 2006), pp. 52–3.
36 Ibid., pp. 52, 53, 393, n67.
37 Suzanne De Brunhoff argues, paraphrasing Marx, that money possesses three prevalent and contradictory functions, as price (or means to commensurability), as liquidity (or credit), and the supreme equivalence (or a storable essence, most typically gold). De Brunhoff, *Marx on Money*, trans. M.J. Goldblum (New York: Urizen, 1973), pp. 19–47. For 'promise of use', see Wolfgang Haug, *Critique of Commodity Aesthetics* (Oxford: Polity Press, 1986), p. 17.
38 Postone, *Time, Labor, and Social Domination*, pp. 52, 88.
39 Christian Marazzi, *Capital and Language: From the New Economy to the War Economy*, trans. Gregory Conti (Los Angeles: Semiotext(e), 2008), pp. 21, 24.
40 Bryan and Rafferty argue that current globalisation, though seeming to operate in the absence of 'a formally recognized monetary anchor' (be it gold or the US dollar as hegemonic norm), finds in the derivative (as a measure of risk, of which more later) its 'flexible gold', or means by which 'capitals manage their exposure to financial instability', operating 'as if the global financial system were stable '. See Bryan and Rafferty, *Capitalism with Derivatives*, pp. 105, 133–4.
41 Nicholas Shaxson notes that 'the offshore world is the biggest force for shifting wealth and power from poor to rich in history, yet its effects have been almost invisible' (*Treasure Islands: Tax Havens and the Men Who Stole the World* [London: Bodley Head, 2011], p. 28). Ronen Palan adds that 'due to opacity of tax havens, with their bank secrecy laws ... no one truly knows the size of the phenomenon', though (circa 2003) the US IRS estimated that between one and two million Americans used offshore credit and debit accounts (*The Offshore World, Sovereign Markets, Virtual Places and Nomad Millionaires* [Ithaca, NY: Cornell University Press, 2006], p. 46).
42 See Zygmunt Bauman, *Liquid Modernity* (London: Polity Press, 2000). See also Moishe Postone, 'Anti-semitism and National Socialism', collected in

Germans and Jews since the Holocaust, ed. A. Rabinbach and J. Zipes (New York: Holmes and Meiser, 1986), pp. 302–14.

43 Marx, *Capital*, Vol. 3, p. 461.

44 Marazzi, *Capital and Language*, pp. 24, 26, 33, 40. See Brenner, *What' Is Good for Goldman Sachs*, p. 1.

45

> There was no real check on how far this circular flow could go. For under-standable reasons foreign central banks did not wish to go into the U.S. stock market and buy Chrysler, Penn Central or other corporate securities. This would have posed the kind of risk central bankers are not supposed to take. Nor was real estate any more attractive. What central banks need are liquidity and security in their central reserves. This was why they had tra-ditionally held gold, as a means of settling their own deficits. To the extent that they began to accumulate surplus dollars, there was little alterna-tive but to hold them in the form of U.S. Treasury bills and notes without limit. (Michael Hudson, *Super Imperialism: The Origins and Fundamentals of U.S. World Domination* [London: Pluto, 2003], pp. 17, 23, 17)

See also page 21 for a graph indicating an exponential rise in the ownership of US public debt as financed by foreign central banks.

46 Marx, *Capital*, Vol. 3, pp. 460–4.

47

> A note from chapter 22 suggests that Chris Fogle knows a string of numbers that, when recited, give him the power of total concentration, but nowhere in the chapters we have does Fogle display this power. Perhaps this ability is the reason Fogle has been summoned to meet Lehrl in chapter 49. (Michael Pietsch [editor], p. 539)

48 Our account of Drinion's 'hum' depends heavily on Garrett Stewart's exemp-lary exploration of 'the reading body' in its response to the 'micro linguistic '. See Stewart, *Reading Voices: Literature and the Phonotext* (Berkley: University of California Press, 1990), particularly 'Prologue' (pp. 1–34) and ch. 4, 'The Ear Heretical' (pp. 100–41).

49 We borrow a form of words from Geoffrey Hill, 'Rhetorics of Value and Intrinsic Value', *Collective Critical Writings, Geoffrey Hill*, ed. Kenneth Haynes (Oxford: Oxford University Press, 2008), p. 477.

50 Alfred Sohn-Rethel, *Intellectual and Manual Labour: A Critique of Epistemology* (London: MacMillan, 1978), p. 20. See also Alberto Toscano, 'The Open Secret of Real Abstraction', *Rethinking Marxism: A Journal of Economics, Culture and Society*, 20.2 (2008), pp. 273–87.

51 Max Haiven, 'Finance as Capital's Imagination: Reimagining Value and Culture in an Age of Fictitious Capital and Crisis', *Social Text*, 108 29.3 (Fall 2011), p. 116.

52 Martin, *Empire of Indifference*, p. 93. Martin also speaks of 'economic self-management'.

53 Paul Ricoeur, 'The Metaphoric Process as Cognition, Imagination, and Feeling', *Critical Inquiry*, 5 (1978), p. 145. For a fuller account of the relation between metaphor and money, see Richard Godden, 'Labor, Language and Finance Capital', *PMLA*, 126.2 (March 2011), pp. 412–21, and David McNally, *Monsters of the Market* (Leiden: Brill, 2011), pp. 119–21.

54 Fredric Jameson, *Representing Capital: A Reading of Volume I* (London: Verso, 2011), pp. 20–1.

55 Jameson's point, recast via Ricoeur on metaphor, translates the bid for equivalency into that moment when the tension involved in 'seeing relationally' gives way to 'seeing as' (Ricoeur) or an act of substitution, whereby money (or the optic of metaphor-denied) displaces that which it prices, yielding capitalist realism.

56 Martin, *Empire of Indifference*, p. 11.

57 Edward LiPuma and Benjamin Lee, *Financial Derivatives and the Globalization of Risk* (Durham, NC: Duke University Press, 2004), p. 105.

58 Michael Pryke and John Allen, 'Monetized Time-Space: Derivatives – Money's New Imaginary', *Economy and Society*, 29.2 (May 2000), p. 280. Bryan and Rafferty, *Capitalism with Derivatives*, p. 13.

59 James A. Clifton, 'Competition and the Evolution of the Capitalist Mode of Production', *Cambridge Journal of Economics*, 1 (1977), p. 148. Since service to the financial pools lying at the structural core of a transformed corporate body increasingly necessitates the substitution of knowledge workers for industrial workers, and of information technology for knowledge workers (witness Lehrl), we may assume that corporate managers, increasingly caught up in the need to co-ordinate 'an ever-more-complex-and-hurried command and control network' (Joshua Clover, 'Value Theory Crisis', *PMLA*, 127.1 [Jan 2012], pp. 107–14), become directors of Personnel, dedicated neither to production nor finance, but to the processing of more and less autonomous instruments for the extraction of credit from deficit.

60 Kliman, *Failure of Capitalist Production*, p. 24. Kliman points out that during the first two years following the collapse of Lehman Brothers, the total debt of the US Treasury increased by 40 per cent, a sum equivalent to a personal debt of $12,500 per US citizen. The yearly value of financial derivatives stood at $100 million in 1980 and $100 billion in 1990; the estimated values of derivatives approached $100 trillion in 2000, when some 1.5 billion contracts were traded. Such figures offer some measure of the pervasion of risk throughout the financial system. See LiPuma and Lee, *Financial Derivatives*, pp. 47–8.

61 Bryan and Rafferty, *Capitalism with Derivatives*, pp. 15, 131. See also, ch. 5, 'Anchoring the Global System', pp. 105–34.

62 Ibid., p. 13.

63 Ibid., p. 15.

64 Ibid., p. 36.

65 Karl Polanyi, *The Great Transformation: The Political and Economic Origins of Our Time* (Boston, MA: Beacon Press, 2001), pp. 3–20, 61–127. See also Giovanni Arrighi, *The Long 20th Century* (London: Verso, 2002), p. 269.

66 As T.J. Clark puts it, writing of 'the most intense materialists – Poussin, Valas-
quez, Vermeer, Cezanne' –

> it would not be bearable, for human subjects, to have the world offer itself
> every second as a fully material thing, a constant proximity, a presence, a
> place of mere events, all of them physically impinging on us – part of us,
> touching us, winding themselves into our subjectivity. Materialism, in
> this sense, is a great and intolerable vision. (T.J. Clark, *The Sight of
> Death: An Experiment in Art Writing* [New Haven, CT: Yale University
> Press, 2006], p. 237)

67 We depend heavily on D.A. Miller's account of innuendo. See his, 'Anal
Rope', *Representations*, 32 (Fall 1990), pp. 114–33.
68 Marazzi, *Capital and Language*, p. 33. For his full argument, see pp. 22–35.
69 http://www.newyorker.com/books/page-turner/d-f-w-tracing-the-ghostly-
origins-of-a-phrase [Date accessed: 14 September 2013]. Wallace claimed that
Terminator 2 inaugurated 'a new genre of big-budget film: Special Effects
Porn'. The movie is porn, he writes,

> because, if you substitute F/X for intercourse, the parallels between the two
> genres become so obvious they're eerie. 'Just like hard-core cheapies, movies
> like *Terminator 2* and *Jurassic Park* aren't really "movies", in the standard
> sense at all. What they really are is half a dozen or so isolated, spectacular
> scenes – scenes comprising maybe twenty or thirty minutes of riveting, sen-
> suous payoff – strung together via another sixty to ninety minutes of flat,
> dead, and often hilariously insipid narrative.' (Wallace, 'The (As It Were)
> Seminal Importance of *Terminator 2*', in *Both Flesh and Not* [New York:
> Little Brown, 2012], p. 177)

See also Wallace's essay 'Big Red Son', on the porn industry's annual award
ceremony; collected in Wallace, *Consider the Lobster* (New York: Little
Brown, 2006), pp. 3–50.

70 Reference to 'Good Old Neon' from David Foster Wallace, *Oblivion*
(New York: Back Bay Books, 2004), p. 179; David Foster Wallace, *Everything
and More: A Compact History of Infinity* (New York: W.W. Norton, 2003), pp.
140, 149; hereafter cited in text.
71 As instruments designed to negotiate exposure to risk, derivatives amount to
forms of insurance and may be taken out against anything. The Chicago Mer-
cantile Exchange trades in weather futures; for a short time, in 2003, the Pen-
tagon opened a terrorism futures market. See Bryan and Rafferty, *Capitalism
with Derivatives*, pp. 1–16.
72 http://blogs.reuters.com/commentaries/2009/08/07/what-derivatives-porn-
have-in-common/ [Date accessed: 15 November 2013].
73 David Foster Wallace, *Infinite Jest* (New York: Back Bay Books, 2006), p.
1063.

74 David Foster Wallace, *A Supposedly Fun Thing I'll Never Do Again* (New York: Back Bay Books, 1998), p. 3; hereafter cited in text.

75 D.T. Max, *Every Love Story Is a Ghost Story: A Life of David Foster Wallace* (New York: Penguin, 2012), p. 293.

76 In the final hours of his life, biographer D.T. Max reports, Wallace

   had tidied up the manuscript so that his wife could find it. Below it, around it, inside his two computers, on old floppy disks in his drawers were hundreds of other pages – drafts, character sketches, notes to himself, fragments that had evaded his attempts to integrate them into the novel over the past decade. (See Max, *Every Love Story Is a Ghost Story*, p. 301)

77 Bryan and Rafferty, *Capitalism with Derivatives*, pp. 96, 98.

Emily Apter

Shareholder existence: on the turn to numbers in recent
French theory

This essay takes stock of recent tendencies in French theory (from Alain
Badiou and Quentin Meillassoux to Bruno Latour, Frédéric Gros, and
Luc Boltanski) that focus on the metaphysics of financialisation. The
notion of shareholder existence, drafted from Gros' book on 'the security
principle', emphasises how experience has become comparable to an investment, stock option, or credit swap. This condition exceeds the familiar
notion of the self-interested individual who is constantly on the lookout
to extract money, social capital, or power through political manoeuvring.
The shareholder exceeds the character of the Machiavellian schemer, à la
Frank Underwood in *House of Cards*, who, by dint of cunning and calculated risk, becomes lethally adept at turning political setbacks to personal
advantage. Shareholder existence is modelled on the well-managed investment portfolio, in which the subject is at once the resource to be invested
and the accounts manager of the resource. By way of Meillassoux's reading
of Mallarmé's *Coup de dés*, the essay argues that the critique of this
phenomenon points to theories of unaccountable experience as the basis
for a new existentialism.

The increasing financialisation of every aspect of life is the presumptive precondition of what follows: a census-taking of salient tendencies in contemporary French theory that emphasise the existentialisation – one might go so far as to say metaphysics – of calculation and the count. I take my cue on this from a tranche of growing bibliography that includes Alain Badiou's *Mathematics of the Transcendental* [published only in English], Bruno Latour's *Enquête sur les modes d'existence* [An Inquiry Into Modes of Existence], Frederic Gros's *Le principe sécurité* [The Security Principle], Luc Boltanski's *Enigmes et complots: Une enquête à propos des enquêtes* [Enigmas and Conspiracies: An Investigation of Investigations], and Quentin Meillassoux's *Le nombre et la sirène. Un déchiffrage du Coup de dés de Mallarmé* [The Number and the Siren: A Decipherment of Mallarmé's *Coup de dés*].[1] To group these works and thinkers together is a stretch given their discrepant foci and approaches. But while they differ in genealogy, each may be seen to represent an iteration of French critical thought that continues in the vein of '68 theory, marked by Althusserian Marxism, structuralism and deconstruction'. Latour's latest work follows Foucault in charting fact/value distinctions within distributive spatio-temporal networks. Gros extends Foucauldian biopolitics beyond state security apparatuses to futural subjective investment strategies. Boltanski sees 'political metaphysics' in investigative consciousness and the hyper-vigilance to detail characteristic of detective fiction. In his work there are clear parallels to Foucault's tentacular, paranoid constructions of correctional architectures and postures of subjugation. Meillassoux echoes Badiou in his fascination with the 'numerological' Mallarmé, erecting him as the avatar of radical contingency.

These authors diverge to be sure, but what draws them into orbit is their common focus on calculated existence. This harks back to Georg Simmel's calculability of modernity in *The Philosophy of Money* and beyond that (and here I paraphrase Jason Barker glossing Althusser) to the way in which 'capitalist reproduction binds humanity to the scourge of calculated interest'.[2] Theories of the 'count' and punctualism – key concepts that surface often in this constellation of texts – lead me to the following hypothesis: that recent French theory is responsive to, if not unified around, a shared concern with what Badiou often refers to as 'the society of calculation', with its actuarial approach to experience and projections of managed life.

All published in the last decade, these texts were written in the context of neoliberalism's global economic crises, whose manifest scenarios, all too familiar for some time, include bank failures and insider trading, a spike in unemployment and unequal income distribution, a surge in subprime mortgage debt, the radical downgrading of credit and bond ratings for entire national economies, and extreme economic volatility (Shumpeter's 'creative destruction') treated as the natural way market equilibrium is righted. Is there some direct connection, one wonders, between market volatility and the 'mathematical turn' in theory? Certainly the themes of 'management', 'insecurity', and 'financial hazard' which underwrite the work of Latour, Gros, and Boltanski resonate with the condition of an emergent class that has been dubbed the economic *precariat* – the class of the socio-economically insecure – whose rallying movement has been 'Occupy', and whose galvanising texts have included Stéphane Hessel's *Indignéz-vous!* (2010), David Graeber's *Debt: The First 5000 Years* (2011), Maurizio Lazzarato's *The Making of the Indebted Man: An Essay on the Neoliberal Condition* (2011), and Franco 'Bifo' Berardi's *The Uprising: On Poetry and Finance* (2012). Graeber sees loan payments to rich nations as a tribute exacted on a permanently indentured underclass. He references the consistently villainous character of the moneylender in world literature – with Jews, the common surrogates – as the expression of a complex western value system that repudiates the creditor while subscribing to 'a sense of morality and justice' that reverts 'to the language of a business deal'.[3] Graeber challenges the myth that money is predicated on primitive barter by arguing that 'virtual money came first', and the logic of barter or what economists call 'the double coincidence of wants' came later (D 34). Nonetheless since Adam Smith, he reminds us, barter has been the prevailing model of thought and discursive interaction: 'Even logic and conversation', writes Graeber paraphrasing Smith, 'are really just forms of trading, and as in all things, humans will always try to seek their own best advantage, to seek the greatest profit they can from the exchange' (D 26). Where Graeber analyses barter as the pre-eminent form of reason, Maurizio Lazzarato, in *The Making of the Indebted Man*, portrays debt as a mode of being: 'Debt becomes a debt of existence, a debt of the existence of the subjects themselves. A time will come when the creditor has not yet lent while the debtor never quits repaying'.[4] Capitalism, he insists, 'has abandoned the epic narratives it constructed around the supposed freedom, innovation, and creativity of the entrepreneur, the knowledge society', and replaced them with narratives of self-servitude: 'of poor people charged with managing assistance and menial jobs, and labour conditions that entail greater dependency on institutions' (MIM 95). His Nietzschean genealogy of indebted man, hobbled by long hours, poor compensation, precarious employment, and diminished life expectancy, reads the debt economy as a form of social subjection and as the expression of a moribund capitalism's desperate effort to stay alive.

These works by Graeber and Lazzarato, alongside David Harvey's many incisive critiques of neoliberalism, are important counterparts to the French texts I listed at the beginning, their impress more significant in the Anglophone world than in France. But they highlight a problem that is also engaged with in recent French theory and which concerns how financialisation, informed by a long history of Marxism and post-Marxist economies of the subject, connects to what Christopher Nealon has described as the desire among key thinkers on the left to reorient a philosophy hitherto 'enmeshed in linguistic and literary problems' towards mathematical formalism.[5] Even if one remains sceptical of the hypothesis that the so-called mathematical turn effects a clean break with the linguistic turn (where semiotics, deconstruction, and close reading held sway), it seems evident that much contemporary French theory is engaged with reworking the Lacanian *matheme* and formalist ontology more generally. The harder call consists of working out the relation between numerical subjects and the 'quant' subjects of political economy.

Badiou distinguishes clearly between the uses of number in his preface to *Le nombre et les nombres* [Number and Numbers], a book published in 1990 shortly after *Being and Event*. Normally he devotes the big philosophical tomes to formal ontology (*Theory of the Subject, Being and Event, Logics of Worlds,* and the middle books on number in Plato's *Republic* which, in his free translation, he groups under the heading *Des mathématiques à la dialectique*) and the shorter polemical treatises to politics (*Metapolitics, Can One Think Politics?,* and *Circonstances*). But in *Number and Numbers* he considers them together:

> we live in the era of number's despotism; thought yields to the law of denumerable multiplicities; and yet (unless perhaps this very default, this failing, is only the obscure obverse of a concept-less submission) we have at our disposal no recent, active idea of what number is.

Underscoring this last point, he reiterates: 'But we don't know what a number is, so we don't know what we are'.[6] Badiou poses the pure mathematical number against 'numerical exegesis', that is, the number that

> governs our conception of the political, with the currency – consensual, though it enfeebles every politics of the thinkable – of suffrage, of opinion polls, of the majority. Every 'political' convocation, whether general or local, in polling-booth or parliament, municipal or international, is settled with a count. ... Political 'thought' is numerical exegesis. (NN 1–2)

As Peter Hallward notes, politics for Badiou represents 'the imperatives of communication and interest, of communal relations or links, of a mere [and here he cites Badiou's book on ethics] "preservation in being"'. The results are nefarious: truth, and thought are reduced to particular interests, interest groups, or, as Hallward notes as he cites these phrases from

Badiou's *Saint Paul et la foundation de l'universalisme* [Saint Paul and the Foundation of Universalism], 'subsets of the oppressed' that defer to the 'false universality of monetary abstraction', which Hallward qualifies as the 'undivided rule of capital'. Hallward glosses Badiou:

> There is no place for truth in such a world: culture takes the place of art, technology replaces science, management replaces politics, and sexuality replaces love. The resulting cluster, culture-technology-management-sexuality, is perfectly homogenous with the market it feeds.[7]

The grip of particularism and partitive identity may be impossible to escape, but it cannot entirely foreclose the idea of what Badiou calls 'a subject to truth' 'counted as one'. The 'count as one' (the English term commonly adopted to translate *Il y a de l'Un*) is an 'inexistent', that is, a non-appearing, subject whose presence is registered as a 'void in the situation'. Hallward explains it this way in relation to Badiou's arguments in *L'Etre et l'événement* [Being and Event]:

> The subject is inexistent, and yet, it is a one or part of a group of ones that are made to be: '*L'un n'est pas*' – There is no be-ing of the one – but '*Il y a de l'Un*,' a statement whose meaning might be best rendered as 'There is a One-*ing*.' The one is not, but there is an operation that 'one-ifies' or makes one. There is no one; there is only an operation that *counts* as one. (B 61)

Badiou's 'count as one' is qualified as a situational inconsistency that ensures that multiplicity can be, even if projected only as an invisible force field awaiting appearance. One can think of this 'count as one' as a manifestly unaccountable or non-accounted-for subject. In a book by Badiou that has only just come out, *Mathematics of the Transcendental: Onto-logy and Being-there* (a text conjoining two works published previously in neither French nor English, *Topos, or Logics of Onto-logy: An Introduction to Philosophers* and *Being-There: Mathematics of the Transcendental*), the theory of the subject is even more explicitly grounded in set theory and logic. Badiou, according to A.J. Bartlett and Alex Ling, 'subtract[s] "being itself" from ontology', referring to a discourse

> which prescribes the rules by which something can be presented or 'counted' as one – its sole operation being that of the count – and the 'one' thing that necessarily *fails* to be counted is nothing other than inconsistent multiplicity, or being itself.[8]

Subtractive, non-consensual, and multiple, the subject is an unaccountable number divorced from politics as usual. Extrapolating here, one could say that Badiou's *metapolitics* (which presupposes an unaccountable subject) stands against *metadata*, the newest currency of capital, fully congenial to the regime of capitalo-parliamentarianism. Badiou nicknames this regime 'Thermidor', or 'the long Restoration'; both refer to sequences characterised by the equation of interest and property; or more precisely, as Badiou puts it, 'the idea that every subjective demand has an interest at its core' (as cited by Hallward, B 28).

While Badiou and Foucault are rarely compared, one could say that Badiou's notion of the 'society of calculation' is not incompatible with Foucault's notion of the 'micro-physics of power', inasmuch as both endeavour to undo logics of interest and optimisation built into political orders. In *Surveiller et punir* [Discipline and Punish], Foucault derived this 'micro-physics of power' from the disciplinary regulation of time. In addition to religious orders, deemed by Foucault to be 'the great technicians of rhythm and regular activities', there was the army's 'chronometric measurement of shooting' and the labour management of a wage-earning class that necessitated a 'partitioning of time', techniques of 'time-management that optimised production and minimized time wasted'.[9] This temporal microphysics, complemented by a comparable spatial microphysics, is together constitutive of what Foucault called 'cellular power'.[10] Raymond Depardon's 2004 film *10e chambre, instants d'audience* [The Tenth Judicial Court: Judicial Hearings] seems plucked from Foucault's playbook. The film's title underscores the distribution of time and space. What comes through so palpably is how juridical subjects are *instantiated* through the application of statistical metrics of crime and punishment, which vary according to the judge's measure of comportment on the stand. The grandmother's testimony, in contrast with that of a male traffic violator who observes the courtroom protocols and is contrite to a fault, shows how behaviour and attitude are factored into judicial calculus. By trying to impose on the judge her personal measure of injustice, and by speaking out of turn, she throws her case disastrously off course. Her miscalculation of *kairos* (political timing) earns her a sentence disproportionately high for drunk driving, especially when compared to the lenient penalties meted out later in the film to wife-beaters and drug dealers.

In *An Inquiry into Modes of Existence*, Latour is similarly attuned to how impolitic timing derails politics: 'The principal infelicity condition of the political', he states, 'is to have its course *interrupted*'. Latour moves his 'anthropology of the moderns' into the ontological territory. He catalogues the micropolitics of systems of enunciation; the 'crab-wise moves' of the political mode associated with the Machiavellian 'Prince of twisted words'; the behaviour of corporate bodies; the way attachments fluctuate according to the 'temperature' of 'passionate interests'; and the 'astonishing immanence of organizations' in all facets of existence and expression.[11] In a chapter titled *Parler organisation dans sa langue*, Latour identifies 'a mode that asks what it means to act and to speak *organization-ally*'. Management-speak is not business lingo, but rather a direct expression of calculative *techne* (IME 389). The word 'stock ticker', pre-served as an English word in the French text, becomes a prime example of an object that transcribes 'economy with a small e'. It belongs to a class of objects

> through which economics transits: account books, balance sheets, pay stubs, statistical tools, trading rooms, Reuter screens, flowcharts, agendas, project management, software, automated sales of shares, in short, what we can group together under the expression ALLO-CATION KEYS, or under the invented term VALUE-METER [*valorimètre*]. (IME 406)

The stock ticker is the quintessential evaluative instrument, a 'measuring measure' (IME 408), a universal key 'with the function of distributing both *what* counts and *those* that count' (IME 406). It goes to the heart of the proprietary drive in possessive individualism ('This is mine') and points to

> an entangling of scripts and projects [that are] *measurable, accounta-ble, quantifiable,* and thus *calculable*: how [Latour queries] are we to allocate, distribute, share, coordinate? The scripts are still there, but *equipped with devices* that will necessarily produce quantitative data, as the stock ticker example shows. Without equipped scripts, such interweaving would be impossible: we are too numerous, there are too many quasi-objects and quasi subjects to put in series. ... We would get lost. (IME 408)

Adhering to his principled refusal to divide the worlds of things and humans, discrete objects, and processual phenomena ('without an appar-atus for calculating, no capacity for calculation'), Latour treats the stock ticker as a timer of the new existent, part-subject, part-object:

> The stock ticker does not measure prices in the sense of reference: it gives them rhythm and pace, it visualizes them, arranges them, accel-erates them, represents them, formats them in a way that brings to light both a new phenomenon – continuously fluctuating prices – and new observers and beneficiaries of these prices, new exchange 'agents,' new entities 'agenced' or 'agitated' by these new data. And

with each apparatus we see the emergence of both new (quasi) objects and new (quasi) subjects. (IME 408)

Latour's metrics of agency, his vision of stocks as a measure of modes of existence, complements Frédéric Gros's notion of 'shareholder existence'.

A political theorist who has edited Foucault's Collège de France lectures, Gros argues in *Le principe sécurité* that 'techniques of protection and control have put into motion logics of permanent solicitation, in contrast to the ancient ideal of interior stability'.[12] Gros maintains that 'biosecurity presumes constant vigilance, proper to maintaining the system at maximum tension, like a body that in order to stay alive must remain hyper-sensitive to its milieu' (PS 232). American neoliberalism, with its history of organisational complexes, has ushered in a new ontology, 'une managerisation des existences'. This brings in its train an even more specialised form of subjectivation that Gros dubs 'share-holder existence':

> Each subject is called on to report to him or herself as one might to a business, constructing a life like a series of investments that one counts on to make a profit. Finance capitalism encourages a shareholder-like existence (*une actionnarisation de l'existence*). Each entity, every individual becomes a financial agent (*un actif financier*), in a supporting role for speculation. The problem is no longer knowing one's price, but anticipating the arc of one's value. The securitization of identities, institutions, and businesses involves continuous processes of evaluation. At every moment there must be an accounting of the future in order to determine values and decisions in the present. This alienation of the present in the future may be found in inverted form in indebtedness. Whether it is household or state debt that is stake, indebtedness is the reverse of financial speculation insofar as the present engulfs the future. ... The future serves to pay down the expenses of the present. ... Individuals no longer have acquisitions, they define themselves instead by their capacity to alienate their future. (PS 236)

Gros, like Graeber and Lazzarato, situates debt and indebtedness as a condition of contemporary life pervading every small transaction and facet of thinking. Debt goes hand in hand with a market model in which you trade in futures (your own future), to cash out the present. There is a dramatic reshuffling of the progressive temporal blocks that divide the lifespan into past, present, and future. The future takes precedence over the past, and the present is either indebted to the future or part of its debt. Either way, life is financialised, whether as deficit or pay-it-forward.

For Gros, 'share-holder existence' makes experience fungible like an investment, stock option, or credit swap. In this case, we are well beyond the familiar notion of the self-interested individual who is constantly on the lookout to extract money, social capital, or power through political man-oeuvring. The shareholder exceeds the character of the Machiavellian schemer, à la Frank Underwood in *House of Cards*, who, by dint of cunning and calculated risk, becomes lethally adept at turning political set-backs to personal advantage. Shareholder existence is modelled on the well-managed investment portfolio, in which the subject is at once the resource to be invested and the accounts manager of the resource. Roland Barthes associ-ated this subjective mode with 'the daily grind' in his seminar on *La Prép-aration du roman*, complaining that the writing subject had been reduced to 'his own manager' and that life tailored to the 'ready-made box' involves 'counting against the tide', which is to say, remaining hyper-conscious of 'the use of Time Before Death' or 'Doing Time'.[13] Like Barthes, Gros emphasises 'managerization' as a kind of totalised subjectivity. Passing over the French term *gérance*, which implies a top-down administrative style characteristic of CEOs rather than existential optimisation, Gros aligns his 'security principle' with time management treated as no mere organisational best practice, but as a way of thinking 'actuarily' (risk assess-ment) and non-stop (always open for business). As Jonathan Crary observes in his recent book *24/7,*

> markets and a global infrastructure for continuous work and con-sumption have been in place for some time, but now a human subject is in the making to coincide with these more intensively. ... 24/7 announces a time without time, a time extracted from any material or identifiable demarcations, a time without sequence or recurrence. In its peremptory reductiveness, it celebrates a hallucina-tion of presence, of an unalterable permanence composed of inces-sant, frictionless operations.[14]

There is a parallel concern with managed life in Luc Boltanski's *Enigmes et complots: Une enquête à propos des enquêtes* [Enigmas and Con-spiracies: An Investigation of Investigations], but with a big difference: capitalism, as it emerges in the nineteenth century, is pitched against the nation-state. The 'volatility of fortunes' linked to the financial fluctuations of the stock market (*'les aléas de la finance'*) and the career meritocracy's shake-up of class entitlement destabilises the normative hierarchies that keep 'reality' in place.[15] The ascendency of detective and spy fiction in the nineteenth century is attributed by Boltanski to the nation-state's need to reassert control over capitalism by extending reason's mastery over the 'plasticity' of the external world (EC 49). The state tamps down anxiety around the 'reality of reality' by subjecting the unknown to a mass of fact-checking, mathematical calculation, and scientific analysis (and we must not forget that it is during Thermidor, year 11 of the republican calendar, that the numeration of French society acquires bureaucratic momentum, buoyed later by Napoleon I's introduction of numbered addresses and Louis-René Villermé's statistics on mortality rates in Paris) (EC 41). For Boltanski, investigative procedures, and the paranoid psychic disposition that can be fostered by them, belong to a larger process of securitisation and management. The representation of crime-solving also bolsters the state's desire to stimulate national *bildung* and national conscience. For Boltanski the *roman policier* and the *roman d'espionnage*, along with the journalistic *forme affaire* and *forme scandale* (which elicit strategies of spin and damage control), are constitutive of 'une métaphysique de la politique', 'a political metaphysics', that neutralises the revolutionary side effects of capitalism by making the enigma accountable to reality (EC 42).

In isolating the enigma as both symptom and target of investigative consciousness, Boltanski provides a thematic bridge to Quentin Meillassoux's *The Number and the Siren: A Decipherment of Mallarmé's Coup de dés,* a text that on first reading comes off as a set of the puzzle-game *Enigma* or a spy-worthy exercise in code-breaking. Meillassoux is, of course, not theorising the enigma as part of capitalism's threat to the society of control or nation-state. Neither Marx nor Foucault casts a shadow. The enigma grows out of the mysterious numbers that Mallarmé encrypted in *Le Livre* [The Book] and his poem *Un Coup de dés* [A Throw of the Dice]. For Meillassoux, the enigma matters because it helps to resolve the question of how to make pure Chance possible, a problem of 'divine inexistence' tackled in his as-yet unpublished 1997 thesis, and which contained the sentence: 'One can thus compare the free act to a throw of the dice. A throw of the dice never guarantees chance, but is that alone which makes chance possible'.[16] Meillassoux's goal is to free Number from Calculation, and to this end he sets out to rescue the 'advent *ex nihilo*' from frequential law; from necessitarianism and the causal overdeterminism of the Principle of Sufficient Reason.[17]

In *The Number and the Siren*, Meillassoux explicates the procedure of encryption housed within Mallarmé's famous 1898 poem. He argues that the poem is coded and that to decode it is a condition of elucidating the workings of its 'Unique Number', which in turn proves that 'Mallarmé never renounced – in principle, anyway – the calculative project of the Book'[18] (NS 6, 9). The code of *Un Coup de dés* is demonstrably indebted to calculations found in Mallarmé's notes on *Le Livre,* an unfinished life-work commenced in 1855, projected as a five-volume project in 1866, then slimmed down to a volume of verse and prose poems in 1867. Hailed by

Roland Barthes as a premier example of the 'Book-as-Guide' ('the unique, possibly secret book that directs the life of a subject'), it contains an array of opaque computations, including instructions for the seating chart at spirit-channelling séances that Mallarmé planned for posthumous communications with his friends.

Meillassoux locates part of the key to *Coup de dés*' secret calculation in the poet's program for 'an absolute Literature of elementary arithmetical operations concerning all possible aspects of the publication and the public reading of the Book' that would have 'a purely symbolic rather than utilitarian meaning' (NS 6). The Master of the poem 'infers' the advent of Number in the Master's hesitation to throw the dice; an expression of the 'expectation of a unique Number potentially contained in the situation of shipwreck' (NS 20). The looming prospect of 'radical disaster' is deciphered as 'a superior metrical necessity' (NS 37).

Meillassoux sets out to determine whether there is a Meter intrinsic and specific to the *Coup de dés*, and, if so, what it numbers. Soon the number 7 comes up ('medium term between the classical metric and pure chance'), embarking us on a numerological adventure (NS 45). In Mallarmé's 'punc-tilious calculations' in notes for *Le Livre*, he discovers the equation '$12 - 5 = 7$: The Number internal to the Book will be the reciprocal of 5 to obtain 12' (NS 48). This is interpreted as a formula for Mallarmé's sacrifice to pure poetry, a sacrificial subtraction that allows Meillassoux to associate the decapitated head of the Master ('whose "head" and crest alone were left float-ing above') with the word 'Si' ('perhaps') typographically set off in capital letters, and thus a singularised 'majuscule' or floating head (NS 61). 'Si' also corresponds to the musical note that sits at place number seven on the 'sol-fa' scale. Meillassoux treats this as the metaphor of 'essential Song' deposed 'into the lap of poetry' and deployed '"in *silence*", as it is written, making of it a mental and no longer an instrumental melody' (NS 65).

Meillassoux's road to Damascus leads to the number 707. It is con-strued as 'the Number of the demon'; 'an encircling structure for the abyss of O'; a 'cyclopean Number whose central eye, but an empty socket, is the source of all beauty'; a negation that figures a secret of poetics; a scale model of the Number's relation to the Poem; and the heralding of a new sacred (he notes that the word *sacre* is the 707th word of the poem) (NS 76–80). Taking stock of the metric count in several octosyllabic sonnets often clustered with Coup – '*Salut* [Toast/Sal-vation]', '*A la nue accablante tu* ... [Beaneath the Oppressive Cloud]', and '*Sonnet en-x*' – and calculating that the odds are that they share a common count ('there is one chance in nine that a Mallarméan sonnet has, merely by chance, 77 or 70 words' [NS 86]), Meillassoux bets the store on the chance that *Coup de dés* hews to the same 'premeditated' numerological code as the sonnets (NS 113). They all, as it were, get with the program, which is to say, they identify 707 as *the* incomparable number, synonymous with infinite Chance (NS 117).

One way to take the code's gesture is as 'a nihilist version of Christ's Passion': 'The *Coup de des* would then reveal, with a calculated delay', writes Meillassoux,

> the discreet drama of a man ready to sacrifice himself for the nullity that he knew was the foundation of his art. And the reader could be shaken by this proof of extreme love – heartrending love – for a Literature whose central vanity would have been symbolized by the prosaic operations of a pointless code. (NS 125)

This idea of sacrifice to 'pointless code' is intended quite literally: the Mallarméan negation defaults to 'the count', and to the computing of ones and zeros that are themselves dumb numbers of the algorithm. On another level though, the 'calculated delay' imbues the count with meaning, giving rise to a 'quavering number' keyed to Igitur's hesitation. The delay registers mathematically as a plus or minus one.

What is Number doing here exactly? Coding a premeditated 707 or decoding a meter with unaccountable feet? In a perverse act of table-turning, having spent the whole book proving that 707 is the unique Number, Meillassoux reveals in the appendix that to arrive at a word count of 707 he has had to cheat, counting *quelqu'un* as two words rather than as one. There is much equivocating in this finale; we are told that the number One is duplicitous, and thus counts for two, though it would seem to count only for one.

What Meillassoux affirms with this 'one that is not one' is his faith in the bifid siren (or 'si-ren', who conflates the subjunctive, conditional 'if' with the musical note 'si', or note 7 on the scale). This is an amphiboly that, as he puts it, 'unfetters Meter from its arithmetical truth' (NS 193). Meillassoux wagers on the compound word *peut-être*, whose hyphen instigates uncertainty in the count-as-one, while serving as an index of 'other lines' (dashes, punctuation marks, and strokes), all of which unsettle the perfect count. He also wagers on the futural condition embodied in the phrase *ne jamais abolira le hazard*:

> the title does not affirm that a throw of dice cannot abolish Chance, *but that it can never abolish it again*. ... Everything is necessarily contingent except contingency itself *and* the unique act of the Poet who incorporates himself into it – once, once only, and forever. (NS 166)

'Once, once only, and forever' – this dictum bespeaks an incantatory, militant adherence (reminiscent of Badiou) to numerological convictions.

Standing back, we might take away from this reading a house of cards geared towards accounting for 'divine inexistence' by projecting a subject that is unaccounted for. Where Latour, Gros, and Boltanski are interested in the critique of accountability, associating it with forms of managed life (or shareholder existence) coincident with specific historical iterations of finance capitalism, Meillassoux identifies unaccountability with pure number, with the discipline of mathematical ontology. And lest one assume that there is nothing political about this philosophical numbers game, Meillassoux builds into his theory a politics of adventism irreducible to the kind of prognostics that is by now familiar in discourses of a 'communism-to-come'. Meillassoux elaborates a futural aesthetics reliant on the clairvoyance of numbers. They are numbers that encrypt life in poetic meter and gesture towards a possible repunctuation.[19] An other-worldly metrics, a book on Mallarmé that goes crazy with numbers, all this may incline you to think you are wasting your time on frivolous cal-culations, but you just might be thinking about how to think another count; a mode of existence in which the meter is not always running.

New York University

Notes

1 A more comprehensive and comparative consideration of the existentialisation of finance would also engage with Bernard Stiegler's 'pharmacology of capital' (*What Makes Life Worth Living: On Pharmacology*) and Frédéric Lordon's 'anthropology of sovereign interest' (*L'Intérêt souverain*), as well as *Willing Slaves of Capital: Spinoza and Marx on Desire*), Georg Franck's 'mental capit-alism' (*Mentaler Kapitalismus*), and Peter Sloterdijk's psychopolitical reading of the American construction of 'actually existing escapism' (*In the World Interior of Capital*).

2 Jason Barker, Translator's Introduction to Alain Badiou, *Metapolitics*, trans. Jason Barker (London: Verso, 2005), p. xxi.

3 David Graeber, *Debt: The First 5000 Years* (New York: Melville House Pub-lishing, 2011), p. 13. Further references to this work will appear in the text abbreviated D.

4 Maurizio Lazzarato, *The Making of the Indebted Man. An Essay on the Neoliberal Condition*, trans. Joshua Jordan (Los Angeles: Semiotext(e), 2012), p. 87. Further references to this work will appear in the text abbreviated MIM.

5 Christopher Nealon, 'Value/Theory/Crisis', *PMLA* 127.1 (January 2012), p. 104.

6 Alain Badiou, *Number and Numbers*, trans. Robin Mackay (Cambridge: Polity Press, 2008), pp. 1 and 3. Further references to this work will appear in the text abbreviated NN.

7 Peter Hallward, *Badiou. A Subject to Truth* (Minneapolis: University of Minnesota Press, 2003), p. 25. Further references to this work will appear in the text abbreviated B.

8 A.J. Bartlett and Alex Ling, Translator's Introduction to Alain Badiou, *Mathematics of the Transcendental*, trans. A.J. Bartlett and Alex Ling (London: Bloomsbury, 2014), p. 5.

9 Michel Foucault, *Discipline and Punish*, trans. Alan Sheridan (London: Penguin Books Ltd., 1977), p. 154.

10 Ibid., p. 149.

11 Bruno Latour, *An Inquiry into Modes of Existence: An Anthropology of the Moderns*, trans. Catherine Porter (Cambridge, MA: Harvard Univeristy Press, 2013), pp. 388–9, 336. Further references to this work will appear in the text abbreviated IME.

12 Frédéric Gros, *Le principe sécurité* (Paris: Gallimard, 2012), p. 232. Translations are my own. Further references to this work will appear in the text abbreviated PS.

13 Roland Barthes, *The Preparation of the Novel*, trans. Kate Briggs (New York: Columbia University Press, 2010), p. 6.

14 Jonathan Crary, *24/7* (Verso: London, 2013), p. 29 and pp. 3–4, respectively.

15 Luc Boltanski, *Enigmes et complots: Une enquête à propos des enquêtes* (Paris: Gallimard, 2012), p. 48. Further references to this work will appear in the text abbreviated EC.

16 Quentin Meillassoux, *Divine Inexistence*, as translated by Graham Harman as an excerpted appendix in Graham Harman, *Quentin Meillassoux: Philosophy in the Making* (Edinburgh: Edinburgh University Press, 2011), p. 216. Cited and commented on by Harman, p. 111.

17 On the abandonment of 'real necessity' and the irruption *ex nihilo* of an immanent metaphysics, see Quentin Meillassoux, 'Potentiality and Virtuality', in Levi Bryant, Nick Srnicek and Graham Harman (eds.), *The Speculative Turn: Continental Materialism and Realism* (Melbourne, Australia: re.press, 2011), pp. 233–6.

18 Quentin Meillassoux, *The Number and the Siren: A Decipherment of Mallarmé's Coup de dés*, trans. Robin Mackay (New York: Sequence Press, 2011), p. 6. Further references to this work will appear in the text abbreviated NS.

19 On the aesthetics of punctuation, see Peter Szendy's *A coups de points: La ponctuation comme expérience*. In tying his notion of punctuated experience to the graphemic trace, Szendy follows through on a Derridean impetus, treating onomastics as the source of *différance* and as a site of the subject's encounter with his own death.

Index

Note: Page numbers in *italics* represent figures

Printed in the United States
by Baker & Taylor Publisher Services